IT'S TIME!

MY 360° VIEW OF THE UFC

sphere

BRUCE BUFFER

IT'S TIME!

SPHERE

First published in the United States in 2013 by Crown Archetype
First published in Great Britain in 2013 by Sphere

A CIP catalogue record for this book
is available from the British Library.

ISBN HB 978-1-84744-561-2
ISBN CF 978-1-84744-562-9

Printed and bound by CPI Group (UK) Ltd, Croydon, CR0 4YY

Papers used by Sphere are from well-managed forests
and other responsible sources.

MIX
Paper from
responsible sources
FSC® C104740

Sphere
An imprint of
Little, Brown Book Group
100 Victoria Embankment
London EC4Y 0DY

An Hachette UK Company
www.hachette.co.uk

www.littlebrown.co.uk

To my father, Joseph Buffer,
my mother, Constance Buffer,
my brother Brian Buffer,
this book is lovingly dedicated.
With you at my side, I learned to live and love, laugh and cry,
fight and win.
Throughout life I have strived to honor you with my
presence and passion.
Now I honor you with my words.

And to my brother Michael Buffer:
Thank you for believing in my dreams, as I believed in yours,
during our historic journey into the world of sports and
entertainment together!

CONTENTS

TORONTO

Like everyone else on the planet, I was looking forward to UFC 129 in April 2011. It was, just from the looks of it, a phenomenal card. You had the great Randy Couture taking on the much younger Lyoto Machida. And the bout everyone in two nations was sitting tight for was the main event: Georges St-Pierre taking on a contender from the U.S.A., Jake Shields.

Well, of course that bout was going to attract attention. We were playing in the Rogers Centre in Toronto. The Canadians snapped up the tickets as soon as they went on sale, giving the organization its biggest sellout crowd in UFC history, in North American history. Everyone, from Dana White down to the freshest newbie, was looking forward to it.

But for me, a funny thing happened on the way to Toronto.

About a week before the fight, I was playing at a two-day poker tournament at the Hustler Casino in Gardena, California, the one owned by the famous magazine mogul Larry Flynt, and fortune was spinning her wheel in my favor. I was up a few thousand dollars in tournament winnings and had high hopes I'd finish with a title.

But as I was walking around the casino, I rolled my ankle when I stepped on an uneven spot in the carpet. I didn't think much of it because it used to happen all the time in my kick-boxing days. You'd roll your ankle, you'd regain your balance, and maybe you'd get a little sprain that you'd walk off in a few minutes or so.

But that day, for some reason, it didn't play that way at all.

By the end of the evening, the ankle was hugely swollen and I couldn't stand on my leg. The next morning, during a break in the action, I rushed to the doctor. He drew blood, not water, out of the ankle. Not a good sign. I'd obviously traumatized the joint. That afternoon, there I was, showing up at the Hustler Casino walking with a cane. But okay. No big deal. I returned to the tables and finished third out of 1,500 poker players and walked away with $30,000.

That was a fantastic win, so I was not about to let a little ankle injury throw me off my game. Clearly I still had it. Luck was spinning in my favor again. Look, I always tell people today, I wasn't born on the twenty-first of May for nothing. Twenty-one is the sign of blackjack, one of my best games, and 21 will always be my lucky number.

For the next few days, I did everything I could to get that ankle back in shape. I would not, under any circumstances, walk into the Octagon with that cane. This was going to be the UFC's hugest night yet. *I've worked fifteen years to get where I am tonight,* I told myself, *and now I can't put weight on my leg.* Maybe that's not a big deal for most fight announcers. My brother,

Michael Buffer, can stand in the center of a boxing ring without moving a finger and entrance a crowd. He's debonair and stylish, with those drop-dead good looks. His voice, his image, and his signature line, "Let's Get Ready to Rumble," are known and recognized all over the world.

But that's not my style. I've taken my work in another direction. More than eighteen years ago Michael and I took a gamble on each other. I signed on to become his manager and business partner, and set out to do what many people told me was impossible: I took his voice, already famous in the world of boxing, and solidified his signature catchphrase into a solidly protected federal trademark that has grossed more than $400 million in retail sales from the licensed products and ventures we developed and created. Yes, $400 *million*.

Along the way, I was able to carve out a niche for myself. I'm known for being the most physical, the most intense announcer the sport of mixed martial arts has ever seen. To do what I do, to absorb all the energy of the fans and channel it into a 180 or, God help us, a 360, I need to be at the top of my game. The tiniest injury can easily derail me. So I nursed that ankle as best I could. Babied it. Iced it. Worked out carefully at the gym. Then I got my stuff together for the flight to Toronto.

That night, I called about six hours of fights. Then came the main event. GSP and Shields were in the Octagon, and the place was going wild. The Canadians were out of their minds.

I took the microphone in hand and said:

"LADIES AND GENTLEMEN! THIS IS THE MAIN EVENT OF THE EVENING!"

The crowd screamed.

I love it when the crowd is pumped and each new fight

builds to a crescendo of raw energy. It's my job to radiate that excitement back to the crowd, to take what they've given me and pay it all back in homage to the two warriors who have trained weeks to get here.

When I'm in the Octagon, I speak from the heart. My heart, and yours.

My message to the fighters is simple: We honor you! We pay tribute to you. You deserve every ounce of recognition for being here, and I'm going to give the raw power of my voice, my lungs, my physical energy, and my passion to get you ready for this match.

GSP and Shields were loosening up.

I held up my cards and marched through the names of the judges and referee and sponsors . . .

"AND NOW, THIS IS THE MOMENT YOU'VE ALL BEEN WAITING FOR . . ."

I spun into a 360-degree turn and roared like a lion:

"IIIIIIIIIIIIT'S TIMMMMMMMMMMMMME!!!!!!!!!!"

The audience went wild.

I did a three-foot aerial jump. I hit the ground, whipped off a lightning-fast 180-degree turn, and locked eyes with Jake Shields as I read his name and credentials.

Then I did an aerial 180, and as I landed, I yelled:

"FIGHTING . . ."

I had never done this before off the ground, and it went perfectly.

"FIGHTING OUT OF THE RED CORNER!"

I stalked over to Georges and locked eyes with him.

"THE REIGNING, DEFENDING UNDISPUTED UFC WELTERWEIGHT CHAMPION OF THE WORLD."

"GEORGES—"

I thrust my body at him.

"RUSH—"

Getting into the spirit of things, Georges lunged at me.

I leaped back as I roared . . .

"ST-PIERRE!"

But as I leaped back, my foot wobbled and I felt a searing pain in my right knee.

It was the loudest *"St-Pierre!"* I ever shouted in my life. A boom and a scream all wrapped together, with a little bit of my body as a sacrifice.

Oh, I thought, *that is not good. Something just blew.*

I left the Octagon as the warriors entered the heat of battle. I watched from the sidelines, horrified that my right knee was wobbling from side to side. I don't think anyone could tell how concerned I was.

But inside, I had only one thought: *Shit, shit, shit. My knee is destroyed. I'll never be able to announce my way again.*

I limped over to Stitch Duran, the UFC's legendary cutman, and lowered myself into a chair. Without a word, he brought over an icepack. Stitch watches everyone in the Octagon like a hawk. It's his job to spot pain, and he knew I was hurting.

Big John McCarthy, one of the sport's pioneers and one of its most recognizable referees, caught my eye. "How you doing?" he said.

"Not good."

"I didn't think so. I saw the way you moved up there. I think you blew your ACL."

Shit, shit, shit.

Look at the crazy irony here, would you? Two of the world's

best fighters are going at it in the Octagon in front of 55,000 people, and the guy in the tuxedo has ice clapped to his knee. What's wrong with this picture?

The record will show that I did my job that night. I announced St-Pierre as the winner by unanimous decision. Later, as Joe Rogan was interviewing GSP, I got a chance to speak with Lorenzo Fertitta, one of the owners of the billion-dollar empire that is UFC. "Awesome night of fights," I said to him. "But I think I blew my ACL. Do you mind giving me the name of the doctor in L.A. that you send the fighters to?"

He said no problem.

After the main event, I was leaning against the safety gates in the arena's aisle and said hi to Dana White, the UFC's leader, as he walked by.

"Awesome show tonight, Dana," I said. "But I think I blew my knee introducing GSP."

He nearly laughed out loud. "You?"

As soon as I left the arena, I became busier than I'd ever been after a fight. This was the largest arena at which we'd ever appeared, with the largest number of fans, and as I limped away from the Octagon that night, this became my longest walk ever. Every corridor and atrium was lined with photo- and autograph-hungry fans. I couldn't really care about the condition I was in. I simply focused on walking slowly and carefully, posing and signing autographs for every single person who asked me for one.

I was supposed to hit the after-parties that night with the fighters, same as always. It's one of the things I love to do. But that night, I passed. I couldn't risk being jostled by someone. A few days later, the doctor gave me the worst news of my life. I had torn a meniscus, one of the two critical pieces of cartilage in the human knee, in three places, and completely ripped my anterior cruciate ligament. The ACL is one of four ligaments that connect the thighbone to the shinbone. It's a common injury for sportsmen; a good, wrenching twist after a lifetime of activity will rip that precious cord. You can live without an ACL; Hines Ward had a spectacular career as a wide receiver for the Pittsburgh Steelers, hardly missing the ACL he snapped in childhood. But the rest of us mortals can't begin to do what we do best without getting it replaced, usually when you're more than thirty years old, with an Achilles' heel tendon taken from a cadaver.

My life of athleticism flashed before my eyes. When I was training as a kickboxer as a younger man, that leg had been freakishly strong and fast. I could kick at your face and stop within an inch of your skin without hurting you. That's how agile that right leg was.

Now, sitting on the doctor's bench, I felt like my body had betrayed me.

"You *must* get the meniscus done within three to six months," the doctor said. "If you don't, it will wear away. You'll be bone on bone, and you'll ruin your knee and you will absolutely need a replacement when you're older. But I do also recommend getting the ACL done."

"How much time do I need to recover?"

"Fully? Six months to a year. To be able to walk up the stairs into the Octagon and do what you do, two to three months with a brace," he said.

I didn't have three months. I had a show in three weeks, and I was also booked to appear in a major motion picture with actors Kevin James, Salma Hayek, and Henry Winkler. Our ten-day film shoot started in Boston in a week's time. Looking ahead at my schedule, I didn't have a good long break from the UFC for three months.

Not long ago, I'd seen another doctor for shoulder pain. After a lifetime of throwing punches and surfing like a madman, my shoulder bone was no longer round but flat. By the time I reached my late sixties, the doctor said, I'd be a good candidate for a shoulder replacement.

Great, I thought angrily. *Knee, shoulder, what else is gonna happen?*

I was worried about my future. I had spent a good chunk of my life in service to the UFC. I'd loved the sport from the moment I'd watched it, and I'd fought hard for the chance to become the sport's preeminent announcer. Over the years, I'd used every connection I'd made in the world of sports and entertainment to up the UFC's profile with fans, sports journalists, and TV producers. Those were all things I did behind the scenes— things people never saw or heard about. But for me, the highlight of any fight was being able to walk into the Octagon and do the job I love.

And now, if I couldn't walk into the Octagon, what would happen to everything I fought for?

Worse, I'd done it all to myself. And that really pissed me off.

I needed to get the surgery done, and fast. The thing was, I had five UFCs in the next two months, one nearly every week. The doc could work on me ASAP, but if he performed the surgery now, I'd break my perfect attendance record. For fifteen years, nothing had kept me out of the Octagon. I hated to ruin that streak.

I had designed my life around my role as the "Voice of the Octagon," or the VOTO, as my brother Brian had nicknamed me a few years back. If I took off now, who knows? Maybe I could lose my job. I could lose everything that mattered to me.

To understand my pain, you must understand how hard I've worked to get here. More than a decade and a half ago, I took a gamble on an incredible partnership with my long-lost brother. Then I gambled my livelihood on a dream of announcing for a living. I felt like the luckiest guy in the world to have achieved everything I set my mind on.

How did I get here? How did I come to manage my brother Michael's career and make him his first million? How did I talk myself into a job I coveted? How did I earn the right to be in the Octagon? How did I get to surround myself with some of the world's most talented athletes? How did I get to travel the globe in service to the world's greatest sport?

It's time I told you.

1

PUNCHED IN THE FACE

You don't know who you really are until you've been punched in the face.

For me, that magic moment happened when I was about thirteen years old. My younger brother Brian and I were living with my folks in Glenside, Pennsylvania, about twenty minutes outside downtown Philly. It was the middle of winter, one of those miserably cold days when any snowball you scraped together from the dirty mound of whiteness on the sidewalk was sure to have a couple of hard chunks of ice in it. I packed one of these monsters together and lobbed it at this tough, stern-faced Italian-American kid named Glenn. He and his friends used to terrorize students, especially Jewish kids, at school. They mistakenly thought I was Jewish, so they singled me out for their brand of punishment.

I was hanging out with his crew and mine, and the moment

the iceball whacked his face you could hear everyone get real quiet.

Glenn didn't say a word.

He stomped over to me. Before I knew what was happening, he hit me with a few well-placed right and left hooks. Boom, boom, boom, all knuckles to the face.

Now, you have to realize something: I was no angel.

Wherever we lived, the kids were always pretty territorial. *This is our turf. You're either in or out.* Well, I thought, if they didn't want me in, I would just carve out my own turf. I had already formed my own gang when I was about six or seven years old. I actually got in trouble at school for it, and my parents had to come in and have a talk with the principal.

Being a kid then was different. My father raised us to be very independent. When we were seven and nine years old, my brother Brian and I were taking the bus or train into Philly in the morning, going to museums or a movie, and coming home around five o'clock or later. You won't dare let your kids do that today. Times were different, and I think kids and parents were different, too.

I was Joe Buffer's kid. I'd been conceived in Las Vegas and born in Oklahoma. I'd spent my childhood bouncing back and forth between Dallas and Philly as my father changed corporate VP jobs for a variety of Fortune 500 companies. He traveled extensively during those early years, and many times it was just my mom, Brian, and me alone for a week or two at a time while he was gone.

Nominally my father was a salesman, but he was so much more. He had always tried to instill some street smarts in the two of us. He taught my older brother, Brian, and me basic self-defense moves at an early age. Good thing, too, because the first time I was jumped was at age six. A kid grabbed me from behind, and I remembered something Dad had just told me. I raised my foot and stomped on the kid's instep. *Crunch.* The kid ran away. He never messed with me again. I was attending a tough school in Philadelphia at the time. I needed to know how to handle myself, because even though we were young, now and then we still had to fight to hang on to our lunch money.

Barring the occasional fretting principal, using your fists back then had none of the stigma it might have among parents and teachers today. The manly art of pugilism was an accepted part of American culture. When we were living in Dallas, we had a gym teacher who encouraged us boys to settle our differences by pulling on some boxing gloves and taking swings at each other. Every Saturday night our mom would cook us a great meal— New York strip steaks and baked potatoes, with lemon meringue pie for dessert—and we'd sit in front of the TV and watch the fights. I'd even fallen in love with a scene in an old movie where the great movie star James Cagney, the original little tough guy, tossed a much bigger man using a number of judo moves. I loved it.

But the day I got pummeled in the face, something went wrong. I got caught off guard and paid the price. More than anything, I'll never forget thinking how the punches felt. I think the biggest fear most kids—and most *adults*—have is, if someone punches me in the face, it'll hurt badly and I'll be horribly wounded or disfigured.

Well, no, you won't.

Chances are, the person throwing the punch doesn't know what he's doing and doesn't know how to connect very well.

Chances are, those punches will sting or bloody your nose, but not do much harm.

This kid had worked me over. All I could do was lie there and mull over the experience in a strangely analytical way. *Huh—that didn't hurt as much as I thought it would,* I thought. The second thing I thought was, *It's never happening again. I'm going to learn how to defend myself for real.* I had been taking judo class, but now I wanted to be very diligent.

All the way home, I asked myself what I could have done to stop him. My dad had always told us, "If a bully threatens you, you hit him first. Don't wait for him to touch you. Don't let him get the first punch. Just punch him in the nose. Make him see his own blood, and I promise you he'll never come after you again."

That was good advice, and if I ever had a kid myself someday, I'd teach him or her the same thing. The surest way to stop most people is to make them bleed. Because they are not expecting that. Anyone who picks a fight is in love with his own sense of power, and he's probably never had anyone stand up to him. That's how most bullies get away with the crap they pull. No one has ever pounded them good.

That day on the playground, I had messed up. I hadn't seen the punches coming. I hadn't reacted very well, and I got beat. After that, I recommitted myself to judo.

My old man was delighted to see that I was getting serious about self-defense—and no wonder. Joseph Buffer had boxed in his youth, served fifteen years in the Marines during World War II and served again during the Korean War. He'd served as a drill sergeant and drill team leader at Camp Pendleton in San Diego. He'd trained young soldiers in hand-to-hand and knife combat. This was intense stuff, where you could look right into the eyes of the man who wanted you dead, feel his breath in your face, and smell his sweat. He'd also served as the master sergeant in charge of the guards assigned to the brig at Camp Pendleton.

He was a tough SOB, and he wanted his sons to share that toughness.

He was a tall, handsome, dark-haired, hazel-eyed man who was John Wayne, Errol Flynn, and Steve McQueen all rolled up into one. When he walked into a room, women wanted him and men envied him.

Side by side, my parents made an odd couple. My mom, Connie, is a sweet, beautiful Italian-American lady who stands four foot eleven. My dad, on the other hand, was a six-foot-tall monster who was absolutely brilliant and half nuts to boot.

How nuts?

Imagine a guy who, on his very first date with our mother, got hassled by a panhandler and tossed the guy through a plate-glass window.

Imagine a father blindfolding you when you're ten years old, and having you break down and reassemble one of his German Lugers while he times you with his watch.

Imagine him teaching you to shoot rifles and pistols at six years old.

Imagine him teaching you to play poker and blackjack when you are eight.

Imagine him teaching you to mix stiff drinks when you're ten.

Imagine him teaching you at the earliest age possible that you should never, under any circumstances, bet on a horse. If you were going to gamble, you were going to do it with your own skills, your own brains, and your own smarts. Horse betting was for idiots. "The only way you follow a horse is with a shovel," my father told us, and we never forgot it.

And he always said, "Walk into a room like you own it!"

There was something remarkably convincing about his sayings. We gleaned the message that we could pretty much accomplish *anything,* if only we had the balls to follow through with it and we were scrupulously honest.

What was the point of cheating at cards? If you learned to be a good cardplayer, you'd rarely lose. And if you're going to fight, then know how to fight. On the street, he saw the point of fighting dirty to survive because, in that situation, you must do whatever it takes to win that fight. He taught Brian and me many tricks we needed to know, because he knew them all.

I carry these lessons in my heart today.

Fighting was actually part of our DNA. Our grandfather, Johnny Buff, my father's father, was a world-champion boxer in 1921. His real name was John Lesky, and he fought in New Jersey and New York, and later other parts of the country in the bantamweight and flyweight divisions through most of those early Prohibition years. Buff was his nickname, and for some reason I'll never know, he passed that name, albeit modified, to my father.

Growing up in a tough neighborhood in New York City, my dad got by on his smarts and his fists, and channeled what he learned into the Marine Corps. But like a lot of guys who leave the military, he struggled to find himself when he hung up his uniform. Between the wars he was a debt collector. Later he became a businessman, an entrepreneur, and a VP of sales of various companies. He did not graduate from high school or college to achieve any of this. He was self-taught. He had a knack for salesmanship, but it didn't make him terribly happy. You could say that behind my father's tough-guy persona dwelt the soul of an artist. In those days, when you didn't have a billion cable channels on TV, families hung out after dinner and did activities. Dad taught me how to draw. And I remember him reading to us.

"You ready?" he'd say, and he'd launch into reading one of the world's most famous poems.

"'If you can keep your head when all about you are losing theirs and blaming it on you,'" our father intoned. "'If you can trust yourself when all men doubt you, but make allowance for their doubting too . . .'"

The words are from a poem called "If," by Rudyard Kipling, one of my father's favorite writers. Kipling was the same Brit who wrote *The Jungle Book*, "The Man Who Would Be King," "Gunga Din," and *Captains Courageous*, some of the greatest adventure stories ever written.

BUFFERISM NO. 1

"BIG CHEERS AND NO FEARS FOREVER."

You can't live in fear. Live in such a way that you're always celebrating life. Wake up every day happy, knowing you're the best that you can be. If you can banish fear, you'll rest easy, knowing that you can handle anything you come up against. When an athlete succeeds, everybody cheers. So why not do that for yourself? You kiss a pretty girl? Cheers. You landed a commission at work? Cheer for yourself.

But Kipling's poem was something else entirely. It was a code of honor, the words of a father offering wisdom to his sons. We would hear that poem all through our childhood, until the words seeped into our brains and we could practically recite it from heart. I especially liked how the poem ended. The father tells his son, if you can do all these things, then: "Yours is the Earth and everything that's in it, and—which is more—you'll be a Man, my son!"

To this day I carry a copy of that poem in my wallet. If you are the parent of young sons, I urge you to share that poem with them.

But as much as he loved the expression of the written word, my father clammed up about his childhood and his mysterious parents. For example, Brian and I never met our grandfather, Johnny Buff, or our grandmother. In our entire lives we never saw a single photo of our father and grandfather together. My mom's side of the family was no mystery. She was 100 percent second-generation Italian; her dad was from the Abruzzi, in central Italy. But we were never sure about our ethnic heritage on our father's side. What nationality was Johnny Lesky—Polish, German, Italian?

Our father waved off discussing such matters, promising to come clean someday. That day never came. But here's the thing: whatever mysteries my father locked away inside him, one of those family secrets would one day bubble up to the surface and lead me on a path to the UFC.

But before all that, I had a debt to settle with Glenn the bully. When I was fourteen years old and our shop class teacher stepped out of the classroom for a bit, I gave him a solid dose of payback punches.

Case closed.

2

FIGHT! FIGHT! FIGHT!

W hen I was in high school, some friends of mine planned a ski trip. All I needed was seventy-five dollars to go along, and I'd have a fabulous weekend on Mammoth Mountain in Yosemite.

I asked my mother for the money. She was and is a beautiful woman, who has a sort of Elizabeth Taylor quality to her. Dark hair, and beautiful eyes that she fixed on me now with a kind of despair.

"Sorry, honey," she said, "we don't have that kind of money to spend on ski trips."

I was cool with that. Absolutely. A lot had been going on in our lives in the last couple of years. My father got a job offer that took us west to California, land of sunshine, movies, endless beaches, and beautiful girls. My parents rented a house in Malibu, of all places. That probably sounds glamorous, but in the 1970s Malibu was not the bastion of wealth it is today. In fact, it seemed to be full of beach bums and a lot of middle-class families like ours. The movie stars were the ones who had the houses on the beach.

One of our neighbors was Steve McQueen. I used to hang out with his son Chad. We were hanging out in the family's kitchen one day when Steve and Ali McGraw came home from shopping. They had just appeared together in Sam Peckinpah's film *The Getaway*, about an ex-con and his girl on the lam. Ali was as beautiful as she was in that movie. Steve shook my hand and said I was always welcome in their home but had to follow one rule: call first before coming over. He seemed like the coolest dad ever. Drank beers with us on the beach when we were older, and told us some hilarious stories. When we got to know each other a little better, he'd let me use his deck and the awesome sauna downstairs in his house after I was done surfing the beach in front of his house. I regarded him with a mixture of awe and respect. McQueen probably was the coolest of all the leading men at the time. The writers of the day dubbed him Mr. Cool.

California opens people's eyes to bigger and better things. No sooner had my father gotten settled in L.A. than he got tired of being a suit. He itched to try something new. He announced one day that he was quitting his job to pursue one of his passions: writing. My mother supported him one hundred percent, even though this decision left our family without a guaranteed source of income. She knew my father needed to make a go at this or he'd never be able to look at himself in the mirror. When you have that kind of dream inside you, you can't look away. Denying it only makes you feel worse. Ask any fighter in the UFC. If you want something so bad that you can taste it, you're better off ditching your old life, getting your family to accept who you really are, and going balls-to-the-wall trying to make that dream happen. It does you no good to let your kids see you live your life as a frustrated person, with your dreams quietly dying inside you.

BUFFERISM NO. 2

"REACH FOR THE STARS WHEN FULFILLING YOUR DREAMS."

Don't just take one step forward. Take it to the highest level possible. Don't be half-assed in anything you do. Believe in yourself and your ability. Don't just reach for the stars— *be* a star yourself.

Eventually, my mom's faith in my dad proved to be a good bet. In the coming years, my dad would build a successful career as a writer. He wrote nonfiction articles for magazines like *Guns & Ammo*. I was much older when I unearthed stories he'd written even earlier in his career, for men's magazines such as *Playboy* and *Argosy*. They were macho guy stories about womanizing, swaggering tough men who brawled their way through a series of crazy adventures. Dad basically wrote about himself, and in the world of fiction, he always got the dames.

And on the side, he and my mother began displaying his collection of antiques and collectibles from World War II and earlier. They reserved booths at gun collector shows held in Vegas, and over time managed to learn a lot about buying and selling collectible weapons and artifacts to the public.

But the success of all those ventures was off in the future.

Right then I was a kid who wanted to go skiing with his friends, and my family didn't have seventy-five dollars to throw away on my trip. I was fine with not going; I really was. I'd never been skiing before, so I didn't know what I'd be missing. I'd spend the weekend with my brother and my parents, like always. No big whoop.

But a day later, when I came home from school, my mother took me aside and handed me a wad of cash. "You take this and you have fun," she told me.

Hey, great, I thought, and I went on my ski trip after all.

A week or so later, at about two o'clock in the morning, I awoke to hear my parents talking in the kitchen. The month was almost up, and they needed money for the rent and other bills. They were coming up short, and were at their wits' end trying to figure out how they were going to get over that first-of-the-month hump.

I huddled in my room. I felt terrible. My mother had given me all that money and now they didn't have what they needed to pay their bills. How selfish had I been? Who the hell was I to ask for seventy-five dollars when my parents were trying to make ends meet?

It was a pivotal moment in my life, one that nearly brings me to tears when I think about it today.

I resolved never to ask my parents for money ever again. I would find a way to make money and keep making it. And if I could figure out a way to help them, too, then I would.

From that moment forward, I devoted my free time to conceiving, building, and marketing a business to my fellow high schoolers. Never in a million years would you guess, knowing me today, what I sold.

Jewelry.

I made it myself, in my bedroom, cranking out beautiful necklaces and earrings using turquoise stones and various metals I got at a craft store. The girls in school loved it. The boys loved buying it for them, and plenty of people even bought them to give as gifts to people in their families. Soon I was doing well, earning about $800 to $1,000 a month in 1970s dollars. I remember my jewelry once getting me out of trouble with my gym coach. In my senior year I had cut a number of gym classes and used to go to breakfast at the diner across the street instead. And now I was in danger of failing gym, of all things. So I built the world's most beautiful necklace and presented it to the coach.

"This is for your wife," I said. "No charge."

He was flabbergasted and accepted it gratefully.

"But there's just one thing," I said.

"You're failing," he said. "This doesn't change anything."

"I know, but couldn't you please just give me a passing grade? I know I don't deserve anything better."

"You don't!" And then he softened and added, "I'll see what I can do."

I know you probably don't want your kids doing this at school, and I expect he was going to pass me anyway, but it shows that at a young age, I was already learning how to make deals.

THERE was no high school in Malibu, so my brother and I went to Santa Monica High School. Weekends, all of us kids used to hang out on the beach. Finding the right spot was usually a hassle. Our school had a fierce rivalry going with nearby Venice High School. If there wasn't a football game on the weekend, there was a street fight along that strip of coast between the kids from those two schools. Beach culture naturally seems to breed turf wars.

One night we were all hanging out at a big party on a stretch of Northern Malibu Beach called Zero's, in front of a number of houses that were scheduled to be demolished because the county was turning this small stretch of surfing paradise into public beach access. It was a big night for us local kids. Almost every teenager from Malibu who went to Santa Monica High was there, plus a bunch of kids from other locales, as fate would have it. We had a bonfire. A live band. Beer. Girls. Everything a teenager could want.

No one had shown up to hassle us. Everything was going great. And then, all of a sudden, a guy from another school started arguing with people on the beach, including a female friend of mine. None of us knew what it was about. All we saw was the football player punch and drop my friend's boyfriend in the sand. My friend started yelling at him. The football player hauled off and punched her, too. Down she dropped into the sand.

Everyone was shocked. *Oh my God, how could this happen?*

But no one, no one, stepped forward.

This guy just loomed over these two kids and kept taunting them while they held their faces. The girl was crying. Her girlfriends were afraid to go over and get her out of there.

Then someone walked out of the crowd and said to the big lug, "I think you should leave now."

The teenager who had spoken was me, and I was plenty pissed.

I'm sorry, I don't care what the situation is. In my book, a man does not hit a woman, much less his girlfriend or his wife. Ever. Even a wimp tends to have more power than the girl he's dating. And this guy was no wimp. He was a 225-pound monster. Think of a guy the size of Tito Ortiz or Randy Couture, but with none of their class or brains.

The guy looked at me. "Fuck you, boy. This is none of your business."

"No, fuck *you*," I said. "You're leaving now!"

The kids around us loved this. Two kids from two different high schools were about to face off against each other. That was cool. At least, this is what they thought in their adolescent minds. Some of them started chanting, *"Fight! Fight! Fight!"*

More people came running over and gathered around, just like in the movies.

That did not help matters much. I didn't want to touch this guy. I had no idea where this would lead. He was bigger than I was, but that wasn't the issue. I felt sorry for him. He was too stupid to know that it was wrong to punch a girl in the face.

Back then, I was not an unknown entity in high school. I was pretty built for a senior. I worked out. I practiced martial arts. I was a lifeguard. I was the guy who made jewelry. I had started for both the Santa Monica High water polo and swim teams for two years, and although I elected not to compete in my senior year, I was in top shape and ready to fight if I had to. But as far as this meathead was concerned, I was a nobody.

I told him again, "Just go now, and leave them alone."

A bunch of the kids started chanting, *"Buff! Buff! Buff!"*

The big kid yelled "Fuck you!" and threw a wild right hook.

As I blocked it, I punched him full force, right between the eyes. He went back but recovered, and then swarmed me like a football player. He picked me up and dropped me to the sand and started throwing punches. I managed to work my way on top and up to the mount. Though I didn't know the term then, I ground-and-pounded him into bloody submission.

"Fight over due to strikes," or a KO, as we would say in the Octagon.

When I was done with him, he was not a pretty sight. His blood was everywhere—in the sand, on my clothes. My new Pendleton shirt was ripped to pieces and hanging from my shoulders.

The crowd was cheering, but there was no glory in it for me. I didn't ask for this. But a glimmer of wisdom in my head said, *No, but he did.*

When I saw that he wasn't getting up, I grabbed my girl-friend and left. I knew it was also time for *me* to leave.

I wasn't thinking too clearly when I got home late that night. I only knew I had to get out of those clothes, which were torn and covered with the guy's blood. I left everything on the washing machine, washed my face and hands, and crashed in my bed.

The next morning, when I came down for breakfast, my parents were waiting for me. Their eyes were heavy with concern. My mother held what was left of my shirt, now stiff with dried blood.

"What happened, Bruce?"

I could never lie to my parents. It just wasn't in me. They were such straightforward, honest people; lying didn't make sense in our house. I told them the truth. I didn't like what had unfolded, but I felt like I didn't have any other choice.

My mother was shocked but not surprised, as this was hardly my first rodeo. She came over to shower me with love.

My father, on the other hand, was ecstatic. You'd think he'd just won the lottery. He was so proud his son had fought the good fight, defended a woman's honor, and taught a brute a lesson.

The phone rang. My father went to take it. I heard him talking to one of my friends in the next room. I didn't hear much of the conversation, but only a few highlights. "Yeah?" he said. "Yeah? Okay . . . you let them know. We'll be there in twenty minutes."

When he reappeared in the kitchen, he was sticking a snub-nosed Colt .38 Detective Special revolver into his waistband. He looked at me and nodded. "You," he said. "Get dressed. We're going out."

"Where are we going?" I said.

"That was Bob Ryan. The kid you beat up last night is looking for payback. But he doesn't know where you live. Him and his loser friends pulled a knife on Bob in back of the super-market where he works in downtown Malibu. They know Bob knows where we live. So we're going into town and we're going to settle this, once and for all."

My mother said, "Joe, please, why—"

"Quiet," my father said. "You heard me. Get dressed."

"What's with the gun, Dad?"

"Simple," my old man said, "You're going to fight this guy in the parking lot, where everyone can see that you beat him again, fair and square."

"Yeah, but what's with the gun?"

"I'm gonna hold off all his friends while you take care of business," he said.

"Are you fucking crazy?" I said. "No way."

Something similar to this had happened once before. When

I was only fifteen years old, I was at the movies with my father when a group of four young thugs broke into the theater exit door. My father hated that someone would just knowingly flout the law like that. He hated how morality was going to hell in a handbasket in this country. He saw himself as one of the last true White Knights, although a bit crazy at times.

When the gang broke in, my father told me to wrap my belt around my fist with the large buckle dangling down as a weapon. He instructed me to stand behind him and back him up if things went south. Then he marched over to the gang and confronted them, ordering them to leave. Not a single person in the theater got up to help us. It was four potentially armed gang kids against the two of us.

But, of course, they left.

And the day we were supposed to meet the linebacker in the parking lot, I'm happy to say that showdown never took place. When we got down to the appointed spot by the beach, the other guys were nowhere to be found. The guy never bothered me again. That was the end of that, except for one thing: I now knew just how far my father was willing to go to settle a score.

THE story of that fight and its aftermath touches on several important aspects of my character: my instinct toward justice, toward righting wrongs; my instinct to protect those who need it; and my struggle to be myself when pitted against my equally strong-willed father.

For every bit of toughness my father instilled in us, I believe my mother taught us kindness and compassion. My father did, too; he could be the kindest and most caring man in the world, but he had no time or patience for A-holes of any kind. My goal as a grown man is somehow to live up to both their examples, to take the good from each and leave what isn't me behind.

I'll never forget the day I was hanging out "downtown" at the Malibu Country Mart, one of the nation's first outdoor shopping centers. I was a high-school junior and decked out in my lifeguard swim trunks. I had probably just come off duty and was planning not to do too much for the rest of the afternoon. I glanced over my shoulder for a second and spotted my mom coming out of one of the shops. She waved. I told my friends to hold up a second as I ran over to give her a hug hello and a rundown on my plans for the day.

She wasn't in a rush to get back home, and was thinking about hanging out herself.

"Do you want to stay a little while and have an ice cream with me?" she said.

"Nah," I said, scrunching my face into the sun. "I gotta get going." After all, I had places to go, things to do. I couldn't waste time at an ice-cream counter with my mom. I was not a little kid anymore.

She smiled. "That's fine. I'll see you later, okay?"

I nodded and ran off.

I don't know how long I hung out with the guys. There was always something happening or a chance to go surfing. And a little while later, as I ran off with my friends, I happened to swing past the ice-cream place. There, on the other side of the window, I saw my mother sitting alone at a table, digging into a cup with a spoon.

I thought nothing of it then, but the human mind is funny,

what it remembers, what it forgets. I'm telling you, I sometimes wish that I could go back in time and sit in that shop with her, if only for a few minutes, so she would not have to sit there alone.

The part of my character that makes me want to stick my neck out for a high-school girl I wasn't dating, or grab innocent people out of harm's way when people start brawling on the sidewalk, is somehow tied up in the love I have for that woman in the ice-cream shop.

When she married my father, she set out on a hell of a ride. A few years into their marriage, they split up and she took Brian and me to go live with her mom in Philly. I don't remember those days, and I've never fully learned the cause of the split, but I remember the day he came back, standing tall in the doorway, dressed to the nines.

For all his toughness, the man was a dreamer. And she helped him live out every one of his dreams, even if it inconvenienced her to do so. A few weeks after that infamous ski trip when I heard them talking about coming up with enough money to pay the bills, they were forced to put an ad in the paper offering my mother's diamond wedding ring for sale. Someone called, offering to buy it, and my mom went alone to the parking lot of the Country Mart to meet that buyer. I can only imagine how she felt that day, selling her ring so her family would have food to put on the table. And sure, when they made a success of their business, my father bought my mother another ring to make up for the one she'd sacrificed. But no woman should ever have to sell a token of her love.

When I got older, I sensed that my mother needed more purpose in life. Later in life, with her in mind, I would start a business, SportsBuff Enterprises, with the idea of asking her to help me out. She was remarkably effective handling the phones, booking venues, and managing and selling my merchandise. In fact, one year she earned $50,000 in commissions and took my father on a trip to Europe. It was her way of saying, "Look what I did! Now let me treat you to something."

My mom was nothing if not a devoted, supportive wife and a loving human being. In her eyes, Joe Buffer could do no wrong. I had a more objective opinion, of course. My dad was tough. There were days when I hated him. Hated how stubborn he was, how hard he was on my mother and Brian and me. It was always his way or the highway. And once his anger got up, watch out. His emotions were too hot to handle.

He got into an uncomfortable conversation once with one of my early girlfriends, Rosy, a girl I loved dearly. They did not argue, mind you. It was just enough of a discussion for my father to decide that he didn't care for her. And after that, Rosy was banned from the house forever. It tore me apart inside. I went to have an angry word or three with my father about it, and he practically kicked me out of the house. He was not interested in opinions that didn't agree with his. But after much thought, he came to understand how important she was to me, and he and I worked it all out between us.

3

BOILER ROOM

When I got out of high school, I enrolled in business and film classes at Santa Monica College. One day I was scanning the job board in front of the guidance office and saw a flyer that promised, MAKE $250 TO $400 A WEEK SELLING OVER THE PHONE! That didn't sound hard at all. I needed to make money doing something that wouldn't interfere with studying—and martial arts training and, of course, surfing.

I interviewed with these people in Santa Monica, who explained that they sold office supplies, mostly paper and photocopier toner, over the phone. They offered me the job on the spot.

"Be here tomorrow at five o'clock."

"I'll be in class then," I said.

"Not 5:00 p.m." They laughed. "Five o'clock in the *morning*. We have to get here early every day because we're selling to the East Coast."

I don't know many college kids who would have enjoyed

getting up that early, but I thought this would be perfect. If I could put in some hours before class, I'd be making money without having to skip classes.

My parents and my brother Brian weren't convinced it was a smart opportunity. Who bought office supplies over the phone? The job sounded like a joke or, worse, a scam.

I was the first one at the office the next day. I watched as the owners and the salespeople started arriving in their Porsches. Beautiful cars. *Well,* I thought, *they must be doing something right.*

They set me up in a cubicle with a headset and taught me what they called the "Reroute Pitch." It went like this:

Phone rings.

"Hello?"

"Yes, this is Bruce. I'm calling from U.S. Toner in California. How are you doing this morning?"

"Whatever you're selling, I'm not interested."

"I understand that. Can you tell me one thing, though? What's the model number on your copier in your office?"

"Our copier? Uh, lemme see. It's right here. Uh, it's the Xerox 3100."

"Really? Oh, hey, listen, you're gonna like this. One of our accounts down the street has the same model copier as you do, only they just got rid of their machine. We just shipped them a fresh order of the Xerox 3100 toner, and instead of sending the toner bottles back, we can sell it to you at a very substantial savings."

"Uh, I dunno." Pause. "How much of a savings, exactly?"

When the Reroute Pitch worked, it worked like a charm. It was simple, persuasive, effective. When it dawned on me that every no brought me closer to a yes, I dialed those numbers like a maniac. I was motivated to be Number One. By the way:

logging tons of noes in order to get to a yes still applies to selling today, no matter what the product.

One day the owner came out and said, "Okay, during the five-to-eight-a.m. shift, the person who makes the most sales gets a buck."

I know what you're thinking: Who cares? What's a dollar? It's nothing. True, you could buy more with a dollar *then* than you could today, but that wasn't the point. The dollar was really a carrot, an *incentive* to get people to try harder. Everyone wanted to be the one to win that dollar and wave it in everyone else's face. Hey, buddy, you think you're a salesman? How many of the dollars have *you* won?

That's when I realized that just working for a paycheck is not enough. In fact, you could almost say that is *non*-motivational. But if you give people a carrot, someone will always, always, always distinguish himself or herself to take that carrot home. This is true no matter who you are. It's not about the dollar. It becomes a point of pride. People love incentives.

BUFFERISM NO. 3

"I'D RATHER HAVE ONE PERCENT OF OTHER PEOPLE'S EFFORTS THAN 100 PERCENT OF MY OWN."

The billionaire J. Paul Getty said this. He was talking about delegation. You can only do so much on your own. If you're successful, you'll ultimately get to the point where you're relying on other people's efforts. If you can build a team and get everyone to chip in, you'll go further. If not, you'll be micromanaging till you're blue in the face.

That very first time, I tied with another salesperson and the owner ripped the buck in half and we each got half a buck. We thought it was hilarious. See? It wasn't about the money.

"Get back to work!" they told us, and we did.

With the Reroute Pitch flowing from my lips and the exhortations of the bosses, I became a top salesman in three weeks. I was making something like $500 to $800 a week, not the piddling $250 to $400 they had promised.

I'm sure by now you've figured out that the products we sold *weren't* overstocks from a previous client's order. In fact, they weren't even brand-name toners, but generics. I knew that every time we picked up the phone, we were technically telling a lie to the people we were calling. But I rationalized it to myself by thinking of it this way: the generic toner worked just as well as the real ones, and customers were happy with their products because we got few complaints and cheerfully accepted all returns. We weren't telling the truth, but we were selling a decent product at a good price, and at the end of the day, nobody was getting hurt.

Besides, it wasn't my job to worry about the legalities. It was my job to sell.

One time I looked up from the cubicle while on a call and saw the sales manager looking at me. He was pulling down a thousand a week. *I'll have your job someday,* I thought.

And two months later, I *did*. The bosses loved me. I had a way of motivating the newbies, getting them to produce like no one had ever dreamed. I was like Alec Baldwin in that scene from *Glengarry Glen Ross*: "You know what it takes to sell real estate? It takes brass balls to sell real estate!"

The day I drove home in my new black 1975 Porsche 911S, Steve McQueen saw me and hailed me down. Came over to check out the car. He was such a car nut, *such* a car nut. He loved anything that had an engine: dirt bikes, planes, motorcycles, and Porsches. He walked around that machine and gave me a handshake.

He was *so* proud of me. "Congratulations, kid, you're doing great."

My father was over the moon. I was probably pulling in more monthly than he was at the time. He was devoting himself wholeheartedly to his craft, writing short stories, novels, screenplays, and magazine articles. He landed himself a literary agent and saw his first book published during this time. It was a hell of a book, a fast-paced, gritty thriller about a hit man with a heart of gold called, simply, *Skull*. In 1975, the *New York Times*'s crime fiction critic praised it as one of the best books of the year. "The writing is tough and earthy, and the book is not for the squeamish, but it is far better than the average," the paper wrote. (Another reviewer said if you wanted to know how to write sex scenes, you had to read *Skull*.)

On weekends, Brian and I would either travel with my parents to Vegas and other states to help them exhibit, buy, sell, and trade their guns and collectibles at various shows, or we'd handle them on our own. Brian and I fast became experts in gun collecting and developed our own collections over time. Brian swiftly became an expert in the field, and I still look to him for advice and expertise. He is a trained sniper who would proudly show you the penny he shot clean through at a hundred yards—scary! I'm passionate about guns, but I'm not a hunter. I always tell people that I could more easily shoot a two-hundred-pound man who was climbing in my window to rip me off than I could blow away Bambi. It's just not in me.

The gun shows started out a little shaky, but my father was a quick study. Pretty soon he and my mother had a wonderful business for themselves. For fun we'd hit the gaming tables and play blackjack.

I remember those days with great fondness, my father and mother in their prime, happy to be out with their sons after a hard day of pulling in cash at their shows. After all that, nothing could be better than eating a thick steak, winning at the blackjack table, and then, still dressed in your finest, catching a show.

This was my new world, my new reality. It was like I was living a scene out of a Martin Scorsese movie. Think *Casino* or *Goodfellas,* and picture me walking through the gaming tables in Vegas with a soundtrack blaring along to the tune of my life.

With the money I was pulling in, I bought my first piece of property, a beachside town house in Port Hueneme, near Ventura, California. It cost me $98,000. I actually didn't live there, because I chose to live at home in Malibu. But my brother moved into my town house when he first became a police officer in Santa Paula, California, before doing a lateral transfer to the Redondo Beach Police Department. I felt I had the best of both worlds. When Brian worked nights, I could have the place to myself. When my parents were out of town, I had *their* place to myself. If I wanted a romantic weekend with one of my girlfriends, I'd book a suite at the Hyatt House on Sunset Boulevard, below the Hollywood sign.

These were the great old *Almost Famous* days of rock 'n' roll, when the Hyatt became notorious for famous bands partying and tossing TVs out the windows. It wasn't unusual to see a rock star like Carlos Santana or Rod Stewart walking in and out of the lobby. My dates and I used to hang out at the Comedy Store next door, where we spent many a night watching the likes of David Letterman and newcomers like Jim Carrey, Jeff Foxworthy, and Andrew Dice Clay. Giants of comedy like Robin Williams and Richard Pryor dropped by on surprise visits to work on their new material. It was a wonderful place to take dates for dinner and a show. I sometimes wonder if I don't have to thank those great comedians for improving my closing ratio with the ladies.

My father's friend was the manager at the Hyatt at the time, and I'd be able to swing a beautiful $150 petite suite for a mere twenty dollars a night. When the mudslides hit Malibu, authorities closed the Pacific Coast Highway, making it impossible to drive down to my offices in Santa Monica. So I moved right into the Hyatt for about four weeks while workers repaired the highway. My employers covered the expenses, and I had the time of my life.

And why not live large? I'd just become a member of a club that would be familiar to many people today: people who sit in cubicles in giant rooms, grafted to headsets and autodialers, selling everything under the sun—copier toner, yes, but also stocks and bonds, real estate, dream vacations, vitamins, protein shakes, cars, and even pets. If you could craft the right pitch, you could sell anything, because people love hearing they're about to save money on something they most desire.

Congratulations to me. I had joined a boiler room.

WELL, of course, everything came crashing down and I experienced one of the worst summers of my life.

I was working for the bosses, turning over these sales like

crazy, when it dawned on me: I knew how to do this now. I could do this myself and keep all the money. A genius idea, and anyone in business would eventually think the same thing. One of the other sales guys convinced me to partner with him. We set up our own shop, and lured all the top salespeople by offering them better commissions. They all came running. I was nineteen years old, and this was my very first corporation.

Things looked good.

And then, one day in 1976, while I was driving around town, I realized that the same car was following me everywhere I went. The same white Toyota. This guy was everywhere. Following me to and from work. Parking outside my home at night. Even following me to lunch. I remember coming back to my car with a handful of burritos for my salespeople and seeing the car parked across the street.

"Hey," I yelled. "What the hell are you doing?"

He looked at me wide-eyed, rolled up his window, and zipped off.

That's when it hit me: I was being tailed by a private eye.

Later my attorney informed me that I was being sued for $1 million by my former employers. Well, sure I was: I'd lured away their entire sales force and I was beating them at their own game. I hadn't expected them to be happy with what I'd done, but I was still a little naïve. Then my partner was accused of stealing leads from our former employer.

Here I was, thinking I was pursuing the American dream, but really it was built on distrust and lies. I was ashamed. And embarrassed. This was not the way my parents had raised me.

I couldn't really take pride driving that flashy car around if I knew someone had good reason to ruin me.

I remembered what my father said when he caught me cheating at solitaire: if you can't do it honestly, there's no point in doing it. Dishonest business is ultimately unsustainable. You can't keep it up, because it always collapses on itself.

I don't know if you've ever been in a situation like that. My girlfriend Amelia and I were at the Hyatt House for a romantic weekend, and I had just found this all out. It was the worst weekend of my life. I didn't know how to handle it. I was just a kid. All night long, I lay in bed thinking, *What's going to happen to me? What if I had done it another way? How can I make amends?*

I got an idea.

I went into my former boss's office early that Monday morning and apologized. I asked him to hire me back. If he did, I'd bring all the salespeople with me.

I mentally crossed my fingers and waited. He bit.

I got about 90 percent of the sales force back. I negotiated a decent deal for myself, too. More money than I was making before, including ownership in the company. The owner even sprung for all my legal bills. As soon as we all started producing like the old days, I got a raise on top of *that*.

It seemed like all my troubles were over. Then, one day, I was summoned to the office of a federal postal inspector. The guy wore a gun on his hip, and leafed through a thick sheaf of federal documents on his desk and had me read them. I didn't quite understand them, but he was a good man, and patient.

"You're walking a thin line," he said.

What a shock—it turned out that the hallowed Reroute

Pitch danced uncomfortably close to fraud. Anytime you mail products sold as a result of a deceptive pitch, you commit mail fraud. If you've used the phone to make your pitch, you can tack on wire fraud.

Fantastic.

Admittedly, the federal codes were debatable. But still, the inspector said, if the feds felt like getting zealous, they could just shut us down. Or they wouldn't. It was all a matter of how a U.S. attorney read the statutes and how hard he or she felt like working.

At one point, telemarketing rooms were such a popular federal investigative priority that the local network news actually sent an undercover reporter to apply and be hired and trained by my staff. One day I got an intercom call from our receptionist that there were people with cameras outside our Venice, California, offices. Three minutes later, the camera crew and the female reporter were walking down the hallway to the salesrooms, asking for the owner. This was actually my "first time" on TV. If you had been watching, you would have seen me walking away to call my lawyer.

All of this scared me. At the time I was hearing of sleazy marketing tactics in other parts of the telemarketing industry—companies that were selling people empty packages or bilking seniors out of their last cents, all because they had answered the phone and gotten caught up in a salesman's enticing pitch. I made a decision. "To hell with this," I said. "I'm quitting."

Don't get me wrong. I loved the money and it was fun while it lasted, but I didn't want to live my life always looking over my shoulder. By now I was twenty-four years old, and rather than be scared about what came next, I felt confident that I would always be able to make decent money by starting businesses, testing them to see how well they performed, and making a decision about whether to continue operating them after a good chunk of data had come in.

For a while I helped develop and manage a company that sold nutritional products. My mom actually became one of my top independent distributors. I dabbled again in telemarketing, using my own pitch—a clean pitch—where we called people and asked about their business needs and told them about our products. I had as many as fifty salespeople working the phones and grossing close to $10 million in sales a year. I was beginning to see the value of the soft sell, of educating consumers and letting them arrive at the decision to buy on their own. I firmly believe that the best salespeople know how to let the customer sell themselves on a product. All the salesperson has to do is educate and excite them by saying as little as possible but *meaning* as much as possible. You create the sizzle and then "close" the deal. I did some motivational speaking at the time, too, sharing what I'd learned about salesmanship and living a healthy life.

BUFFERISM NO. 4

"BSC: BALLS, SKILL, CONFIDENCE."

BSC is my theory of life. You can do anything if you have these three things. Some people focus exclusively on skill—preparing, training, becoming professional. That's good, but don't neglect the other two. Beyond these three, you'll need luck and timing. But if you focus on BSC, that's a strong base to work from.

Outwardly, my life was back to awesome. I'd get up in the morning, stick my surfboard in my new Mercedes 560 SL convertible, and drive to work with the top down and the board sticking up in the front seat, buckled in beside me like a surfing executive. We'd shut the office at 1:00 p.m. and I'd go surfing. On weekends, I still worked with my family at collectors' shows. As I learned that business, I worked with my mom to promote my own SportsBuff Collectible Shows in Vegas and the Los Angeles area. Between the booth rentals and the entry fees we charged people to enter, we could gross upward of $100,000 on those shows in a weekend.

In the background of my life, however, simmering on a different track, was a family secret that was about to change my life forever.

4

SECRETS

E very family has its secrets, things that the adults never discuss with the kids and that you have to piece together for yourself as you get older. Our family was no different. When he was seventy years old, my father finally got a look at his real birth certificate and discovered that he was actually sixty-nine years old, not seventy as he believed. His father, the prizefighter Johnny Buff, had falsified my father's age when they were filling out his military enlistment papers. My father had spent his whole life thinking he was one year older.

There was only one reason my grandfather would have done this. My father had been running around with a tough crowd in New York City. At the age of thirteen or fourteen, he'd been kicked out of Catholic school for punching a priest. He punched the clergyman in the throat and sent him spilling down a flight of stairs. It was a nasty incident, but my father had become enraged when he saw one of his best friends being viciously disciplined by the priest.

It's hard to purge your record after pulling a stunt like that. My father was headed for trouble if he didn't clean up his act. While military service is not right for everyone, it was for my dad. He entered the military and became a stand-up guy.

My brother Brian and I were still coming up empty-handed every time we tried to piece together our family history. Every time we saw photos of John Lesky, aka Johnny Buff, he was depicted with a woman who was not our grandmother, and children who did not include my father. To top it off, we never got a chance to meet him. Johnny Buff had died in East Orange, New Jersey, in 1955 at the age of sixty-six, two years before I was born.

Brian and I wondered: Was our father Johnny Buff's illegitimate son? Or was he the product of a marriage that had ended in a quick divorce? We still don't know the answer to these questions, because my father was not the kind of man who took kindly to being interrogated.

He never told stories of his experiences in World War II. In fact, my father seemed to frown upon such tales. He kept a case that held all the medals he was awarded for his military service. Peeking into that case, seeing his Purple Heart, among others, was all I needed to imagine what he'd seen and experienced. He was a walking military historian and proud of his service. Unlike some veterans, he bore no ill will against his former combatants. His attitude was, "I served my country. You served yours. We should both be proud of that."

That was the world my dad inhabited. He wasn't one to

talk about personal stuff in his past. But when I was a young man, I was struggling to understand his past because so much of it was a mystery. I love old movies, especially those old films noir where characters played by guys like Humphrey Bogart try to sift through lies and deceit and long-buried skeletons in the closet. I had no idea that I was about to become that detective.

In 1987, when I was in my late twenties and running my telemarketing business and my SportsBuff gun and collectible shows, I was watching boxing matches on TV. More than anything, I couldn't help noticing the man announcing those fights. From time to time, they printed his name on the screen.

He was tall, handsome, and debonair. That tuxedo of his gave him a James Bond look.

Every time they flashed his name on the screen, I felt chills run through me.

The guy's name was Michael Buffer.

Now, big deal, you say. What's in a name? But you see, all of us have a sense of how common our names are. If your name is John Smith, you don't blink an eye when you meet another Smith. Dana White is not going to freak if a fan comes up to him, hysterically saying, "Dude, you're never gonna believe this! My last name is White, too!"

But in all my life I'd never met anyone named Buffer. Believe me, by the time I was in my mid-twenties I'd traveled enough, looked in plenty of phone books, and had always come up empty. And now my friends and everyone in my office were asking me, "Hey, is that boxing announcer guy your brother?"

At the time, Michael and I did share certain facial similarities. That and the name were enough to pique my interest.

From then on, whenever I got a chance, I'd make a point of watching the fights and paying special attention to Michael Buffer's mannerisms.

Every time, I'd get the same feeling in the pit of my stomach. *Something's going on,* I thought. *I don't know what it is.*

I didn't know how to bring this up with my parents, so I squelched it. Buried it. Tried to put it out of my mind. But that didn't work. If you liked the fights, as I did, you were going to keep seeing Michael Buffer.

A couple of years passed. I was taking a long road trip with my dad to check out some gun collections for his own collection or the business. We were having a great time, hanging out, talking our heads off about everything under the sun. My job, sports, the fights.

We were on a part of the drive where my father had the wheel. I figured, what the hell.

"You know," I said to him, "a lot of people have been saying that that fight announcer guy must be my brother. We look a little alike and we have the same last name."

My father was stone-faced.

"Isn't that funny?" I said, kind of hoping to lead him out but prepared to shut up now.

Silence.

The man who rarely talked about his past surprised the hell out of me. He looked away from the road and eyed me quietly for a second.

Thinking.

Then he looked back at the road.

Finally he said six words that changed my life: "I think that *is* your brother."

You gotta be fucking kidding me! I thought.

As we made our way north, he began to tell me his story. Once upon a time, he'd met a girl and fallen in love. They were young, and married hastily, the way so many young people of that generation did. My father went to war, and when he returned home he was greeted by his wife and his bouncing baby boy. But the marriage, which had come together in a hurry, fell apart. The young couple had split, and she'd taken their son.

From what I could decipher over the years, my father saw Michael last when the boy was two and a half years old. After that, my father never saw either the boy or his mother again. Shockingly, my mother had known all along about this relationship—and my father's firstborn son—but had never breathed a word of it to us.

Not just one but both of my parents had kept this secret from Brian and me.

I was stunned. I was glad that my father was driving or I probably would have driven us off the road.

How do you like that? I had another brother. He was out there in the world, on TV, making a name for himself. And he knew next to nothing about us.

"Would you ever want to meet him?" I asked my father.

He shrugged it off, suddenly awkward and uncomfortable. I knew the conversation had run into a brick wall.

But I didn't let it die. Together, my brother Brian and I pressed the issue. Sometime later, we had a more serious conversation with my father and he admitted that he had long wondered how his other son had turned out. He was proud of Michael's success, but he was torn. He didn't know if his son, who was now in his early forties, was interested in hearing from him after all these years.

"Don't worry about him," we told him. "Think about *you*. Are you open to meeting him?"

"Yes," he said.

I began working the phones to find out more about Michael. At one point I even called the offices of Don King, the great boxing promoter, to track down Michael. And one night a few months later, Michael was announcing a fight at the Country Club in Reseda, where they filmed the opening club scene in the film *Boogie Nights*. It's just over the hill from our home in Malibu. The show was live, and we were watching in my dad's home.

"Look," we told him, "he's here in town right now. Why don't you call him?"

We handed him the number of the venue.

My father got up and walked to the phone. A short time later he was talking with Michael, who was open to meeting him for lunch. I found out later that Michael had a refreshingly open attitude about the whole thing. A lot of people would have held a grudge after all that time. But not Michael. He probably figured, *Look, let me go meet the guy. If he's nice, great. I'll have two fathers: the man who raised me and my biological father. If I don't get along with Joe Buffer, no harm done. I never have to see the guy again.*

The two met for the first time at a restaurant in Century City. I'm happy to report that they got along very well—well enough to agree to a second meeting with the whole family. With Dad, Mom, Brian, and me.

We met one night at La Terraza, an Italian restaurant on Wilshire Boulevard. I was so excited going into the place. Besides the novelty of connecting at last with a long-lost sibling, I was a huge boxing fan and was starstruck by the guy's charisma and the coolness of his job. We got along tremendously, and

Michael told us that his mom had died when he was still young, and he'd been raised by a foster family for much of his life but had never been formally adopted. Luckily his last name had never been formally changed, or we would never have found him.

It was a further thrill for him, a fight announcer, to discover that the fights ran in his blood. Had my father not reconnected with him, Michael would have gone his whole life not knowing that he was the grandson of a prizefighter and the son of a man who boxed in the military. How it is that he was drawn into this particular profession is one of the great mysteries of life. He'd served in the Army during the Vietnam War. Afterward, he became a professional model and even sold cars. Somehow, one thing led to another, and through his passion for the sport, he became a boxing ring announcer.

The three of us—Michael, Brian, and me—became friends. Every time I watched him, I started to have a new feeling deep down, a feeling I never expressed to anyone. As a young man I had never wanted to be a professional fighter, but I had trained hard like one. But announcing in the ring seemed like a great way to connect with the sport in a way that called upon the traits that I knew I had inside me. A strong voice. An ability to connect with people. And passion for fights.

I wish I could do what Michael does, I thought. *I wish I could be an announcer.*

At the time, it was one of those crazy wishes you make that you don't think will ever come true, and I buried the feeling. Besides, the closer I got to Michael, the more I learned about his career. Yes, it was an amazing job. He got to travel all over the world. He got to hang out with tremendous athletes who regarded him as a classy icon of the sport. And since he was such a good-looking guy, I'm sure beautiful women desired him every time he walked into a room. And let's not forget the fact that his catchphrase drove audiences wild and had become synonymous with the start of every boxing event. Even if you didn't know Michael's name, you knew boxing just wasn't the same without the handsome guy in the tux roaring, "Let's Get Ready to Rumble!"

But the truth was, fight announcers just weren't paid well in those days. In order to make a living announcing full-time, Michael did a large number of events and was traveling almost every week. He made good money, but he'd never had a million-dollar year yet.

Michael and I got to talking about this. For a young man, I was a very successful businessman. I was driving great cars, living on the beach, dating wonderful women, and pulling down six figures a year. Okay, so I hadn't had my own million-dollar year yet, either, but I'd proved my ability to sell my products and myself. A while back, Michael had had the notion to trademark his catchphrase, and had even hired an attorney to handle it for him. The trademark didn't go nearly as far as it had to in order to protect his intellectual property. On top of that, Michael was not actively trying to market it in any way, and no one was pushing him to do so or asking to do so for him. Selling himself was not something Michael felt comfortable doing.

I thought maybe I'd be able to help, but I didn't want to jump in with both feet. If I started telling him what to do, maybe I'd hurt the relationship that was still growing. And I was probably intelligent enough to know that I still needed to learn a lot more about the sports and entertainment industry before I tried my hand at managing someone's career. In Los

Angeles, everyone gets this idea that they can manage people. God knows, there are many people out there who *need* managing, and if you have any business sense at all, it occurs to you, *Hey, I should take someone under my wing and see if I can make us both some money.*

So it wasn't a far-fetched thing.

It just wasn't time.

Then one night I drove to Vegas with Mom, Dad, and Brian to catch the Evander Holyfield–vs.–Riddick Bowe fight at the Thomas and Mack Center in Las Vegas. Michael was announcing. The date was November 13, 1992. It turned out to be a pivotal night for Holyfield, the first time he lost to anyone in his career.

It turned out to be pivotal for me as well. I was sitting in my seat watching Michael announce live.

"LET'S GET READY TO RUMMMMMMBBBBBBLLLLLLE!"

The sound of the crowd flowed over me like a wave. It was so deafening, so powerful, so filled with freaking potential that I could barely concentrate on the fight.

Suddenly my mind was filled with ideas. One after another after another. I could not stop thinking where Michael's career could go. It suddenly seemed so clear to me that it was possible to harness his fame and push it beyond the squared ring of boxing. Michael was not *just* a ring announcer. I wanted to establish him as the world's most renowned *sports* and *entertainment* announcer—that was my goal.

If you could somehow build on that, you could—if you were smart—create a ripple effect to other financially rewarding opportunities.

After the fight, I rushed back to my hotel room and started pouring out my thoughts onto a legal pad. Page after page after page.

In a flash I had seen what kept so many announcers from making it big. They were trapped. They had booming, powerful voices that they didn't know what to do with.

But I did.

Not long after, we talked and I laid it all out for him.

"I want to make you richer and more famous than you've ever dreamed. You give me a chance to manage you, and you'll have more chances to announce than ever, in all forms of sports and entertainment. All we need to do is put together a little seed money, sign some papers, and I'm ready to go to work."

BUFFERISM NO. 5

"STOP DREAMING—TAKE ACTION."

Only 2 percent of the world's dreamers successfully put their thoughts into action and achieve their goals. They become leaders and top earners. The other 98 percent keep dreaming. Think like the minority.

I also conveyed that after I made him rich, I wanted to fulfill my dream of being an announcer, too.

It was out! I had just uttered my secret dream . . .

"There's no money in it, and I'm probably the only one making a full-time living from it!" Michael told me. "What have I been telling you?"

"Hey, no worries," I said. We agreed that it was a conflict of interest for me to announce boxing. I agreed then and there that I would never announce boxing without his blessing—a pledge I have never broken. I knew in my heart that someday something would come along that would be a perfect entertainment arena for me to fulfill my dream.

5

SELLING THE VOICE

Now that I had Michael on board, I took my parents out to a nice dinner and told them my plans. They were fascinated but worried about what I was proposing. The biggest thing on their minds? I was earning six figures a year at the time. If I divested myself of all my businesses to focus on Michael, wouldn't I be shooting myself in the foot? If I was making this much money, why would I ever jeopardize it?

If anyone could understand why I wanted to do this, it was my father. After all, here was a man who had quit his VP job to chase a dream as a writer. But even he was confused.

"How are you going to do it?" my father said, unaware that he was echoing Michael's own words.

"Trust me," I said. "Believe in me. And I'll make it happen."

I definitely had a lot on the line. I had a beach house with a $5,000-a-month mortgage. I was rolling the dice with just the money in the bank and a dream. But I had started enough businesses to know how easy it was to make a comeback. I just basically said fuck it, let's *do* this . . .

It would not be easy, but I was working from a few basic principles that are obvious to anyone who had ever run a business: If you're good at selling, you can sell anything. In my life, I've launched companies that sold everything from home and business security systems to water filtration systems, clothing apparel, direct-mail solutions for businesses, and of course telemarketing companies that sold products to individuals and businesses. One of my mantras has always been *All business is the same; only the products are different.* If I could sell toner and nutritional supplements, I could certainly sell my brother's voice. I just had to convince customers why they would want to pay to license such a thing.

To me it was obvious. Michael's image was known to millions of people who followed boxing, but the catchphrase was elastic enough to apply to almost any other sport, event, or product. When people heard "Let's Get Ready to Rumble," they thought things like, "Let's get down!" "Let's party!" "Let's rock and roll!" "Start your engines!" There was something infectious and fun and exciting about the phrase and Michael's delivery. It seemed to apply to everything in life—not just fighting. I saw it as a clarion call to the competitive spirit. It seemed logical to me that if a company wanted to evoke those kinds of feelings in their patrons, customers, and fans, they'd want to use Michael's line.

I would need some help locking down Michael's trademark, so I hired a lawyer and put him to work making sure that Michael had the strongest possible protection under the law. Then I designed a promotional kit, a little folder with tons of information about Michael and what we were offering, and had copies printed for about thirteen dollars a pop. That wasn't cheap in 1994 dollars. At the beginning I didn't have much money to play with, so I worked alone out of my home office, doing everything from packing boxes to cold-calling.

One day I flew to New York to attend a licensing trade show, and I walked the floor with those promo kits under my arm. I had never done anything like this before, and I wasn't even sure what I was looking for. I just thought, *When I see something that fits, I'll know it.* If anyone seemed like they might be a good fit, I'd walk up to them and go into my pitch.

I got three types of responses:

"I see that guy all the time when I watch the fights!"

"Hey, yeah, I don't watch boxing, but I've heard of that line!"

"Michael who?"

I was deliberately soft-sell. If they hadn't heard of Michael, I didn't want to push the explanation; too much explanation always puts you at a point of weakness. I educated them just enough to start thinking about the phrase. Then, some weekend, when they were sitting at home and heard Michael say the phrase on TV, they'd make the connection and suddenly get a "brilliant" idea. And I'd get a call from them the following Monday. There's an old saying in Hollywood that Michael and I both agreed with: If it's not their idea, it's not going to happen. That was exactly my mentality.

I was tenacious. If I read a boxing magazine and saw an ad for some kind of apparel or nutritional drink, I put them on my list. If I saw a company mentioned in the business section of the *Los Angeles Times,* on the list they went. I'd prowl the aisles at the local Toys"R"Us or Spencer's Gifts, looking for toys and little gadgets that might be a good fit for Michael's brand. I'd flip the packaging over and make a note of the companies I liked. Everything went on my list, and then I'd get back to the office and start researching the companies. These were the pre-Internet days, so I often had to do my homework by making a few calls or running out to the library to look them up in the business directories. But eventually it all came down to picking up the phone and making that call.

My first hit was with a little company called Funomenon. They had some nice gift-shop novelties. I liked them because their products were so inexpensive that people of any income level could buy them. Funomenon loved the idea of doing a Michael Buffer key chain and coffee mug. You press a button on a little plastic microphone and it screams at the top of its electronic lungs. Ditto for the coffee mug.

As soon as I had dozens of those samples in my office, I was no longer selling from an empty shelf. Anyone who does sales will tell you that sometimes people suffer from a lack of imagination. If they can't picture what you're trying to sell them, they won't buy it. But what's more memorable than a key chain that sounds like Michael Buffer?

Eventually I was able to persuade the merchandising people at World Championship Wrestling to use Michael in their licensing and merchandising of WCW products. We agreed to licenses for action figures, an electronic wrestling ring, and a WCW Thumb Wrestling toy implanted with audio voice chips of Michael's voice, among other products. Their sales were huge. But then the big one hit.

I'd been a big video game player since the days of Pong and Space Invaders. I was crazy for the stuff. I pitched a few companies, but they all wanted to pay a flat fee up front and go their merry way. That didn't sit well with me. I remembered the story of how Sylvester Stallone turned down multiple offers to buy his script to *Rocky* because he wanted to star in it and to own a piece of the movie.

10 TIPS FOR STARTING YOUR OWN BUSINESS

1. Be an "OPMer"—invest with other people's money (OPM).
2. Keep it legal!
3. Check out the competition and incorporate their success formulas into your own.
4. Teach your employees by example. Be the best, and teach them how to teach others.
5. The secret of success is delegation. You can't do it all yourself.
6. Have PASSION for what you do, or don't do it.
7. Building your own business is not work, it's a lifestyle. Enjoy it!
8. Do NOT sleep with your employees.
9. "Fake it till you make it." You can look and feel successful without lying.
10. Winners concentrate on winning. Losers concentrate on getting by. Be a winner!

That got me thinking: *If I sell people the rights to Michael's likeness and voice, we'll get a little money now and we'll never see much more than that. How can I get on the inside? How can I position Michael to become essential to a video game and become his own brand-name game?*

I envisioned a Let's Get Ready to Rumble video game, and shared the concept with everyone I talked to. The game ought to have fictional boxing characters with funny names mixing it up in a ring with a Michael-like character calling the fights. The game should use a name that was a play on Let's Get Ready to Rumble. Above all, our company had to own a piece of the profits. Otherwise, we couldn't do the deal. Midway, the company known for Mortal Kombat, made us an offer on those terms.

Ready 2 Rumble Boxing was released in 1999, bundled with the new Dreamcast video game console along with nine other Dreamcast video games. The reception was huge. How huge? Within the first twenty-four hours, the Dreamcast console and its ten video games racked up $97.5 million in sales. *Variety* magazine noted that this package set a new record in Hollywood history, racking up the most sales of an entertainment product in a twenty-four-hour period ever.

It was a huge success for me, the biggest mark I'd made in my business career up to that point. One day, our first royalty check from Midway arrived at the offices of the Buffer Partnership. Kristen, my vice president, opened the right side of the envelope and pulled out the check *s l o w l y . . .*

First we saw five numbers: 168.40.

Then we saw an 8.

Then a 2.

I thought, *This is great! We just made $28,000!*

That would certainly be a nice chunk of change for our first video game endeavor.

Kristen whipped the rest of the check out of the envelope. At the head of all these numbers was the number 6.

"Oh my God," she said. "It's for $628,000!"

The two of us were jumping up and down in the office. It was a long while before we were calm enough to phone Michael.

Later I realized what a tremendous accomplishment this was. To my knowledge, no one had ever taken someone's voice and trademarked phrase and sold it so successfully and so profitably. If I had not taken this shot, it probably would never have happened, because no other manager would have seen the potential and taken on a fight announcer as a client. No other manager in Los Angeles would have seen the potential. In fact, a number of Hollywood people cautioned me that it was a bad idea to take on just one client. It only worked if your client was a superstar. One of these naysayers was Michael's own attorney, who told me that he himself would not be able to survive representing just one client like Michael. It seemed clear to all the players in Hollywood: If you wanted to earn a healthy six-figure income and set yourself up in the good life in L.A., you could not bank on one client.

This only made me hungrier for the success I had envisioned. My response to the naysayers? "I will blow you all away!"

But I was no ordinary manager. I was connected to Michael by a bond stronger than the contract we'd signed. I knew my parents and Brian were watching me, too. I could not allow myself to fail. I was acting out of passion, out of love of family, and out of the conviction that I could make his voice and catch-phrase a part of American culture.

That was just the beginning. We also started making money from various court settlements for copyright and trademark infringements. I don't like to dwell on it because so much of what goes on in such matters is acrimonious. Everyone feels bad, everyone feels embarrassed. But let's put it this way: If you have a trademark or copyright, it's your duty to defend it. If someone uses it in violation, you have to call them on it or you're setting up a dangerous precedent where you're allowing people to abuse your rights. So we let it be known that we would pay a reward to anyone who informed us of infringements, and we started getting calls almost immediately.

A company called Tommy Boy Records had licensed the right to add Michael's voice saying "Let's Get Ready to Rumble" as the opening track of an album of theirs called Jock Jams. You can still pick it up. Michael's voice is the first track on the album, running twenty-five seconds. We thought it was a great honor to be the first track, sort of kicking things off, so to speak.

As soon as that album came out, everyone, from DJs to TV sports shows, was playing that track to kick off games and their drive-time morning radio shows. At the beginning, when we were still operating on a shoestring budget, I did a lot of the trademark enforcement on my own, without an attorney. I'd call TV networks, radio stations, and others and say, "Look, you may not realize this, but that track is formally protected by trademark. You need to license it separately from the album."

And they'd say, "But we *paid* to license the performance rights to this album." And I'd say, "Read your contract again." I purposely did not give Tommy Boy the rights to license that track. And I purposely did not register the track with BMI, ASCAP, or any of the other organizations that ordinarily collect and pay royalties for public performances of songs. I knew that if I had gone that route, the phrase would have been played without my control and it would have had its fifteen minutes of fame and died like so many other catchphrases, such as "Where's the Beef" or "Three-Peat." I knew early on that I had to act to protect *Rumble* from just such a fate.

If people wanted to play Michael's track publicly, they had to make a separate deal with us. Football franchises, for example, routinely licensed the rights to play a recording of Michael twice per game—at kickoff and halftime.

Most people were agreeable about it, but occasionally we'd get producers who arrogantly insisted that they had the right to do whatever they wanted simply because they had bought a ten-dollar compact disc, and because they were used to getting their way.

Next thing you know, I was dropping off my clothes at the dry cleaner's and the man behind the counter said, "Hey, your brother was on the Don Imus radio show this morning!"

I sent Imus a letter asking him to please stop using Michael's catchphrase until he'd worked out a license deal with us. As was typical of Don, he went on the air and announced that he'd just gotten a stupid letter from some jerk named Bruce Buffer. Then he proceeded to play Michael's phrase, saying afterward, "Oops, I guess I shouldn't do that." I had our attorney, Mark E. Kalmansohn, draft a complaint for Federal court and send it to Imus, stating that if he did not stop his infringement, a lawsuit would be filed to protect our trademark rights.

One morning just days later, I got an early-morning freakout call from Michael, who was in New York City on business. He had just opened his *USA Today* newspaper and read that Infinity Broadcasting, the CBS subsidiary that owned the Imus show, was suing Michael Buffer over the right to use our trademark and recording. If they won such a suit, it could result in releasing the phrase (and even the recording) into the public domain, where it could be used by anyone who wanted to use it.

"What the hell is going on?" Michael demanded. "Did you know this was going on?"

"I'm on it," I said.

Well, I have to say that this was scary for us. We didn't have the kind of money to be involved in a lawsuit with CBS. I had to decide: Do I cave? Or do I fight?

If I didn't fight, people would just assume they could push us around because, let's face it, people are accustomed to pushing around talent in Hollywood. The average person assumes that performers have all the control and power. That's not true. Artists—actors, performers, musicians—are the lowest people on the totem pole. In the eyes of the power brokers, they are dispensable, interchangeable. It they don't play ball, the power brokers just move on to someone who will.

It was David-and-Goliath time. I asked our lawyer to file our own lawsuit claiming infringement by CBS and Infinity Broadcasting. He wrote it up on the very afternoon Michael called me, and filed it the next day. Lo and behold, within forty-eight hours one of the largest media corporations in the world offered us a settlement and dropped their countersuit. That caught the eye of *Variety* and *The Hollywood Reporter,* which began covering these lawsuits because, for some reason, they considered it to be so unusual that a fight announcer should have a marketable property. Imagine that.

We've been involved now with 300 to 400 matters where we have pressed claims of infringement. The vast majority of those start and end with a letter or two: Please stop doing this; contact us if you want to *license* it. We've only had to file a dozen or so lawsuits, and most of those have been settled quickly by the other side. I'm not out to ruin anyone. I just want to protect our trademark. There's a bright side to this: if people are stealing something, it's a sign of how popular it is. If people *stopped* stealing Michael's phrase, that would be a sign that perhaps the phrase's time in the sun had waned. Thankfully, he and his phrase are still extremely popular all over the world.

The best stories we have about Michael's catchphrase have nothing to do with violations by big media corporations or hot-headed DJs. They have to do with ordinary people who reach out to us with a special request: What's it going to cost to play this at my son's or daughter's bar/bat mitzvah, or my wedding?

One wealthy gentleman hired Michael to fly to his wife's birthday party. Michael hid behind a curtain, and the guy said to his wife, "Hey, honey, remember that man on TV that you enjoy so much?" And then out came Michael to announce her birthday. The woman got a kick out of it, her husband looked like a prince, and Michael collected a few bucks.

Amazing.

Another time, Michael was hired to visit a megachurch. There he was, walking out in front of a huge congregation of people dressed in their Sunday best to announce the pastor, and none other than Jesus Christ!

Hallelujah, indeed.

Within five years I had made a lot of Michael's dreams come true. We started that business with a $5,000 check from each of us, and we never had to put in a dime financially after that. I'd helped make my brother a rich man and cemented his place as the best-known sports and entertainment announcer on the planet.

It was time for me to make good on the second promise I made the day we clinched our deal. A promise to myself.

6

TAP OUT

"Tap," he said.

I was about thirty-five seconds into a sparring session with a skinny Brazilian kid I'd never heard of. He was on top of me, cradling my head while forcing my own arm against my throat so I could not breathe. It's called a side choke, and it's pretty effective. I felt myself slipping out of consciousness. So did he.

"Tap," he repeated. "If you don't tap out, you're going to pass out."

There was no use keeping up the charade. A smart fighter needs to know when he's beat. If you don't know your limits, you have nothing to shoot for in your training. If you pretend you don't have any limits, if you try to stick it out just a little bit longer, you can get seriously hurt because your opponent has no choice but to escalate the fight to the next reasonable level. Like knocking you out or choking you to the point of unconsciousness.

I patted the mat with my fingers.

It was 1991, a few years before Michael and I cemented our business partnership. I had recently relegated myself to a training regimen of gym work and light sparring. When I was a kid, I learned to box, and went on to earn a black belt in Tang Soo Do, and dabbled in a couple of other martial arts, trying to build my repertoire. I'd fallen in love with kickboxing and had committed to training and sparring in that one sport multiple times a week for many years. But the demands of business had sidetracked me. I was happy with the way my career was going, but I hated losing time in the gym. To make it worse, I was getting older, and taking on crazy sparring sessions just to convince myself that I still had it.

One day I had a sparring match with a guy who had about twenty-five pounds on me. I won the match, but incurred a concussion in the process. The next morning I woke up with blurred vision and I was slurring my words. I went to the doctor that afternoon.

"Do you fight for a living?" the doctor asked, frowning.

"No," I said.

"Then stop," the doctor said.

"What—why?" I'd been sparring weekly for the past seven years. Though the dream was dimming, my image of myself as a person who worked out by sparring was still pretty strong.

"That slurring of words you did this morning . . . you're how old now? Thirty-two? Well, if you keep this up, when you're forty-five it's gonna be a lot worse. Let me ask you again—do you make any money off this?"

"No. I'm a businessman. I do this to stay in fighting shape and because I love it."

He was incredulous. "Love?" he scoffed. "Work out another way."

He was right. If you don't intend to fight for a living, you probably shouldn't be going toe-to-toe in the ring on a weekly basis—especially when you have family members depending on your brainpower. I had my business with Michael and the business with my parents to consider. I wouldn't be able to do either of those jobs if I got seriously hurt. And let's face it, no one wants to be slurring their words when they're sober. So I reluctantly ended my sparring sessions and transitioned over to circuit and weight-training workouts, surfing, beach runs, and various other regimens that kept me in shape.

A family friend, John Milius, called around this time. John is a film producer, director, and Hollywood screenwriter best known for *Apocalypse Now, Big Wednesday, Red Dawn,* and *Conan the Barbarian.* He and my father went way back, and connected through their various passions: writing, movies, boxing, martial arts, guns, guns, and guns. John was younger than Dad, about the same age as my brother Michael. John's a big, strong guy with a beard and sunglasses, and he's something of a legend in Hollywood, even among people who don't adore weaponry. He's said to have inspired John Goodman's gun-toting character Walter in the Coen brothers' hilarious film *The Big Lebowski.*

John loved my mother's cooking and used to come over our house for brunch on weekends. He used to regale all of us with his stories of guns, wars, and movies. He used to invite me over to his offices at Sony Studios on Friday nights, where he'd treat his staff and stuntmen to beer and pizza. One time we went shooting deep in the canyons of Malibu. He took me and a friend out into the middle of nowhere, and popped his trunk, which was just loaded with a variety of weapons. We fired off a ton of rounds and called it a day. It was a highly therapeutic way to blow off steam, and I'd do it myself on my own from time to time—until I realized that I was unwittingly going shooting alone in a canyon where some bodies had reportedly been found. I stopped going real quick, let me tell you.

So, back when John phoned me, he'd been training in Brazilian jiu-jitsu at a fascinating dojo in Torrance. "Bruce," he said, "you gotta come out here and meet these guys. They do a different kind of jiu-jitsu. Submission stuff."

The Gracie Jiu-Jitsu Academy opened its doors in Torrance, California, in 1989. You could call the Gracie family the Kennedys of Brazilian jiu-jitsu, with the ironic observation that the Gracies tend to get hurt less. The family patriarch, Helio Gracie, along with his brother Carlos, perfected their distinctive brand of jiu-jitsu throughout the 1930s and 1940s. The Gracie style of jiu-jitsu relied less on brute strength than on working as efficiently as possible in every fight to force an opponent to tap out. Helio's four sons left Rio de Janeiro for Southern California in the late 1980s, with the goal of introducing Gracie jiu-jitsu to an American audience.

At this point, UFC 1 was still more than a year off in the future. The term *mixed martial arts* had not yet even been coined.

I drove out to the family's dojo with John. One of Helio's sons was training in the gym at the time, and came over to introduce himself.

His name was Royce.

As soon as John told him that I was an avid martial artist and kickboxer, Royce invited me to do some sparring with him. It was an odd request. He was six-foot-one, about 175 pounds, and didn't look to be terribly muscled under his *gi*. I was burly and strong, and had several pounds on him. I was a powerhouse. But what the hell. I agreed.

He led me to a private, padded room, closed the door, and said, "I want you to come at me with all you've got."

"You're sure?" I said. "We're not holding back?"

"No—go all out. I want you to take my head off."

I went at him like an animal. Thirty seconds later, this guy had me bent like a pretzel on the mat. I was sweating like a pig, and he was slowly closing off the air to my lungs.

Hence the tap.

He loosened his grip and rolled off me.

"See," Royce said, straightening his *gi*, "isn't it nice not to get hit in the face?"

"You know what," I said, my eyes refocusing, "it sure as heck is."

BUFFERISM NO. 6

"WARRIOR SPIRIT FOREVER!"

What does a warrior do? He fights to his last breath. When he's knocked down, he gets up and tries to win the war with whatever it takes, until he's dead, physically or mentally. I approach everything I do with that same warrior spirit. It's the only way to live. Otherwise, what's the point?

I didn't know it that day, of course, but all four of the Gracie brothers would become MMA legends and instrumental in the birth of the UFC. The youngest kid, the one who'd mopped the mat with me, would become the tournament winner of UFC 1, UFC 2, and UFC 4, and fought to a draw with Ken Shamrock in the championship match in the UFC 5's Superfight. And my dad's friend, John Milius, would be credited with helping to design—along with Rorion Gracie—the Octagon itself. Actually, and this shows you the kind of guy Milius is, he wanted the Octagon to be surrounded by a moat filled with dangerous fish.

The sport I encountered that day in Torrance was different from anything I'd ever seen. What Royce threw at me upended everything I knew about fighting. I'd rushed to a doctor the other day because I'd fought a guy I shouldn't have, a guy who was way out of my weight class. But Royce had taken on a trained man, me, who was bigger than he was, and he'd kicked that man's ass. For all the two decades I'd spent practicing Tang Soo Do, judo, tae kwon do, and kickboxing, the only way I could save myself in this sparring match was to tap out. Were Royce or any of the brothers Gracie to challenge me in a street fight, I would be at the mercy of passersby to notify the police.

That's not a good feeling, but it taught me something. These guys were thinking about fighting in a whole new way. They were like the genius number-cruncher in the book and film *Moneyball* who realizes that the only thing that matters is scoring runs.

In the fight world, the rest of us were thinking of beating our opponents through brute strength and careful strategy. The Gracies threw brute strength out the window. When they fought, they were thinking of one thing only: *How fast can I get this guy in a choke and get him to tap out?* The Gracies had turned fighting upside down. They'd shown that it was possible for little guys to beat monsters, for fighters of different skill sets to match wits with each other in the ring.

• • •

THE first time I watched a UFC bout on TV, I was floored. Say what you will about the uneven matchups of those early fights—the sumo wrestler getting pounded by a French savate-trained kickboxer, or the wrestler getting his ass handed to him by the karate practitioner—you could not deny that it was tremendous spectacle.

Now, granted, if the sport was going to survive, it had to rise above mere spectacle. But for now I couldn't look away, and neither could anyone else. The UFC looked like one of the most exciting sporting events to come down the pike in a long time. I couldn't *not* get Michael a gig with the organization. That kind of exposure would expose him to a different sort of fan, and who knew where that could lead?

So I called the organization, made my pitch, and landed Michael the most lucrative per-show contract he'd seen until that time, with the exception of the WCW. With Michael locked into a three-fight deal starting with UFC 6, we packed our bags one night in July 1995 and headed for the first UFC we would ever attend, in Casper, Wyoming. Those were the days of the great UFC Tournaments, where fighters could fight up to three times in a single night, depending on how well they were doing. This marked the debut of Tank Abbott, who fought his way through the quarters and semifinals, only to lose by submission to the Russian Oleg Taktarov. Tank and I didn't know each other at the time. We would soon become friends. At the time he looked like one of the most formidable fighting monsters I had ever seen in my life.

It was a great night for Michael, who was introducing himself to a whole new crowd of fans. But come Monday, the hammer fell. I got a call from my contacts at the WCW. They hadn't really minded when Michael took on the UFC gigs, and his contracts with them certainly didn't prevent him from doing the UFC shows. But they were unhappy with the words he'd been given to say at those UFC bouts:

"If it's not in the Octagon, it's not real!"

If you watched and loved the UFC, you knew exactly how true those words were. To the WCW, they felt like a particularly stinging dig, because in 1995 the pro wrestling world wanted people to think that what they were watching was real. When people saw Hulk Hogan pound someone twenty-five times in the head, the audience was supposed to think, *Oh my God, that guy's dead meat! He's gonna die!* Well, folks, no, he's not; you're watching a stunt performance.

I thought that the UFC was the most skilled no-holds-barred fighting you were ever going to be allowed to see. But the WCW was wildly popular at the time. Between Michael's fight appearances and his Ready to Rumble merchandise that the WCW sold, the WCW was Michael's largest source of income. We couldn't afford to jeopardize it. The decision was obvious. I told them that Michael would fulfill his three-fight deal with the UFC but decline further offers.

I realized that this might be *my* chance to try my hand at the UFC. At the time, I had announced only one fight. It was an MMA/kickboxing event named "Clash of the Dragons," held in Kellogg, Michigan, in February 1995. I'll never forget that day. During the undercards, Michael got in the ring and announced to the crowd that he was bringing up his "friend, manager, and brother to announce this kickboxing bout." Before the show started, he and I had hashed out which fight I would announce. I wore a tuxedo for the occasion. I thought I did a good job, but after I announced the winner, the victor came up to me and said, "Thank you, but I've been waiting two months to hear Michael Buffer announce my name . . ."

Oh well. You can't please everyone.

But I didn't want to be a moonlighting announcer. If I was going to announce, I would play for keeps. I would land a good gig and pursue it full-time. And to avoid jeopardizing anything Michael had already carved out for himself, I'd make sure that I stuck to my own little corner of the fight industry.

I just needed to find some takers.

So I started pitching myself to Robert Meyrowitz, who was the owner of the UFC franchise back then. I laid out all my credentials. I knew the sport. I'd connected with it from the very beginning, through John Milius. I knew all the fighters and their records. I'd announced one fight and had enjoyed working with the power of my voice. I had done tons of motivational speaking. I was comfortable in front of crowds. Hell, I had even gotten my ass kicked by Royce.

"How about it, Bob?" I said. "Why don't you give me a shot? You should have a Buffer in the Octagon. And if you get me in the organization, I'll use all my marketing knowledge and media contacts to help you get publicity." I knew that my contacts could help build the UFC into one of the biggest mainstream events in sports and entertainment. It was clear to me that the UFC could potentially go there.

Bob, a good man whom I liked and respected, wasn't buying it. My pleas fell on deaf ears.

As it happened, around this time I had decided to accept an offer to manage a 340-pound monster from Minnesota named

Scott "The Pit Bull" Ferrozzo. I liked Scott's initiative. He had sent me a videotape and résumé, and had asked me to help him realize his dream of fighting in the UFC. Scott was going to fight in UFC 8. I called Bob and said, "Listen. I'm coming down to Puerto Rico for the fight with my fighter. I'm packing my tux. Give me a shot. Let me announce the preliminaries."

Bob was busy as usual, and I had worn him down just enough to get to *yes*. "Yeah, sure," he said. "Let's talk the night before the show, and I'm sure it'll be okay."

I went to the prefight party on Friday night and bugged him again. He was into it. Why not? If I botched it, he could brush me off better the next time. "I said I would give you a shot," he said. "So go. Go for it."

The next day was the first and only time I was nervous before announcing. Rich "G-Man" Goins was the announcer at the time, and he helped me get all set up. I went on and announced in front of 13,000 people and 160,000 pay-per-view takers.

I had a blast, and I thought, *They're going to call me for the next one. Just watch.* Well, they didn't. I was in New York City a couple of times to negotiate deals for Michael, and I'd always phone Bob at his office and say, "How about drinks? How about lunch?"

Nothing.

Then, one afternoon, I'm in the hospital visiting my mother, who's having a gallbladder operation. Serious stuff. My mobile phone rings and it's Bob's right-hand man. "Uh, hi, Bruce?" he says. "Rich Goins's uncle passed away and he's got to go to the funeral. Can you be in Birmingham, Alabama, to announce UFC 10? Are you free in two days?"

I said, "My mom's in the hospital, guys. I'm not prepared for this. I'll call you back."

I hung up the phone and looked at my mom and Brian. It was like something out of *Rocky*. I told them what had happened. My mom looked at me like Talia Shire, the actress who played Rocky's wife, put her finger in the air, and said, "You gotta go. Go! Go!"

BUFFERISM NO. 7

"WHY NOT LOVE TODAY, AS YOU MAY NOT TOMORROW."

I use this to remind myself to seize the day. Life's short, so why would you ever want to put off what's going to benefit you or make you happy in life? Don't miss your chance to fall in love with a job, a business opportunity, a woman, or a special family experience. The window of love is only open for a short time—don't miss it.

So I packed the tux and went down and did the entire show. I gave my all. But lo and behold, I got no phone call after that. *What is it with these guys?* I thought.

The thing is, I knew I could do the job. I'm a big believer in visualization as a way of bringing about success. I had already seen myself in action a thousand times in my head, dreaming of announcing in the Octagon. And I was confident that I had a big voice. And now I had seen myself in action at the UFC. I just needed to perfect my own distinctive style. The last thing

I ever wanted to do was copy Michael and come across like a Frank Sinatra Jr., the younger guy trailing after the success of the better-known performer.

Even though I hadn't done much announcing, I knew how to project my voice. I'd learned from the best: my father. Joe Buffer had a strong voice, even better than Michael's, and Michael had once admitted as much, saying, "Pop has the best pipes of all of us." When Joe Buffer spoke, I listened. My father only hit me twice in my life. He apologized with tears in his eyes afterward. But his voice carried enough discipline to send chills down my spine. If he was mad, he could assemble a string of words in such a way that it was absolutely horrifying. His verbal discipline always drove the point home better than any whipping could have. The man could scare the pope.

He was, after all, a former Marine drill instructor who could intimidate men who were bigger and stronger than himself. He always said that your voice is your most important tool. And if he ever asked me a question that I answered weakly, he'd yell, *"Pro-ject! Pro-ject your voice!"* His training came back to me when I ran those telemarketing rooms, and I had to connect with people fifty feet away, across the boiler room.

I figured that if I had to learn to announce better, I would. It was only a matter of time. But after UFC 10 came and went, I ended up watching UFC 11 at home on the TV. No call. I was like a girl waiting for a date to the prom.

But here's how I gained some leverage on the situation. One day I got a call from Robert Meyrowitz, who said he'd been contacted by the producers of the hit TV show *Friends*. They were doing a UFC-themed show and had written their script to include the voice-over of a UFC announcer. But now they had changed their minds; they wanted the real announcer, in the flesh, to appear on camera. Rehearsals began tomorrow, so whoever was doing the gig had to be on the Warner Bros. studio lot in Burbank, California, the very next morning. I was the perfect man for the job, since I lived in L.A. How did I feel about representing the UFC in that way? How could I say no? *Friends* was the top-rated comedy at the time. During the call with Bob, I agreed to do it but requested that we meet on the set because I had something very important to talk to him about.

The rehearsals took place the next day on the Warner Bros. studio lot. Big John McCarthy was there to play a referee, and Tank Abbott was guest-starring, too. While I was there, Bob and I met to talk.

"Look, Robert," I said, "this show is the biggest on TV, and when it comes out, you're going to get more publicity for the UFC brand than you've ever dreamed. Everyone's going to think I'm your announcer because I'm co-starring as myself with Tank and Big John. Let's make a deal. It's time for me to announce every single UFC from now on."

It was, if I do say so, the best poker hand I've ever played in my life. The next thing I knew, I was on a plane down to Augusta to announce UFC 13. I was in.

7

LOW POINT

We had a couple of good years at the beginning, but soon we were looking down the barrel of a gun. In March 2000, at UFC 24, I was getting ready to announce the main event of the evening when I got a message in my earpiece:

The heavyweight title bout has been canceled.

What the hell?

Kevin Randleman, the two-hundred-pound heavyweight wrestler from Ohio, had been warming up backstage when he slipped, as if on a banana peel, on some pipes carelessly left lying around. He'd whacked his skull against the concrete floor. He was out cold, being rushed to a hospital with a concussion. This was serious stuff, not to be taken lightly. And now the bosses wanted me to announce to this crowd—and those watching at home—that the event they'd all been waiting for was dead in the water.

The crowd at the Lake Charles Center in Louisiana that

night was pathetically sparse. As I looked out in the arena, I saw empty seats everywhere. This was something we'd begun to notice. At UFC 8 in Puerto Rico, attendance had hit an all-time UFC high of 13,000, but ever since, it had been dropping off. In Lake Charles the night Randleman slipped, there were only 1,800 people watching me about to become the bearer of bad news. Every one of those people had paid good money for their seats. Every one had come out to show their pride in the young sport. I knew I'd hear boos, and braced for bottles and cans to be thrown into the Octagon.

That, for me, was the low point of the ambitious organization to which I'd hitched my star. That night epitomized for me what had been happening for the last couple of years. The UFC had come under fire by many who accused it of promoting an inherently barbaric sport. Senator John McCain of Arizona, the future presidential candidate, famously described our sport as "human cockfighting," and throughout the nation he and others were lobbying venues and athletic commissions to have the sport banned.

The witch hunt was working. Venues were locking us out, and management was dealing with legal issues over the right to put on a decent show to paying fans. Now, in retrospect, this was actually the best thing that could have happened to the sport. It forced the powers that be to look at the sport and ask, *Hey, what's good, what's bad, what's getting us in trouble, and what can we drop without tossing out the essence and purity of these phenomenal fights?* Ultimately, the persecution of those early years made the organization stronger. It had, frankly, nowhere to go but up. But hindsight is 20/20. That night, in the dismal light of the stadium, it felt like we were fighting for our survival.

I wasn't relying on the UFC to pay my bills at that point. I think I was making $650 a fight. But my dream of being an announcer and helping build the UFC into a mainstream sporting franchise was on the line.

I wanted MMA to be a respected sport. And I wanted UFC fights to be the premier events in the world of MMA. If the UFC tanked, I would have to reevaluate my dream of becoming an announcer. I could not see myself announcing anywhere other than the UFC Octagon. Sure, I was being approached by other MMA organizations, including K-1 and a couple of boxing promoters who offered me the chance to be their man in the ring, but none of them excited me. I knew that if the UFC failed to exist, then I would lay down the microphone and not pursue announcing anywhere else. No other fight organization did it for me. I didn't want to be just another announcer looking for a paycheck and a free seat. I hadn't signed up for that kind of life. I wanted to be a part of a sport and an organization that I loved and believed in.

Even before the night of the Randleman debacle, from my privileged perspective inside the organization, I could tell that things were not right. When I visited Robert Meyrowitz's corporate offices in New York City, my business sense told me things were in trouble as soon as I stepped off the elevator. Office workers I'd known were now gone. Desks sat empty. The employees who remained seemed in over their heads.

The place was a shell of its former self—clear, irrefutable evidence that the money wasn't rolling in. My guess was Bob was pumping his own money into the franchise to keep it going, hoping for a better break. If he had wanted to find investors to infuse the organization with vitality and much-needed cash, he would have had a hard time convincing them it was a good bet. It was an extremely questionable business at the time. Because of the McCain scare, UFC pay-per-view shows were pulled off the iN DEMAND network, which had access to more than 75 million homes. The only cable network that stayed loyal to the UFC was DirecTV, which had a subscriber base of about 16 million homes at that time. We also owe a huge debt of thanks to the gods of the Internet, because they gave the fans of the sport a forum in which to share their love of the sport. By broadcasting their fascination for these fights in blogs, forums, and bulletin boards, they helped keep us alive until the Zuffa era.

When we lost those iN DEMAND pay-per-views, that was the larger share of the money that was coming in. My guess is Bob had little revenue coming in and just wasn't breaking even. DirecTV's 16-million-home subscriber base didn't tell you how many people were actually going to watch. And how many home sales were you going to make when you were only attracting 2,000 to 3,000 people to the shows themselves?

That's only the beginning of the numbers equation. If only 16 million people have the *potential* to watch your show, it's hard to make intelligent ad buys. Where do you advertise? How do you get people to discover you? It's not as if anyone in the mainstream media was covering us back then. It's not as if you could open the *Los Angeles Times* or *USA Today* or the *New York Times* and check the sports TV schedule to find out what was going on in the sport and where you could watch it tonight. It was an underground sport. You almost had to be in the know to know when it was going to be on and where you could catch it. I know some fans get off on that; it makes them feel special to be in the know. But that's no way to run a business. Business is about making things predictable, so fans know where you're going to be and when. Same bat time, same bat channel.

The underground element concerned me. It meant that it was becoming harder for fighters to make a living. If you have a dream to fight, but one fight doesn't pay your bills, what do you think you're going to do? Fight more fights, of course. And pretty soon you'll be grasping desperately at meager paychecks to make your nut and pay your trainers. That's when fighters fight fights they really shouldn't, when they succumb to the lure of unscrupulous outside promoters who only want to stage a spectacle. The UFC *had* to get better, *had* to get stronger, not only for its own good but for the good of the warriors who were its lifeblood.

I remember hanging out with Frank Shamrock a year or so after UFC 22, when he beat Tito Ortiz by strike submission. Frank's an extremely intelligent man with excellent communication skills, which is why I have always enjoyed his fight commentary and his friendship. Whether in a mental debate or going head-to-head in the Octagon, Frank is a calm cat with a very low resting heart rate. When he fought Tito, he was remarkably calm and spoke into Tito's ear much of the time, psyching him out by taunting Tito about how tired he was getting.

That fight had been pretty dramatic, and they'd both suffered some damage. Frank told me that he pulled in about $65,000 the night of the fight. But after he paid for his medical expenses and God knows what else, he cleared maybe a third of that. That was all he got for the second of only two fights he fought that year. "Tell me, Bruce," he said. "I have to ask, Was it really worth it?"

There's no question in my mind that if Frank were fighting

today, he'd be making millions. Back then, there just wasn't the kind of money fighters can make today under the Zuffa realm, which has helped many fighters become millionaires, if not multimillionaires.

In the back of my mind, there was always a scale, similar to the scales of justice, hanging over the UFC, weighing the difference between *spectacle* and *sport*. I had been fascinated by UFCs 1 and 2 because of the Gracies, and the martial arts component, which had been such a major influence on me when I was growing up. But UFC 3 turned me off a bit. There were basically no rules, no judges, no time limits, and apparently no weight classes. The skill was there, but the matchup was like a heavy-duty street fight where sometimes one guy would clearly have an advantage over someone else. They were touting this as a new, up-and-coming sport and I thought, *Whoa, wait a second. This is completely unregulated and someone could get hurt.* If the sport wanted to go mainstream, it would have to get some rules.

Anytime you're watching an event hoping for someone to get hurt, I think it's ceased to be a sport. Sport is about skill. A spectacle is regressing to the days of the ancient Romans, watching people get torn apart by lions. So I skipped the next show and started watching again at UFC 5. I told myself to appreciate it for what it was. I realized it had potential but that it needed to be fine-tuned. There had to be a way to refine what was taking place, or it would just disappear because it was too violent.

Even today you hear people say how much they liked the old days. Well, sure, so do I. I love the head butt, for example. That's something that we can't do today, but it's a cool thing to watch.

The businessman in me got great pleasure watching Robert Meyrowitz at work. He was a consummate showman who understood entertainment. He made his bones in pay-per-view and the radio industry. Once, he had a venue cancel and had to move the show to Alabama overnight. He got the trucks packed and the fighters and all their equipment on their way in a matter of hours, all without breaking a sweat. Imagine having to pack up the Octagon and all that goes with it overnight! What an incredible feat of logistics and grace under pressure.

If there was a fight on a Saturday in some city, I guarantee you that Robert was in court in that city earlier that week, fighting to make sure that the show went off without a hitch, because people were out to block them.

I give him tremendous credit. He was fighting as hard as he could, but he was on the verge of losing every dollar he ever made in those years, trying to bail out a sinking ship and fighting battles in court that maybe could have been avoided with better planning. The people Robert had working for him toward the end deserve a lot of credit as well. They did what they could to keep the UFC, but the handwriting was on the wall.

It was doubly frustrating for me because I had a business background. As I was watching their slow demise, I thought I could try to offer my services. But it wasn't appropriate for me, an employee, to offer my expertise in that area. Instead I used whatever contacts I had to get the sport noticed by the media. I discovered that because of the McCain ruckus, the media wanted to cover UFC for all the wrong reasons. They were only interested in scandals. I can admit now that I did think about getting a financier to buy the UFC, but that never got off the ground.

During that time I received a call from a New Jersey–based boxing promoter named Gary Shaw, who wanted to meet with Meyrowitz before a show being held in New Jersey, to discuss possibly buying the UFC. The morning of our scheduled meeting, Shaw called me to cancel, and looking back, I am so happy he did.

In later years Gary Shaw entered the world of MMA in a big way with a fight organization known as EliteXC, owned by ProElite. Shaw was their "Live Events President" and worked to get fights on network TV. ProElite promoted a backyard street fighter and YouTube sensation named Kimbo Slice in a series of fights that hurt the sport, setting it back years. Kimbo wasn't ready, and his non-MMA skills were exposed on national TV when he was KO'd in fourteen seconds by a last-minute, lower-weight opponent named Seth Petruzelli, who had stepped in as a replacement for Ken Shamrock. Before that fight, the promoters had allegedly paired Kimbo with fighters he could beat. Had they fought, Ken Shamrock would have taken Kimbo to the ground and ended the fight quickly. After the fight, Seth Petruzelli revealed that he was told *not* to take it to the ground, although he later retracted the statement, and an investigation by Florida state authorities found no evidence of wrongdoing by the promoters. Still, numerous commentators wondered if it was a "work," or predetermined fight, and the controversy could have seriously damaged the credibility of the sport.

Understand, I have nothing against Kimbo. He fights to support his mom and his family, and he has always been polite to me. My issue is with the powers that be who hyped Kimbo to the world as a man who had the skills to compete with the best of the MMA fighters. In my opinion, this just wasn't true. He was a street fighter with boxing skills, but his range of MMA skills were not comparable to those of a B– or even C–level MMA artist. But so many people who should have known better fell for the hype, including *ESPN* magazine, which featured him on their cover.

When ProElite went out of business, I thought to myself, *I told you so . . .*

But still, the UFC was hurting, and a savior was desperately needed. And one day, that savior appeared.

Bob called me one night. "I have some good news and some bad news," he said. "The bad news is, I'm selling the UFC. The good news is, I sold it to Dana White and the Fertitta brothers."

This was a huge, fascinating development, I knew Dana by reputation, of course. He was the savvy fight manager who'd shaped the careers of Tito Ortiz and Chuck Liddell, two of my favorite fighters. Lorenzo and Frank Fertitta were casino and entertainment entrepreneurs reportedly worth hundreds of millions of dollars. (They would later attain billionaire status, as certified by *Forbes* magazine.) They had the cash, and they couldn't have snapped up the show at a better time. They reportedly paid a mere $2 million for it. Peanuts, really, when you think about what it became. They could negotiate well because the franchise was hurting so badly. If they had waited any longer, there wouldn't have been anything left to buy.

"Uh, Bruce?" Bob said.

"Yes?"

"A lot of people are going to be let go," he said.

Okaaaaaay, I thought.

"But you and Big John are staying on. You should expect a call from Dana very soon."

I thanked him and put the phone down. I breathed a sigh of relief. The UFC would no doubt change, but it would survive.

Now I just had to sit tight and wait for a call from my new boss.

8

WHITE KNIGHT

I t wasn't until after the first couple of shows together that the organization flew me to Vegas to meet with Dana White one-on-one.

My nerves were a little on edge going into that meeting.

Just as Bob Meyrowitz had promised, Dana did me the courtesy of a short welcome phone call. To my surprise, Dana offered me a raise on that call because he knew from the books that I hadn't had one since the beginning. I saw it as a gesture of faith and a thank-you for my loyalty. Dana had acquired a business that was near bankruptcy. He could easily have said that we all had to tighten our belts right now. But he didn't. That was classy.

And shortly after that call, he and Lorenzo treated John McCarthy, me, and others to a wonderful dinner in Vegas, where expensive wine flowed freely. Lorenzo and Dana exuded such confidence that night that I couldn't help but swear my loyalty to them. "Whatever you need, whatever you want, just ask," I told them. "If it's in my power to do, it'll get it done. No questions asked."

Despite Dana's warmth toward his new employees, none of us in the organization knew what was in store for us. The first couple of shows we did after Zuffa's buy were business as usual. But little by little we began to notice much more attention to detail on the part of upper management. I personally felt that I was being treated like a teammate, not an employee; UFC headquarters would check with us on a more regular basis before, during, and after each show.

But now, meeting Dana one-on-one for a sit, was different. Like everyone in the UFC, I was wondering, *What happens now?*

Today was my day to find out what Dana had in store for me.

Was I worried when I walked into his office that I'd be walking out jobless? Yes and no. In the back of my mind was the thought, *Hey, what if this goes south? What if this is my last visit to the UFC?* I didn't think they would have given me a raise and flown me out just to dispose of me. But still, I knew Dana was a strong-minded, tough individual. There was a chance we wouldn't see eye-to-eye.

I was grateful he thought enough of my work to want a face-to-face sit. To my relief, he didn't beat around the bush. He was completely frank.

"We're going to do things my way," he said, or words to that effect. There would be big changes, but in the end, the UFC would be the biggest thing in sports. He told me he had a dream, a vision, for how to make that happen.

From the tone of his voice, you could not doubt him for a second.

I was relieved to hear him say that, because obviously, if we were having this conversation, then I was still standing. And then it was time to talk about my announcing in the Octagon.

He wanted to elevate the sport, to bring to it a level of class and stature that it had not yet attained. And that impacted how I was saying the words. He then launched into one of the most perceptive analyses of fight announcing I've ever heard. It was as if he were dissecting the way various announcers had executed their jobs over the years, and he had strong opinions about what he liked and didn't like—what worked, what didn't. Among other things, he thought at times I'd gotten too wordy.

"There were two introductions I thought were the best I've ever seen," he said. "Your brother Michael introducing Evander Holyfield and Riddick Bowe in their first fight ever. I'll never forget that night. He was amazing. The other? The night you introduced Tito Ortiz and Evan Tanner. If you can, I'd like you to keep the tempo the way you announced that fight that night."

It wouldn't be hard for me to get on board with that. The fight had taken place only recently at the Trump Taj Mahal. It was UFC 30, the famous Battle on the Boardwalk in Atlantic City. Tito was amazing that night. Defeated Tanner by knockout in something like thirty-two seconds.

Now, I wasn't exclusive to the UFC at the time, and they were okay with it. They understood that they couldn't yet pay me enough *not* to do other gigs. I knew someday they would. When the time came, I wanted to be able to put the UFC logo on my chest like Superman's *S*, and say to the world, *This is who I am.*

And that was all the business Dana and I discussed. We spent the next hour or more having a nice, friendly lunch, talking about our love of sports.

BUFFERISM NO. 8

"TAKE ALL YOU WANT, BUT EAT ALL YOU TAKE."

My dad always used to say this about food, but it applies to almost anything. My parents grew up during the Great Depression. It taught them a lesson about waste of any kind. To take more than you need is greedy and wrong. Even to this day, I never let a crumb leave my plate. Whether it's a meal or a path choice in life, once you make it and take it, you should finish it!

At the time, the UFC still wasn't paying my bills. Whenever possible I enjoyed doing smaller fights for smaller organizations, which almost always paid me more than the UFC at the time. Finally, starting in 2007, we negotiated an exclusive contract and I stopped doing other MMA bouts.

Occasionally I'd also do cameo appearances as a fight announcer in various movies, such as *Play It to the Bone,* in which Michael also appeared, along with the film's stars, Woody Harrelson and Antonio Banderas. I'd roll onto the set for a day or two, say my lines, pocket a fee. But now and then an offer came along that was just so beneath me and beneath the standards set by the UFC that I declined. Once I was offered a lot of money to appear in a B-list martial-arts film for one week's work. Money aside, I didn't feel it would be a good move for me to appear in a potentially cheesy film, so I declined the offer.

I can honestly say that I've never had a problem with Dana in the decade we've been working together. In fact, the only problem is that he's incredibly busy and it's hard to set up one-on-one time to talk with him. He's jetting around the world, building the sport and making deals.

But the more I've watched the organization flourish, the more I realize Dana really hasn't altered his vision from the day we met, when this young man just into his thirties had an idea about how he was going to refloat a sinking ship. Everything he and the Fertitta brothers have done since then has been unerringly savvy.

The biggest thing, I'd say, is that he knew exactly how to tap into the enthusiasm of the fans. Compared with how other sports connect with fans, the UFC beats them every single time. Unlike the bosses who run various sports franchises, Dana comes off as a living, breathing human being, an authentic fan in his own right. He comes out before many shows at the weigh-ins and does a Q&A with the fighters and the fans. He answers their questions, some of which can be redundant. Yet he shows uncommon patience because he knows today's UFC neophyte is tomorrow's diehard. The teens who fall in love with the sport today will introduce their children to it a decade from now. Go to the weigh-ins, if you can, and watch his interactions. Then come and tell me if you've ever seen such face-to-face from any promoter of any other sport, especially boxing.

He's harnessed the power of social media—a thing that was barely alive when we first met in his office in Vegas—like a pro, and urged the fighters to do the same. He Tweets before bouts and tells fans where they can score tickets. "Meet me here at this time and this place," he says, "and we can make it happen." Or "I left two tickets at the 7-Eleven at this address. First person in gets them." That's fun—and smart.

"Can I take a picture with Chael Sonnen?" a fan asks.

"Sure," Dana says. "Come on down!"

UFC's critics cannot tell me that this kind of thing goes on elsewhere.

It doesn't happen in boxing.

It doesn't happen in baseball.

It doesn't happen in hockey.

It doesn't happen in football.

You see it only in the UFC.

Dana was a genius at this. He somehow grasped that the sport had to move light-years in order to catch up to other sports. So the UFC had to innovate. And now they're beating other sports at accessibility, openness, and transparency.

10 REASONS UFC IS CHOKING OUT BOXING IN THE U.S.A.

1. Dana F****ing White. Enough said.
2. Twice the pain in half the time.
3. Good seats don't mean you have to rent a tux.
4. In the UFC, the best fight the best.
5. Their fighters only have two weapons. Our fighters have twenty-plus—and elbows.
6. Joe Rogan: best commentator since Howard Cosell.
7. Did I mention Octagon girls?
8. Which sounds cooler: "left hook" or "rear naked choke"?
9. Hitting the mat means things are just getting started.
10. Fighters who aren't afraid to Tweet.

Now, sure, Dana's not a guy you want to mess with. The way I figure Dana, he's a guy with a code. You work with him on his terms, and if you try to push him, he shuts you down. Look at what happened when Miguel Torres made a rape joke on Twitter. Dana tossed him out of the UFC, although he later relented and hired him back. The lesson there was yes, it's important for fighters to market themselves via Twitter, but they'd better say the right thing.

Look at what happened with Fedor. Dana fought long and hard, several times, to sign Fedor Emelianenko. When Affliction collapsed and Fedor was a free agent, Dana tried again. The UFC offered the Ukrainian monster a contract worth—so I've heard—$20 million or more to fight for the UFC. At the time, Fedor had it all going on. He was undefeated for a decade, with more than twenty-five wins under his belt. In my opinion, the UFC was the next logical step for him. Correction: it *had been* the next logical step for him for a long time now, but he and his managers never saw it. They never got along with Dana, and told the press they didn't care for his tactics or comments. So what happened? Fedor went with Strikeforce and into an embarrassing trio of losses. The luster was gone and Fedor retired. It's easy to criticize in hindsight, but *maybe* Fedor would have shone a little brighter for a little while longer under Dana and the UFC's tutelage.

Or look how fast Dana cut Jason "Mayhem" Miller loose after UFC 146 in May 2012. Mayhem showed up to the weigh-ins in Vegas dressed in sunglasses, a pink feather boa, and pink shorts, sporting a new hairdo and carrying a pink boom box. He looked like a clown. The night of the fight he got into an argument backstage with UFC site coordinator Burt Watson, who objected to Mayhem's new outfit, which included a paper bag/ gas mask getup he was supposedly going to wear with his camo shorts in a misguided attempt to celebrate Memorial Day. Insane.

I like Mayhem. We've hung out a few times. I remember being with him on Sydney, Australia's, famous Bondi Beach, where I watched him charm the ladies. The guy's got game.

But UFC 146 was nuts. He went out and lost to C. B. Dollaway, and Dana came out to the press conference after the fight and announced Mayhem was done. Just like that. Yeah, I feel bad for Jason. But he should have shown up serious and fight-ready that night, with little fanfare, since he'd just turned in an extremely poor performance at the TUF 14 Finale and was completely overpowered by Michael Bisping.

Then there was that time in 2007 when Dana was going to fight Tito Ortiz in a boxing match. People may have thought it was a stunt, but the two had actually sparred together when Dana was still managing Tito. Dana trained for it like crazy. I think he was eating twelve eggs a day and pushing himself to the limit, and dieting all the while he was running the UFC. It looked like it was going to happen, too. But then it was called off at the last minute when Tito didn't show up at the weigh-in. He later told the press that he thought he should get a producer's credit for putting the fight together. It might have been an interesting fight, by the way, but from my perspective, it was lose/lose all the way around. If Tito had beaten Dana, the world would have said, well, sure, Tito's a fighter anyway. And if Dana had beaten Tito, how would that have looked for Tito's image and his marketing potential in the UFC going forward? That's why I'm actually kind of glad the fight never happened.

There's only one time I can remember when I had to ask Dana to do me a favor. Early in 2008, my brother Michael was diagnosed with throat cancer. He was going under the knife and asked me to fill in for him in an HBO bout. I pulled Dana aside at a weigh-in and asked if he was okay with this. Technically, my contract permitted me to do boxing, but I wanted to make sure Dana was completely fine with it, and he was.

And that's how the Casamayor-Katsidis Boxing Event at the Morongo Casino in California became the first and last full HBO show I have ever done (although I did announce a number of HBO boxing undercards between 2003 and 2007). I was happy to do Michael that favor, and honored that HBO permitted me to do that fight. Consummate pro that he is, Michael had the cancer removed and was back to work five weeks later.

I was glad, too, that Dana gave me the thumbs-up.

It's what you do for family.

9

PATH TO GLORY

Now, I would hate to give the impression that it was all easy street for Zuffa when they took over the organization. They were still hampered by a lack of visibility. The fans knew they existed, but that often is not enough. To grow a sport, you have to have a home, a base of operations where people can discover you again and again. Think of how much baseball, football, and basketball dominate TV programming during their respective seasons. There was no fixed season for taking a man's head off in a steel cage. So Zuffa had to invent it.

From the moment they took over, it was obvious that we were well backed and financially solvent. At the same time, we were also getting back to basics. Dana got rid of the fancy entrance ramp to the Octagon and got us back to having fighters enter directly from the back without the needless pyrotechnics and WWE-type grandeur. It was as if the company was saying that the proof was in the *fighting*. The new entrances were simpler, more stately, and way more dramatic when mixed with the overall production quality.

In those early days, I started seeing more advertising promoting the UFC, such as full-page ads in magazines like *Playboy, Maxim,* and elsewhere. This was great to see from a business ego standpoint, but to my mind it was a waste of ad dollars. This wasn't the best way to attract the ideal viewing market— eighteen- to thirty-four-year-olds who became the heart and soul of the UFC. Zuffa needed something smarter, bigger, and more powerful. They ultimately found it, but it took nearly running on fumes to do so.

One of the early duds was UFC 33. We had five fights on the pay-per-view card, and every one of them ended by decision. It ended up being a night that was, in a word, unexciting. To make it worse, they pumped so much *energy* into this show. It was our first big foray into the Las Vegas fight scene. We had 9,500 people at the Mandalay Bay Events Center, among them tons of fight-savvy press and executives who'd come out to see what this hot new sport was all about. One of my old friends, Jeremy Zimmer, one of the owners of United Talent Agency, was there. After the fights were over, I didn't even have to talk to him. The boredom was written on his face. He told me that he "just didn't see it," and was less interested in possibly working with the UFC now. I felt like we took three steps backward.

What went wrong? Dana and the Fertittas cracked the code. They figured out that when people come out to the fights, they're looking for electric, dynamic action. If the fighters go to ground quickly and stay there, trying to get each other to submit, it can make for some pretty boring entertainment for the rest of us. That disappointment didn't stop the organization.

It only fueled their fire to work out the kinks. That was when they instituted the rule that if the fighters hit the ground and there's no action, the ref has to stand them back up and restart the fight. Now, sure, I know that if you're really experienced in grappling, you're probably going to yell, "Fights like that are the greatest!" Well, sorry, to both the trained and untrained eye, those all-ground fights can look static. We've got to keep them moving for the sake of the future. They were right about that.

Did it work? Some. But not enough.

Four years after their daring buy, Zuffa was reportedly $44 million in the hole. Dana took a call from Lorenzo Fertitta at one point, who gave him the bad news and suggested that perhaps they should sell off the organization.

Sell off the UFC? *Again?*

A few days later they had an offer on the table, but it was reportedly under $8 million. Anyone who can do subtraction knows that that wasn't going to get them out of the hole they were in. But did they cave? No. Depending on your perspective, they did something either incredibly foolhardy or remarkably brilliant. They ponied up another reported $10 million and put the first season of a TV reality show, *The Ultimate Fighter* (*TUF*), into production. You know the concept: sixteen young fighters from all over the country would come together at a training camp, get trained by some of the greatest coaches in the business, and work their way up to a major fight. Each show would end in a fight. Randy Couture and Chuck Liddell, another two of my favorite fighters, would guide the young men through that grueling first season.

In a nutshell, *TUF* was a $10-million crapshoot by Dana and the Fertittas.

It's funny, because around that same time I actually had the chance to work on a boxing TV show but turned it down. One day I received a phone call out of the blue from the office of Mark Burnett, the producer of such hit TV shows as *Are You Smarter Than a Fifth Grader?*, *The Apprentice*, *Survivor*, and *Shark Tank*. My caller started talking about how Burnett needed an announcer for his new series *The Contender*, which was going to be hosted by Sylvester Stallone and Sugar Ray Leonard.

I assumed they were looking to book Michael, and launched into a discussion of what his schedule was like.

"No," the caller said. "We want *you*."

I was taken aback. It was kind of a turning point for me, because until then I had been doing my thing for the UFC and hadn't really thought that my persona, or whatever you call it, was making an impact beyond the world of MMA. But now here I was, hearing that Burnett had personally requested that his office contact *me* with the offer. It was a dream call, as far as I was concerned.

I heard them out, but I politely turned them down. It wouldn't have been a right fit for me, and it would have encroached on Michael's turf. The squared ring is not the world I chose to announce in. *My* world has eight walls. Now, bear in mind, I've never appeared on any of the season shows of *TUF*. I've never once visited the set, to be precise. I'm only brought in for the finale shows, where they fight to become *TUF* season winner. But I'm still pleased to have walked away from that other job, and to have my contribution be my announcing talents at the end of each *TUF* season.

From the start, the Spike TV show actually struck me as far more interesting to watch than *The Contender*. Why? At the end of every show, you saw an entire fight, not a highlight reel, the way you did on *The Contender*. Both five-minute rounds—and a third round if a draw took it into overtime—could now be seen by millions of Americans who just happened to be clicking through channels. Well, shoot, what do you think happened? People who'd never seen the sport were galvanized and frozen to the screen.

That first *TUF* finale in 2005 culminated in the legendary Stephan Bonnar/Forrest Griffin fight in Vegas. The show aired live on Spike, so you didn't have to pay to see it, just tune in. Zuffa made sure that everyone who had followed these men through the full twelve weeks would not have to pay a dime to see how it ended.

The second the fight started, the crowd was on its feet and stayed standing for what turned out to be one of the most amazing fights anyone had ever seen. These guys were balls-to-the-wall, fighting with every ounce of skill they had, punching, kicking, and evading each other ruthlessly. It was amazing to see where this fight was going. You couldn't imagine that they had this much skill, intensity, and desire to win locked away inside them. When it was over, we were all beside ourselves. It was arguably the most *real* conclusion to a reality show that has ever aired in the history of television.

I was so excited that when I got into the Octagon to announce the winner, I made a mistake, at least in my mind. I told the crowd, "You've just seen the greatest fight *ever* in the Octagon." You probably don't think that's a big deal, but announcers are supposed to project an air of impartiality. If you start editorializing, you're entering the realm of sports commentary. (Joe Rogan, God bless him, would later echo my exact words.) But this time, you could say that I had been transported by enthusiasm like everyone else. I could not freaking help myself. So sue me.

You probably know what happened next.

Dana got in the Octagon and awarded a six-figure UFC contract to the winner—a bleeding Forrest Griffin, by unanimous decision—along with a car, a dirt bike, and a high-end watch. But then he stunned millions when he announced that he was also awarding Stephan a UFC contract.

The crowd erupted. It was *insane*. It was a small venue, true, but that was appropriate because somehow this single event, which had nothing to do with the regular run of official UFC shows, had engendered such an emotional connection with fans. They had watched these guys over twelve weeks, and they were ready to come watch them fight to the end.

THE two men hugged each other. Stephan fell to the floor in a gesture of gratitude, hands over his eyes, head back, as if he were about to weep.

In that big, historic moment, I lost all my composure and reacted like a little kid, throwing my arms in the air and shouting. If you watch the video, you can hear and see how emotional I was. It was amazing. I went out of character for the second time in a matter of minutes. I thought Dana and the organization had acted so generously, so chivalrously. In that moment I *was* a fan, along with millions of others who will probably watch UFC shows till the day they die.

Now, of course, the next day Zuffa still had bills to pay, and what was now $44 million to pay off, but they had found the thing that would help them rope in viewers, and they'd cemented a seductive rhythm of shows designed to make the sport accessible while still maintaining its mystique. The formula was simple: free TV, free TV, free TV, pay-per-view, and back to free TV again. And all the while, tons of reruns of *The Ultimate Fighter* aired in marathon chunks to catch the eyes of newcomer fans. Leading into the next season, the show had a huge built-in audience.

That one golden moment will never be forgotten, and it helped brand the sport. The pay-per-view numbers went up from there. And Stephan and Forrest will probably have a place in the UFC forever.

As I write this, *The Ultimate Fighter* is now in its sixteenth season, and I'm proud to say that I've announced at sixteen finale shows. I also think the show has earned its place in the UFC's pantheon of properties. It's the gateway drug, so to speak. It lures people in, gets them hooked emotionally, and doesn't let them go until they've made a commitment to the sport. The show does more than show fighters training. It trains *fans*.

TUF is the only show of its kind. You don't see young men who want to be pro baseball players or pro basketball players on TV. You don't bear witness to their energy and urgency and passion, where they desire something so badly that they can practically taste it. That's what this show is about: getting people pumped about the sport and realizing that if they have what it takes, they can go for it, too. That's pretty special in TV today. *TUF* shows a side of sport that is usually hidden from view.

It also makes for just great TV. The TUF 15 Finale in June 2012 was especially moving, I thought. Like millions of viewers, I could not help but be moved by the heartfelt story of fighter Michael Chiesa. He'd lost his father during the series' filming.

In a touching moment, Dana had told Michael to go home to be with his family; instead, Chiesa came back and ultimately won the whole thing in honor of his dad and his family. Just a great night of TV all the way around: great fights, and great emotional impact, which you can only get from TV.

That's why, when I meet young fighters who ask me how they can fight for the UFC, I tell them to try their damnedest to get on *TUF*. If you dream of being a fighter, and there's a tryout in your weight category near you, there's no excuse not to go. Yes, if you get in, you'll be isolated from your girlfriend, your job, and your family for about twelve weeks, but it's worth it. In return, you'll gain invaluable friends and maybe even a little notoriety overnight. And you'll be light-years ahead of other fighters whom the fans have never seen until they walk into the Octagon.

Yes, it can be annoying to have people all over the world watch your life on parade for twelve weeks. They're going to know what you eat and drink, how you sleep, how you conduct yourself, how you get along with others, and they're going to form an opinion about you based on what they see that may well be negative, cruel, or downright unwarranted.

But that's TV. They'll either love you or hate you. We all go through it, and you have to develop a thick skin to shrug it off and say, "I could care less what people think of me. Say what you want—just spell my name right."

The show is a great way for a fighter to get noticed, but no matter how much persona a fighter has, he will not go far unless he is also a phenomenal fighter. Style is no substitute for skill.

One night, Stitch Duran and I were in Milwaukee watching a young fighter. He came out and he had nailed down his persona beautifully. He had a cool nickname, he had the walk-out costume, he had the music, and he made a great connection with the crowd.

He was, shall we say, highly marketable.

He put in a great fight that night, but he lost.

Why?

We noticed that his cardio sucked. He was gasping the whole time he was in the Octagon. Later I walked over to him just as Stitch, who's seen a lot of fighters in his day, pulled the kid aside and asked him a simple question: "Son, are you doing cardio training?"

"No . . . well, I don't do enough."

We were both shocked. How can you end up here in the Octagon and not be working on your cardio? That's a recipe for getting killed.

You have to get some training, we told him. It's nice to put all this effort into looking great and putting on a nice show for the fans, but you can't rely on personality and marketing to win fights. Costumes and attitude are superficial. That's icing on the cake. You can get away with that only up to the point that you can't fight. Then the crowd will cross you off the list and move on to the next guy.

It was our chance—Stitch's and mine—to impart a little wisdom to a young athlete. Clearly, he got this far because he's got great ability. But right now he's a piece of MMA clay waiting to be molded correctly by the right trainer. We passed along the names of a few trainers for him to look up.

I saw in him something I see in a lot of fighters: a kind of reluctance to make that break with their families and their hometowns. A lot of these fighters come from humble beginnings, and they're afraid to be selfish, to put the focus on their passions and leave a family that perhaps depends on them for an income.

I know it's not easy to make that sacrifice, but if the fighters don't make the effort, they may always be wondering if they could have made it. Or as Brando said in *On the Waterfront*: "I coulda been a contender. I coulda been somebody."

I'm not an active fighter and trainer, so I can't speak from that angle. But I am speaking from the lifetime experience of having trained before, and of watching great fighters rise above not-so-great fighters.

What makes the great ones great?

Why do some spend a career in the Octagon and leave it beloved, while others come and go in the most forgettable manner, never to be seen again?

It comes down to training. Sure, style and personality are factors, too, but if you can't breathe, forget it. You're dead before you start.

Someone asked me once, "Do you see yourself in these young fighters?"

Hell, yes, I do! I never wanted to be a fighter, but I know the life. It's the world's loneliest sport. Every morning you wake up and put your body to a test that most people never do. You chase something most people can't understand. You spend eight weeks preparing to fight a guy who can take your head off. That is all something most humans will never fathom. And to top it off, you have no team members backing you up when you step into that cage.

Good trainers know this. They impart this truth to the young men and women they're training.

When the gate slams shut, you're all alone.

10

THE PEOPLE'S CHAMPION

One night, at one of the early shows, I went into the men's room, and there in every urinal were these little baseball-card-sized cards with Tito Ortiz's picture on it. The card listed his stats and credentials, and promoted his clothing line. I was checking it out as I was, excuse my French, peeing on his head.

Tito Ortiz is one of those fighters who always impressed me, not only for his fighting ability but for reasons that go well beyond that realm. He's a perfect example of a fighter I'd like young fighters to emulate. Tito's a fighter who gets it, and one who will always be remembered as a titan of the UFC.

Submission wrestling is his key skill, but his conditioning is beyond most. Very few people train to the level that he does. In fact, in the past I have worried that he could possibly be over-training. I know: you're thinking, how is that even possible? But you *can* do that.

Come to the weigh-ins sometime and you'll see that as soon

as the fighters step off the scales, their trainers are there with food and liquids, forcing them to suck it down and start taking in some nutrients after working hard to cut weight. Tito has mastered the art of cutting weight. But to do it, he once again pushes his body to an impossible limit. People have even joked that he should shoot a video titled "How to Cut Weight the Tito Ortiz Way." His response? "Yeah, but it would have to come with a disclaimer: 'Following this program may just kill you!' "

One Friday in 2011, the night before he was to appear in the main event at UFC 133, we went to dinner at a *churrascaria*, a Brazilian steakhouse. The waiters were parading around with giant skewers of beef, chicken, lamb, and pork—every type of cut and preparation imaginable—slicing it hot off the grill for you. It was the day before a fight night, so Tito wasn't touching a drop of alcohol and I was drinking moderately.

Earlier that day, he had clocked in at 205 pounds at the weigh-in. Seconds later he was gorging himself on pasta, bread, and fluids. He counted up the calories and offhandedly announced, "I just gained eight pounds." He didn't have to get on a scale; he knows his body so well that he can do that.

Irony of ironies, as we were surrounded by all this meat, he started telling me how he had, on occasion, dropped eighteen pounds in a single day. First he does his workout. Then he takes an Epsom salts bath. He dresses in a nylon sweatsuit and gets in bed under a ton of blankets for thirty minutes with his head-phones on, listening to music. That's guaranteed to lose him seven pounds in two hours. Later, rinse, repeat.

I don't know how many people would be willing to go to such lengths for their profession, but fighters do. Most people would say the human body is not made to be treated like that.

And sure, if you're not under a doctor's or trainer's care, you could easily wipe yourself out from heatstroke pulling a stunt like that. But fighters are not like the rest of us. On a daily basis, they are pushing the threshold of what the human species can tolerate, from pain to sweat. The payoff: Tito is capable of losing an average of ten or more pounds in the last twenty-four hours before he steps onto a scale at the weigh-ins.

Okay, so that's dedication to the regimen. But what about dedication to marketing and self-promotion? The first time I met Tito in 1997 on the set of *Friends*, he was a young, excitable kid who was jumping up and down, proclaiming, "I'll be a champion one day! You watch me!" Back then, I thought, *Who is this kid to talk so big?* He hadn't had a fight yet, but he knew what he was going to do and was not ashamed to do a little pre-publicity for himself.

Eight years later, after some losses and some time off, he was confiding in me and Big John that he had gotten an offer from another MMA production and was planning to leave the UFC.

"Don't do it!" Big John and I told him, virtually at the same time.

"Tito," I said, "whatever you do, or whatever they offer you, don't leave the UFC. You might get a big up-front bounce, but it will all fizzle later. If you want to build your image and your brand in this industry, you *have* to be in the UFC."

Ironically, perhaps, Big John went through something similar a few years later. At one point he decided to retire from being a referee, leaving to work as a commentator and on other endeavors. He was back a year or so later.

I've had my own experiences with this issue. In the past, I've been offered to do all the K-1s and other promotions for much more money than I was making with the UFC, but I turned them all down. I always felt it was more important to stay loyal to the UFC.

But what we were talking about that day I attribute to two things: a young man's desire for bigger and better, and youthful impatience. Tito went on to become the coach of *TUF* and fought three straight wins, two against Ken Shamrock, in 2006. That was a hugely memorable, profitable year for Tito Ortiz on his comeback trail.

The 2006 matchups with Ken and Tito were fights that tipped the scales for the UFC. Think about it: Zuffa was still working its way up a year after their daring move to launch *TUF,* a year after Lorenzo reportedly said they might have to consider selling. And here came these hot fights that everyone wanted to see. Okay, down in Florida where their third and final fight was held, we only had about 3,500 people in attendance. It was a sellout crowd, but a small venue. But at home we had nearly 6 million people watching on free TV. That was huge. It would take us another whole year before we hit a home number that big. Dana had done it. Ken and Tito had done it. The UFC had done it. They'd translated the success of the Spike TV show into a powerful combo of free and pay-per-view events.

I'm sure that, looking back, Tito was happy he did not take a fight elsewhere. It's not always about the big guarantee up front; it's about the long run and building a career. I was happy to see Tito make the right decision. He came into his own, in and out of the Octagon, and he's matured into a successful businessman.

Those trading cards I saw in the bathroom are a good example of his natural-born marketing savvy. He's always been comfortable creating sales tools to promote himself and his clothing line, Punishment Athletics, which he started from scratch and which has done millions in sales. His brand is an inevitable blossoming of the same instincts I saw in that young fighter so many years back, who was so full of confidence and braggadocio.

I admire him for that. I love his charisma. At one point, early on in my association with the UFC, I used my media influence to get Tito on national TV shows such as *National Enquirer TV* and *The Best Damn Sports Show Period* on Fox. I realized that if I wanted this job, I had to do something to help build the sport.

Tito looked to be a major fan favorite, so I coaxed the producers into giving him a shot. I had connections with *The Tonight Show with Jay Leno*, and persuaded them to do a reporter-in-the-field segment with Tito training in Huntington Beach. (The reporter, by the way, was a young Ryan Seacrest, in his pre-$60-million-a-year days.) Normally, those bits end at the clip, but I pushed to get him on Jay's couch. The time was right, for Tito and the UFC. But it's extremely hard to get on the couch. It's the most coveted piece of real estate in the world of publicity. But lo and behold, Leno *did* it. Tito came out, served as the sport's ambassador for a night, and the crowd loved him.

We've got years of friendship behind us. I've been to all of his fights except UFC 29 in Tokyo, when the production didn't have the budget to fly me there. I was upset about it, and called Tito just to say that I wouldn't make it. He said he understood. Believe it or not, that's the only fight that broke our streak.

The next night after our steak-fest, I walked into the Octagon to introduce him by his nickname, the Huntington Beach Bad Boy. He wore an intense look on his face that night. Rashad

Evans connected about forty times, and Tito lost by technical knockout.

Later I went up to Tito's hotel room to check on him. His face was bruised and battered, but not cut. I said nothing about the fight. I've been around fighters enough to know that they don't need my words of comfort.

His eyes brightened when he saw me.

"That's the last time you're gonna call me the Huntington Beach Bad Boy," he said.

A flicker of concern flashed through my mind. "Uh, why?"

"I'm *not* the bad boy anymore. From now on, I'm The People's Champion. Because that's who I am, and that's who I'm going to be in all my marketing. Will you do that for me?"

"You know I will."

11

NO PAIN

I was wary of talking about my knee injury with the fighters, athletes, and trainers I knew. Seriously, how much sympathy was I really going to get from these guys? "Oh, your knee hurts? Fuck you, Buffer. You're the announcer, *we're* the fighters."

It turned out that everyone was giving me really good advice on a wide range of things. But only two pieces of information resonated with me and spurred me to action. Marlon Shirley, the great paralympic athlete, with whom I've played the World Series of Poker main event, pulled me aside and said, "All I can say is, when the nerve-block medication wears off, be sure you're ready for the pain. It'll be the most excruciating pain you've ever experienced in your life." Lots of people concurred with his assessment. *Okay,* I thought, *so how do I prepare for the pain?*

A friend and gym buddy, Flavio de Oliveira, a former Brazilian fighter, has had two ACL replacements in his life. Flavio is a five-foot-eight, 195-pound steel monster who is probably the nicest killer I've ever met. He works as a trainer today, whipping people like actor Jason Statham and volleyball star Gabrielle Reece into shape. He has also trained the great jiu-jitsu fighter Jean Jacques Machado. "Bruce," he said, "I've been watching you train, and you're doing fine. But for this operation you have to train at a much higher level. You have to train like a fighter. You need me. Hire me to be your trainer and I'll make sure that when that doctor goes in to operate, he has a nice, comfortable room to move around."

I know the imagery probably leaves something to be desired, but Flavio was nothing if not persuasive.

"You need to be strong going into this operation," he told me. "The more flexible you are, the more your doctor is gonna say thank you because you made it easy for him to go in and do his work. When this thing is over, do you want to be 100 percent, or do you want to live with pain and scar tissue?"

"Who the hell wants that?" I said.

"Then you have to trust me."

Well, I'm not Jason Statham, but for the next six weeks Flavio put me through some of the most grueling leg workouts I've ever been through, all designed to increase the strength, flexibility, and blood flow to both my legs. I'm talking intense ninety-minute to two-hour workouts. We started with thirty minutes of stretching, followed by an hour or more of nonstop circuit training of multiple weight exercises. I did three sets per exercise, and cardio movements in between, to keep my heart rate up. When that was done, I did thirty minutes of cardio on the bike.

I tell you: I have had many fine trainers, but Flavio truly

tested my mental and physical limits by pushing me to weight levels I had never before attained. Even with one good leg, I was able to work out incredibly hard, as long as I was careful not to attempt side-to-side motion exercises, running, or jumping rope. I discovered that you can actually do a heck of a lot of leg work with a detached or torn ACL.

Leading up to the operation, I cleared my calendar of everything but the essentials. If it wasn't a UFC event, I thought very, very carefully about whether I should cancel. If you saw me announce a fight between April and July that year, you didn't see me move very much. Under my pant leg, I was wearing a leg brace to protect my knee from being damaged further.

I was going under the knife on July 6, and I wasn't due to show up in the Octagon for UFC 133 until August 6, 2011. My window of recovery was four weeks—not a huge amount of time, but enough if I played my cards right and listened to my doctor and rehab trainers. I was determined to do this right and heal right. No way was I going to be Bruce the Gimp.

Dr. Neal S. ElAttrache, who replaced New England Patriots quarterback Tom Brady's ACL and who is head physician to the Los Angeles Dodgers, performed the surgery. This super-doc in the world of sports medicine advised me to do nothing for a week, and as much as I like to be up and about, I'm a guy who listens to my doctors. I checked into a hotel for a few days because I wouldn't be able to deal with the stairs in my home. Alex, the son of my mom's caregiver Daysi, stayed with me in the hotel and later, at my home, for two weeks, acting as my twenty-four-hour nurse. And believe me, I needed his help during that first week. I did nothing for a few days but read books, catch up on old movies, play online chess, play video games like UFC, Call of Duty: Black Ops, and Fight Night, and thumb through a long-neglected pile of magazines. I handled all necessary business via phone and mail. Beyond that, I basically became a kid again and played hooky.

Strangely, in spite of everyone's predictions, I had minimal to no pain. I hate taking prescription drugs and especially painkillers; they're the most highly addictive drugs and the hardest to shake, so I prefer not to go there, if at all possible. The morning after the operation, I went off the heavy-duty drugs and switched to three Advil three times a day. I was walking with one crutch on day five. When the bandages came off on day eight, I got the stitches out and showed up for my first day of rehab at the Kerlan-Jobe Center in Los Angeles. The plan was to work out there three times a week, while also training three times a week with Flavio and my physical therapist, who did body work on me to keep me loose twice a week. So some days I'd literally be training three to four hours a day.

As I stood in the rehab gym reviewing the game plan, I looked around me. I was surrounded by some of the world's greatest amateur and professional athletes. Here they were, all on their off seasons, trying to heal their amazing bodies, which they'd pushed to impossible limits. But to my amazement, some of the men, who were all younger than I was, had had the same operation six months ago and were still having problems.

I had none.

That was either great or terrifying, depending on your perspective. Had Flavio's prescription for pre- and post-op success worked like a charm, or had something gone wrong?

I didn't know, and I was craving professional opinions about where I was in the healing process. It's one thing to sit at home and think your knee is doing well. It's another to hear it from the doctors.

The docs took some images, and left me in a room with my thoughts. I got to wondering: *What if the operation didn't take? What if the graft snapped or slipped off?* Shortly after the operation, I had tried to get on a stationary bike and do just one turn of the pedal, and it was impossible. I just couldn't do it. I realized then just how much work I had ahead of me. *The pain may not be here now,* I thought, *but it is going to come.*

I looked at the door now, waiting.

Maybe I was just kidding myself.

I remembered the conversation I'd had with Dr. ElAttrache just a few weeks before. Everything had been so upbeat, so confident.

"Just promise me one thing," I'd said. "When I get this operation, will I be able to walk in the Octagon in four weeks?"

"Bruce," the superdoc said, "I will have you in the Octagon in four weeks and have you at full force in Rio on August 28 for UFC 134."

But sitting there now, I wondered if it was going to happen.

In walked the doctor.

My parents, Joseph and Connie, in their youth. My dad was brilliant and one of the last true "old breed" warriors, a man who thought nothing of facing down a group of thugs armed only with his fists. By the time I was ten, he had me breaking down and re-assembling Luger pistols—blindfolded.

(below) When I was in high school, my parents moved to Malibu, back when it was a small community made up of mostly middle-class families like ours but also with some movie stars living on the beach—and I promptly became a typical SoCal kid, spending every day I could riding the waves.

When I was in my late twenties, I started noticing a boxing announcer on TV who shared my last name and who, people said, resembled me. When I worked up the courage to ask my dad about it, I discovered I had a brother whose existence my parents had never once hinted at! The friendship Michael and I went on to build would change both our lives.

UFC 8 in Puerto Rico was my first UFC gig. Even after the fight, then UFC owner Bob Meyrowitz wouldn't make me the league's official announcer. It took one of the most high stakes gambles of my life to get him to agree.

(Above) The day after UFC 8, I was with fighter Scott Ferrozzo, who I managed at the time. As you can see, I came out of the evening in better shape than Scott!

I was an avid martial artist and kickboxer while growing up. That's why I knew from the first time I entered the Octagon that if I couldn't announce for the UFC, I didn't want to be announcing at all. Here I'm messing around with MMA commentator Stephen Quadros, a longtime martial artist himself.

The three Buffer brothers—that's my big brother Brian in the guest chair—staking out one of the world's most valuable pieces of media real estate, the *Tonight Show* desk.

At a club with Rampage Jackson: Rampage sometimes jokes that we're blood brothers because for a while he was dating one of my ex-girlfriends. If we are, at least we didn't have to cut our hands to prove it!

Hanging out with Tito Ortiz the night before UFC 133. As we sat there gorging ourselves on meat, Tito described the insane routine he sometimes uses to drop upward of *eighteen* pounds in a single day. That kind of dedication is part of why I love this sport—and why I'm so proud to call these warriors my friends.

Jon "Bones" Jones showing off some Buffer gear at the Buffer Poker Room store in the Luxor Hotel in Las Vegas. I firmly believe that Jon has the potential to be the Muhammad Ali of the UFC—the only adversary who can hurt him is himself.

When Dana White and the Fertitta brothers took over the struggling UFC, it was a much needed change. Thankfully, Dana believed in me as an announcer and even helped shape my style in the Octagon.

There's been a lot of talk floating around about Steven Seagal giving tips to UFC fighters. When I watched him working out with Anderson Silva and Lyoto Machida back in 2011, I got to see the truth for myself.

If you ask me, Chuck Liddell is one of the greatest strikers the world has ever seen, boxers included. As a fan, I'm crushed that I won't be able to watch him in the Octagon again, but as a friend, I'm glad he chose to retire. I'm even happier that Zuffa has since made him a V.P. and an official ambassador for the sport. COURTESY GETTY IMAGES/ZUFFA

Dan "the Outlaw" Hardy is one of my all-time favorite fighters to introduce. He always beckons for me to come closer and to roar my intro face-to-face as he mouths the words with me and shakes his head only inches from the camera. The fans love it—and so do I. COURTESY GETTY IMAGES/ZUFFA

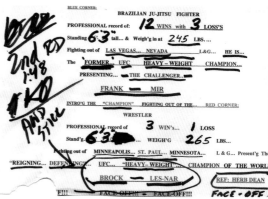

My dad taught me to play poker when I was eight years old. Over time, playing the game has become another career for me. I guess you could say my obsession with it really started when, in only my second tournament ever, I made it all the way through to the televised final table!

This is one of my marked-up fight cards from UFC 100, when I pulled off the 360. I always make a little tear at the bottom to help anchor the card in my hand. The way I move around in the Octagon, I gotta make sure the things don't go flying off on their own.

I enjoy spending time with my godson Henry and his brother, Rupert. Thanks to these boys—and the friendship of their mom, Kristen, who is also V.P. of my company—this old bachelor has learned a thing or two about fatherhood. I might even be ready to settle down sometime.

A couple years after my 360 triumph, everything had changed. I blew out my knee at UFC 129, and during the weeks of rehab and surgery that followed, I wondered if I'd ever be able to announce my way again. I'm putting on a brave face in this photo, but in truth, I was scared.

Being at a photo shoot with the original ladies of the Lingerie Football League is a tough job, but hey, somebody's gotta do it.

If you'd told me thirty years ago that fans would be wearing T-shirts with my name on them, I wouldn't have believed it! And if you ever see me, you better believe I'll be willing to stop and say hi. Trust me, moments like those mean as much to me as they do to you.

Sometimes it's not what you say, it's how you say it. Announcing catchphrases are great, but most of all I want my natural passion for the sport to shine through in my voice—and in my physicality! COURTESY GETTY IMAGES/ZUFFA

12

BRAWL IN THE FAMILY

Pat Miletich, the Croatian Sensation, is a great guy and a tough man, with whom I've always gotten along. But there was one moment between us that I'll never forget. It's hilarious in retrospect, but at the time I wasn't laughing.

Those of us in the UFC share a common bond. We're always traveling on the road together and we share a camaraderie that few co-workers, if we can even be called that, will ever have.

Pat and I were on a flight together that dead-ended somewhere in Texas. It was supposed to be an hour-or-so layover, but of course the flight was canceled, leaving us stranded thousands of miles from our destination.

It had been a long day, and I was not in the best of moods. I started swearing. It was colorful. It wasn't creative. Just an angry stream of F-bombs from a guy who thought he should have been better treated by a multinational corporation from whom he'd bought a ticket.

There were dozens of families in the seating areas. Lots of little kids fidgeting or playing around their parents' luggage. Pat's eyes darted from me to the kids and back.

He glared down at me as I sat in my chair, moping.

"Buff," he said. "I like you, but if you don't stop cursing right now, I'm going to punch you." His eyes flicked to the children again. "You know it's not right."

No way in hell did I want to get punched in the face by the UFC's first welterweight champion in a Texas airport. I piped down.

"I'm sorry, Pat," I said. "You're absolutely right."

"I know I am."

"Won't happen again." Then I paused and looked at him. "Are you still gonna punch me?"

I come from the old school where, if you have a disagreement with someone, you fight it out, then have a beer. You can't do that today, because you never know if the stranger who just mouthed off to you is a gun-toting maniac. There have been times when I've been in crowds and someone will think it's funny to whack me with an elbow. Ha, ha—let's hit the guy in the monkey suit. One time it happened and I was going to deal with the guy, but my friends pulled me out of it, and they were right to do so. I cannot let myself be drawn into altercations of that type, because it's bad publicity for me and the organization. In my father's day, a guy who got what was coming to him learned to shrug it off because he *knew* that he'd brought it all on himself. Times have changed. Today, the slightest altercation can create a lawsuit. I don't need that headache.

But MMA athletes are trained to fight. It's what they do. When they get into the Octagon, they're there because they've been asked to fight. They may not hold a particular grudge against the other man. And yet, look at what they do to each other. Imagine what they'd do to someone who gives them a reason. Unless you've been trained to fight, your first instinct is to shrink away from confrontation. Most of the time, that's the logical and prudent thing to do. MMA guys don't think that way. If the person pissing them off is another fighter, they know the guy can take it. If he doesn't back down, they let him have it. And that has led to some insane moments on the road.

The first time I saw non-Octagon violence on a fight weekend was at UFC 6 in Casper, Wyoming—the first UFC I attended. The Sunday after the show, Michael and I were about to leave the hotel for the airport when I heard a huge commotion, which sounded like a fight. I ran to the elevators, where I saw Pat Smith, a kickboxer who'd fought the night before, on his knees, tearing up and making sounds like a wounded banshee. I later found out that he'd been in a beef with Tank Abbott's crew the night of the fight. Now, as he'd walked out of the elevator the next morning, he'd been coldcocked by one of Tank's cornermen to settle the issue. I have seen a lot of street fights, but the sight of a highly skilled professional fighter holding his head and screaming from unanswered punches has etched itself permanently into my memory banks. Remember—anyone can beat anyone on any given day. It is not always fair and by the rules. It's the street.

Then came UFC 13, my first official UFC event, in 1997. That Augusta, Georgia, event marked the first appearance of Randy Couture and Tito Ortiz. Both had emerged victorious that night. Randy especially, since he'd taken on two opponents and won both times. Really a great night. We had just finished the fights and were hanging around at an after-party in the hotel where we were staying. Bob Meyrowitz always knew how to throw good after-parties. There was a nice buffet going, a couple of good drinks, people having a few laughs. I was ecstatic that night, basking in the glow of my new job and looking forward to great things now that I was part of the organization.

The main event that night saw that big, bearded monster Tank Abbott pitted against Vitor Belfort, who took Tank out in less than a minute. It was a tough time for Tank. He'd picked a fight with the Brazilian fighter Allan Goes at UFC 8, down in Puerto Rico. Bob had banned Tank from the organization for close to a year to teach him a lesson. His loss to Vitor would turn out to be the second in a trio of professional losses.

Tank had started as a bar brawler, tearing apart chumps in Huntington Beach who coughed up money for the chance to take him on. Once, one of those takers whipped out his cash, waved it around, and said, "Where do I put this? Do I give it to *you*, or what?"

"Just stick it there in your shirt pocket," Tank told him. "I'll take it after I knock you out."

He and I go way back and I still consider him a friend of mine, though we've had our differences. He'd call my house late at night and say, "Hey, Buff, let's go out, get drunk, and get arrested. Whaddaya say?" And I'd reply, "How about we do just one of the three and leave it at that?"

Although scary to most who don't know him, Tank can be fun to be around. I used to get a kick out of watching him impress girls back in the day by standing on his head to show off how he can drink a beer upside down. Most people don't know him as well as I do, and don't realize how intelligent he is, or that he has a degree in economics. Like me, he's taken the time to pound out his memoirs. One of these days they'll come out and we'll get to see what goes on behind that gruff, beefy exterior.

He doesn't reserve that personality for strangers, either, by the way. Even his friends are occasionally subject to his wrath. We were sitting outside on the deck of my house one time, watching the beach, and he said to me, "I like you, Buff, but if you ever fuck me over, I'm gonna have to come for you."

You don't want to mess with this guy.

So here we were, drinking and talking with each other, when who should come up to say a few words to Tank but Vitor Belfort's striking trainer, Al "Stankie" Stankiewicz. He's an older gentleman who is in his seventies now. Back then he was maybe in his late fifties. He got his start training fighters when he was still an undercover vice cop in Los Angeles.

I have no idea what Al said to Tank. A few words of commiseration on his loss that night? Better luck next time? A heck of a fight? For some insane reason, Tank bitch-slapped Stankie hard. Bam. Right in the face. Right in front of all of us. Dozens of men and women are standing around, drinks in hand, confusedly looking and asking each other, "What the hell is this, now?"

Well, that touched off a melee. Vitor and the Brazilians came over, and Wallid Ismail sucker-punched Tank with an overhand right to the jaw. Tank fell to the ground in the turtle position; in his defense, he was a bit inebriated. All hell broke loose. The fighters got into it, and the rest of us tender civilians were scattering on the periphery, trying to get the hell out of the way.

I tell people sometimes that I'd rather fight in the Octagon than anywhere else. You're safer in the Octagon because there are no obstacles. No furniture. No glass. No sharp edges. Start flinging heavy men around a room, and there's no telling what'll happen. I remember one fighter beating the crap out of another fighter in a bathroom. The guy had it coming; he'd mouthed off to the fighter about his wife. I would never want to be involved in a bathroom fight. Too much porcelain. Too much tile. Too many ways to split your skull open.

Anytime a fight breaks out in a public place, you're in danger. When people see red, they think everyone's their enemy. They aren't thinking carefully, especially if they've been drinking. I've been in enough fights to know that as soon as it starts, you must reduce your chances of being hit. That's why I immediately grabbed Bob Meyrowitz and pushed him out of the way and got up against the wall. With your back against the wall, you can at least see the punches coming.

In the center of the room was this swirl of tangled men. Then the swirl broke up and a couple of the guys started swinging at people on the periphery. One guy came sailing toward me as if to punch me. There was this funny moment where he did a double take, fist in the air, and saw who I was. "Oh, sorry, Bruce," he said, and then he ran back into the tornado of limbs again.

It was like something out of a movie.

Mind you, this was only a thirty-second melee. That's how fast fights spring up and blow over. Anyone who thinks they'll see it coming and have time to react is kidding himself. It happens fast. Twenty seconds later, it blows over and you're holding a broken nose or jaw because you didn't move fast enough to protect yourself.

Mark Coleman didn't fight that UFC, but he was in town. He walked into the "brawl room" and started swinging, as he's always up for a fight. Big John reacted instinctively, grabbing Mark and subduing him before he could create any more damage.

I watched Bob Meyrowitz, the businessman, talk Tank, the barroom brawler, down from his rage. Big John took the big man upstairs to his room.

And that was the end of that. That was the only time a fight broke out at the after-party in the hotel where we were staying.

Another brawl I witnessed is also the most famous—the one that took place outside the Chinawhite Nightclub in London in 2002, right after the first-ever British UFC event. Fighters and fans still talk about this one, and everyone has his own take on it. It was pretty harrowing, and I doubt we'll ever get to the bottom of it.

None of us were feeling any pain that night. UFC 38 had played to an enthusiastic crowd at the Royal Albert Hall, showcasing the talents of a mix of fighters from all over the globe, but especially a handful of Brits and Australians.

You have to understand something about UK fans. They love watching their warriors go toe-to-toe. Even today, no matter what size arena we're in, such as the O2 Arena in London, which holds around 20,000, UK fans make it sound like 50,000-plus are in attendance. The Manchester fighter Michael Bisping, with whom I've enjoyed becoming friends over the years, has had a couple of hundred street fights and never turns down a professional fight. He took on Chael Sonnen once with only four weeks' notice. One of my favorite fighters to introduce is

Nottinghamian Dan "The Outlaw" Hardy. Whenever I turn to his corner to begin introducing him, he beckons for me to come closer and roar my intro face-to-face. He'll mouth the words with me and shake his head only inches from the camera. The fans love it.

Bisping and Hardy didn't fight at UFC 38, however. That night, Matt Hughes took on and beat Carlos Newton in the fourth round of the main event. A truly wonderful ending to our first-ever show in England.

Afterward, we were at Chinawhite and the champagne was flowing. It was packed to the gills upstairs and downstairs, but we were cordoned off in the VIP area. I was with Tito Ortiz and Chuck Liddell most of the night. All of us were getting off to the music and the beautiful women. Around three in the morning, it was time to start thinking about heading back to our hotel. For some reason, we didn't have a ride back and needed to hail some cabs. We stepped out into an alley to do so. Pat Miletich was horsing around with one of Tito's friends, Bo, who had climbed onto Pat's back and was *pretending* to mess with him. The first thing I saw was another guy come up to them and grab Bo off Pat's back, whereupon Bo fell to the ground. The guy who pulled Bo off was fighter Tony Fryklund, who was a friend of Pat's and apparently didn't realize that the two were just horsing around. Years later, Tony would tell me that when Bo dropped off Pat's back, someone else—who Tony believed was fighter Lee Murray's bodyguard—started punching Bo. Tito saw his friend Bo getting punched out and ran over to deal with it. During the ensuing melee, a taxi actually ran over Bo's arm.

It was as if someone lit a powder keg. Next thing you knew, everyone in the alley was throwing punches. I followed Chuck as he mowed through the crowd. I watched him bring a hulk-like hammerfist down on someone's head and swipe him with a right. It was bad news for anyone who got in front of Chuck at that moment. A ring girl who was partying with us was just standing there, looking confused. I grabbed her and pulled her out of the way. Lorenzo Fertitta's assistant was trying to calm things down, too. I got her out of the way. You don't want to be going past that swarm of swinging limbs.

On the other side of the alley, Tito was trading punches with Lee Murray, the Moroccan-British MMA fighter. Tito went down and Murray reportedly kicked him viciously in the head. Murray was a tough guy, a hothead best remembered today for later orchestrating a £53-million bank heist that put him in prison. (He's still there.) For some reason, that night he had it in for Tito, of all people.

All of us, the Americans at least, were having trouble defending ourselves that night. Most of us had never fought on a cobblestoned surface; our ankles were wobbling every which way, giving the Brits the home-court advantage.

The fight blew over fast. Lee and a few other people disappeared before the British bobbies showed up and threatened to arrest us all.

When I finally saw Tito, his mouth was bleeding and he was pissed as hell. I wanted to leave, but he wanted to wait for Pat, who was talking to some of the cops.

"Bruce," Tito said. "Can you talk to them?"

I introduced myself and Tito to the bobbies in their tall

helmets, and gave them my version of the events. In a nutshell, what happened appeared to be a freakish misunderstanding. All we wanted to do was get back to our hotels and go to bed. The cops took our statements and let us go. On the way back in the cab, Tito was pissed and openly emotional. I had never seen him like that in my life.

Back at the hotel, Tito sat in the lobby waiting for Pat and his crew to return. I knew that he was pissed enough to start a fresh brawl, which would inevitably involve me as well. It took me a while to convince Tito to let it go and get up to his room, which he finally but reluctantly did.

The London brawl affected me in ways I am still discovering.

10 TIPS FOR SURVIVING A STREET FIGHT

1. Never bring a club, knife, or gun to a street fight unless you're prepared to be clubbed, stabbed, or shot, too.

2. Never have your girlfriend or wife throw the first punch—unless you're dating MMA Champion Ronda Rousey!

3. Hit first and ask questions later—unless it's a police officer!

4. Stay alert! If you see trouble brewing ahead of you, walk away.

5. Elbows hit harder than fists, knees hit harder than elbows, and head butts rule!

6. As soon as the fight starts, get your back up against a wall. It's easier to defend yourself from three angles than four.

7. Anything goes in a street fight. When in doubt, BITE!
8. Bar fights are bad. Flying glass cuts deeper than a punch, and leaves scars, too.
9. When fighting in the street, assume the attitude "Kill or be killed."
10. The best self-defense is to avoid street fights in the first place. As Bruce Lee said, master "the art of fighting without fighting"!

Just a for-instance: In 2011, after UFC 135 in Denver, I was at an after-party with Rampage Jackson after his loss to Jon "Bones" Jones. Everyone was there: me, Damian McLawhorn, Michael Bisping, Chuck Liddell, Rashad Evans, Jason "Mayhem" Miller, and a couple of other fighters. The night before, a bunch of us had gone out with MMA journalist Ariel Helwani and Arianny Celeste, the Octagon girl, to a fabulous steak place in Denver, where I'd proceeded to get them all tipsy on port, which was a novelty for some of these folks.

Tonight, I was marveling at the camaraderie of the sport. Think of it: fighters like Mayhem and Bisping, for example, who were destined to meet in the Octagon in December 2011, were hanging out like brothers. That was a truly wondrous sight, I thought.

But at the end of the night, we had to go out the back alley of the club, and as we did so, everyone was joking back and forth, and there was the usual booze-fueled grab-assing. The local cops were watching us from the top of a nearby parking garage, flashing lights on us and urging us to disperse. I looked around and spotted another huge crowd of partiers also leaving the club. We were surrounded.

Suddenly I got this weird feeling: *Uh-oh, it's going to be London all over again.*

Nothing actually happened that night, after all. But I've learned that if I'm going to hang out with fighters, I need to stay alert, because you never know when something like the Chinawhite incident will happen again. I firmly believe that professional fighters don't purposely cause fights of this magnitude. When they let loose, they more often are trying to defend their honor or protect a loved one.

That said, I'm always on the lookout for a "London vibe." When the party's going late, when everyone's been drinking, and when musclebound men start giving each other affectionate, brotherly punches that are just a tad too forceful, maybe it's time to call an end to the night.

YOU want to talk fights? When I once went to Hawaii with my brother Brian, we were hanging out at Waimea Beach on the north shore of Oahu, watching surfers tackle twenty-foot waves. Later some young Hawaiian guys chased these *haoles* (white guys) off their turf and commenced to kick the crap out of them. Needless to say, if my brother and I were thinking of surfing on that beach, we quickly found a new spot. It was not the last time we saw that happen. It's a tough culture.

My friend B.J. Penn embodies what I call true Hawaiian warrior spirit. He is ferocious, tenacious, and unstoppable. I got to know B.J. Penn and his brother J.D. Penn when B.J. started to fight in the UFC. We all became friends and they started inviting me to come announce their Rumble on the Rock Shows, which were fights promoted by J.D.'s Rumble World

Entertainment, and I jumped at the chance because I love them, I love the sport, and I love Hawaii.

I did four shows with them in all, three Rumble shows and one joint show with the K-1. In this way I got to know the two brothers and their family. B.J.'s mother Lorraine is about five-foot-five, beautiful and stylish. Tom Callos, B.J.'s first instructor, tells a story about how Mrs. Penn, or "Mom," as I call her, is a good grappler in her own right, who once flattened Callos's wife in a sparring match. I'd go to these fights, and there was B.J.'s mom, sitting in the front row with her sister and their extended family, cheering B.J. on. At the Expo she'd be manning the booth with her crew of ladies, selling products from their T-shirt and clothing line. Lorraine and B.J.'s dad, Jay Dee, were there every night of those shows, helping out, even if it was something simple like setting up chairs for the crowd. It reminded me of the times I worked together with my mom, dad, and brother on those collectors' shows. Mrs. Penn, in particular, reminds me a lot of my own mother, working hard to bring money into the family.

Okay, so much for the sweetness and light. Here's what I have to tell you: if you cross the Penn brothers, watch out. They will kick your ass. When you're out with the Penns, it's time to party, but you have to be aware that they never back down from a fight. Once the drinks start flowing, you don't want to piss anyone off, because you'll be brawling before the night's out. That's the essence of the culture: don't let the other guy get one over on you. Go out, have fun, but if someone gets in your face, don't hesitate to take him down. Those islands made B.J. the man he is today, a down-to-earth, warm man—who will not hesitate to take on someone bigger than himself if the guy pisses him off. Imagine having that kind of balls from the day you're born. Imagine coming from a place where that was accepted and celebrated.

Some guys will fight because it's just what they do.

In an appearance on my radio show, B.J. once announced that he wanted to fight at least five times a year. He thought that was a pretty good schedule to have. I was incredulous. B.J., I said, that's way too many times. In fact, by UFC standards, it's insane. If you train a minimum of eight weeks to get up to speed for a UFC bout, you'd be working your body at full tilt for forty weeks out of the year. No one fights that many times in a year. It's a *very* punishing schedule. But B.J. figured, look, I have to stay in shape anyway. I may as well be training hard and do some damage while I'm at it. True to his word, he fought three times in 2010 alone, twice against Frankie Edgar and once against Matt Hughes.

After one of those Hawaiian fight events, we were all out having a good time at a nightclub in Waikiki. It got late. I was tired. I figured it was time to turn in. So I said good night to everyone and left. The next morning I checked the news on the Internet and found out that a little after I left, B.J. had tussled with the cops—had actually fought with a police officer—and had ended up arrested for his bad-boy behavior. Needless to say, given his fame, it was a huge story in Hawaii. Sad as I was for him, I was thankful I hadn't stuck around or I probably would have been arrested along with him. You have to back up your friends.

ONE other incident, which I am asked about by interviewers and fans all the time, involves me and the veteran UFC/MMA fighter Frank "Twinkle Toes" Trigg. Frank and I are friends, but one night Frank got a little too cocky and did something he shouldn't have done, to me or anyone.

In June 2006 we had two UFC shows in five days at the Hard Rock Hotel in Vegas, and after the first show I was hanging out with Trigg, who was between fights, and weighing in at around 195 pounds. We had a round of vodka tonics in Mike Goldberg's room, then the three of us headed out for the night. When we reached the elevator, the doors opened, and who should be inside but Dana White and his security man, Tom.

At that point in his career, Trigg had had five UFC bouts. The previous year, 2005, he'd fought twice and lost both times. He was two for five, and itching to get back in. We got on the elevator, and before the doors even began to close, Trigg was asking Dana, "When are you going to let me fight in the Octagon again?"

I'm a wristwatch freak, and I couldn't help noticing that Dana was wearing a cool watch. I stepped in front of Trigg to look at Dana's watch as the two of them were speaking. Probably not a smart thing to do. For some reason, as I was looking at Dana's watch, Frank—who was standing off to my side—suddenly hit me firmly in the throat with a ridge-hand strike. The inside part of his hand, between the thumb and his wrist, was right at my Adam's apple.

I was blown away. You do not hit an announcer in the throat. My voice is my livelihood. It's like capping a runner in the knees or smashing a surgeon's hands. I turned around and said, "Frank, why the fuck did you hit me?"

"What are you gonna do about it?" he said.

Well, that's the wrong thing to say to me. Talk is cheap. I

hit him twice in the stomach at about 70 percent power, which sent him back against the wall. Why did I pull my punch here? Because I knew Frank hadn't hit me at full power, so I made it a point to hit him with less power, too. It's the basic rule of sparring: you train with your partner at a strong tempo, but not to hurt or KO the other guy. But if he hits you harder, then you hit back just as hard.

I will say that Frank's on record as saying that I still hit him so hard he almost shat himself. I guess there's a compliment in there somewhere.

As the elevator doors closed, he immediately came back at me.

We were locked in that elevator for ten floors now, and the fight was on.

Dana, Tom, and Goldie were plastered against the wall of the elevator as Trigg and I punched, blocked, and hit each other. At first we knew enough not to hit each other in the head, but our anger was mounting, and the fight was escalating into 100 percent power. I knew it was only a matter of time before he started pounding my head. I got myself ready to bring it if that happened. Either I knocked him out, or he was going to knock me out.

Frank tried to knee me in the balls at one point—but missed. Instead, he hit one of the other men. I don't remember who, but I knew it must have hurt. I knew I had to shut him down. So I shoulder-turned him and shoved him to the wall, and when he bounced back I began to slip in a rear naked choke, which I knew was the very same move Matt Hughes had used to submit him in two of their Octagon wars.

I was so angry that in the millisecond that I had him in the hold, I was tempted to say, "Call me Matt Hughes, bitch!"

But suddenly the doors began to open. I knew that the lobby was full of glass display cases. Not cool. If we kept fighting, we ran a risk of crashing through them and hurting ourselves as well as innocent passersby, and racking up some terrible publicity for the UFC.

I threw my hands in the air and roared, "Frank, we're done, we're done!"

I looked at Dana. He was smiling; he seemed to have enjoyed this little altercation. So had Frank. And to tell the truth, so had I.

But now I looked down and saw that my expensive new silk shirt was drenched in blood. *My* blood. The skin over the knuckle of my right thumb was peeled back, and you could see the slick white membrane above the bone. My hand was bleeding profusely. I must have caught it on Trigg's belt, or one of the large rings he was wearing. I excused myself and went to find the UFC paramedics. I asked them if they could glue the skin shut, using the liquid bandages they use in a pinch on fighters, but they insisted that I go to a local emergency room. There, I received five stitches, a tetanus shot, and a bill for $500.

Funny thing: When the doctor walked into the emergency room and saw me, he did a double take. "A bunch of us were just in the other room watching you on TV!" he said. Of course, he was blown away by the fact that he was treating *me* and not one of the fighters from that night's show.

When I went back to the Hard Rock, Frank had calmed down and was *so* apologetic. I told him I was fine, but for the next three days he kept calling me to see how I was doing. Later that night, I decided to go out to Tryst nightclub. There, I ran into Joe Rogan and Eddie Bravo, who were partying with friends and a trio of beautiful women. One of the ladies was free, and she and I hit it off.

At the time I was forty-nine years old, and all I can say is that I felt twenty-five years old all over again. It was one hell of a memorable night: I announced the UFC, watched the fights from the best seat in the house, had a friendly go with one of the world's top MMA welterweights, got stitches, partied, and enjoyed the company of a beautiful woman for the evening.

Hell—even as I write this at age fifty-five, it still sounds like a fun-filled evening to me.

Aside from a few close friends, I didn't tell anyone about the incident, but a few days later veteran UFC fighter Mikey Burnett came up to me and said, "Hey, I heard you took it to Trigg. Good job!"

I was surprised. I asked Burnett how he had heard it. He said Dana had told someone who told him. Eventually the story would leak out and go viral.

Months later, while in the UK for a show, I had the pleasure of hearing Dana relate the entire story to Lorenzo Fertitta, of all people. Dana cheered me and gave me props as we were all having a drink together.

It made me proud. My UFC Heads of State seemed glad that they didn't have a wimp announcing their Octagon Warriors.

13

ON THE ROAD

A big reason I love my job is that it gives me a chance to travel the world and have some fun in exotic places. In the beginning the UFC stayed close to home, but over the years, as it has grown more and more successful, we've branched out. Today I am happy (and exhausted) to say that we're on the road more than thirty weeks a year.

In the early days I took on some strange announcing gigs unrelated to the UFC. Overseas promoters would hire some fighters and me, and fly us halfway around the world to put on a command performance.

I do mean *command.* In 1999, I was hired by Sheik Tahnoon Bin Zayed Al Nahyan, son of the former United Arab Emirates president, to go to Abu Dhabi for the Abu Dhabi Combat Club (ADCC) Submission Wrestling World Championship. The rules were a little different: no punching, no kicking, just jiu-jitsu and grappling. If you've ever seen either of those classic movies *Enter the Dragon* or *Blood Sport,* you have some idea what this was like: a bunch of great fighters from all over the world coming together to do battle.

The promoters sent me a $12,000 first-class seat on Lufthansa to Abu Dhabi, sparing no expense. The flight crew brought out a bowl of beluga caviar for us to share. There were only five of us seated in first class, and none of the other guys wanted any. I was the only one who enjoyed the caviar, so believe me, I had a ball!

The first day of the fight event was like the opening of the Olympics, with all these fighters divided into their home nations. One by one they walked in under their flags.

Now, from the way I'm describing this, you'd think it was taking place in a massive stadium filled with tens of thousands of people. But no, it was just sort of a private party at a private compound, which was home to a racetrack and a horse stable. The sheiks themselves, and maybe some close family members and friends, were there. About two hundred people, tops. Just imagine luxury heaped upon luxury. These men sat in big chairs fit for kings, with endless drinks being poured for them and huge bowls of chocolates sitting in front of them. There was an expansive buffet table in the back, and people could take a break from the spectator sport and gorge themselves on incredible dishes of lobster and salmon and intricately prepared vegetables and drinks. These kings treated us like kings.

I *sat* at a table for two days, announcing fights literally nonstop from about 10:00 a.m. to 5:00 p.m. It was an absolutely intense atmosphere. I usually do all my own data organization of fighter stats, but in this case it was coming so fast and furious that I actually had to have a feeder, someone who passed me the names and figures throughout the day. I walked out onto the mat only once, for the main event.

A lot of the great fighters had signed on for this adventure: Royler and Renzo Gracie, Mark Kerr, Jean Jacques Machado, Caol Uno, Matt Hughes, Josh Barnett, Evan Tanner, Ricco Rodriguez, you name it. Kareem Barkalaev, the Russian, was there, as he was personal fight instructor to the sheik. During one of the fights, Kareem threw a punch and he was barred from the competition and sent home the next day.

Now, we all know today that in 2010 Sheik Tahnoon would acquire a 10 percent share of the UFC for an undisclosed sum. That didn't come out of nowhere; he's been a fan of these fights for a long time, even before Dana White and the Fertittas owned the organization. Even after the sheik's investment in the UFC, the ADCC went on to do a submission tournament in Nottingham, England.

It was probably inevitable that the fighters would be invited to perform in other nations in the Middle East. In 2001, when a bunch of the top fighters and I were asked by one of the sheiks of Kuwait to perform in that country, the Abu Dhabi trip was still fairly fresh in our memory. A lot of us jumped at the chance. This was close to when the organization was being bought by the Fertittas. Here, too, the sheik wanted a throwback to the old-school days of MMA tournaments, when one fighter would fight multiple times in a single night. With tournaments it always felt as if they were drawing names out of a hat, and you fought whomever they drew for you, with little regard for height, weight, or skill set. It was fun, it was fascinating, it was a whole lot of nuts. You'd fight someone, and if you beat him, they'd say, okay, take a break, you'll be fighting again in a little while. If you had an injury, you probably fought anyway.

I flew over with Big John McCarthy and his wife, Elaine. We were joined in Kuwait by fighters such as Matt Hughes, Carlos Newton, Dave Menne, and, from Russia, Kareem Barkalaev, about a dozen fighters in all. Everyone gets there and they're all exhausted from the long flight and so begins this very weird, otherworldly experience.

People are praying in the streets everywhere we look. Buildings look battled-ravaged. There's a military base only a few miles away, and a lot of tension in the air. I'm thinking, *I wonder if we're going to get out of this country alive, let alone get paid.* We arrive in the middle of this, and are ushered to a very nice hotel. The second we get there, the word goes around, "Stay away from the Russians." For some reason, they were not getting along with anyone. John went to check the cage, and he's walking around the posts, shaking them to see that they're solid, and it's clear that if a fighter flew into them, he would hurt not only himself but possibly spectators as well.

We had a good-sized crowd for the show, but sure enough it ended with Russian fighter Kareem Barkalaev losing to Dave Menne in the final fight. In an angry gesture, Barkalaev gestured as if he wanted to take everybody on. The next night, Sheik Naif, one of the royal family members, invited us all out to dinner and we went through a ceremony where each of us was presented with gifts. I was given a curved Yemeni dagger, a really gorgeous piece of weaponry that spoke to my love of weapons and collectibles. Kuwait was certainly different, but most of us were pretty tense during the whole four days, and happy to head home.

• • •

THERE were two experiences in other countries that I can only describe as transcendent. They were remarkable, almost spiritual encounters that made me understand just how much fans in other places revere fighters and the pleasure of sport.

The UFC 134 in Rio de Janeiro in summer 2011 was a turning point for me. I stepped into the Octagon to do my thing.

"LADIES AND GENTLEMEN," I said.

The crowd screamed.

"WE . . . ARE . . . LIVE!" I said.

A rumble ripped through the stadium that was deafening, awe-inspiring, and humbling. I got through the rest of the preliminary cards and the crowd was insane. Dana was out back getting ready, and later said he thought the fans were going to punch a hole through his dressing-room wall.

From the response of the crowd, you'd have thought I was doing a concert.

It was only later, after announcing the main event, as I was walking back to my desk, that Stitch Duran stopped me. "Did you hear that?" he said.

"Sure, it's a crazy crowd tonight!"

"No, Bruce," Stitch said, "they're repeating what you say!"

"Really?"

Remember: When I'm working, I don't pay much attention to the crowd. I'm focused on the fighters and the cards in front of me. So I didn't realize until Stitch pointed out to me that 17,000 Brazilian fans—many of whom are not English speakers—were nevertheless repeating many of my words as soon as I said them.

I'd never seen anything like that, especially from a non-English-speaking audience. Not even when Michael was roaring "Let's Get Ready to Rumble!" had I seen fans react this way. When I got to the end of my announcements, they applauded and stamped their feet, which I also had never seen done by the vast majority of fans in North American stadiums.

Later, when I got home and was able to watch the videos, I confirmed what Stitch was saying. I was blown away. From the start of my career, I've tried not to be phrase-driven. It wasn't until early in 2010 that I even trademarked the phrase "It's Time" and another line I originated, "We are live!" And now, to hear an audience go insane at those words was remarkable, and a huge compliment.

I didn't know it yet, but it was an indication that I had somehow clicked in a big way with Brazilian fans. In the months that followed, my office would start getting calls asking me to do various promotional campaigns—TV commercials mostly—in Brazil. That was great to hear, but I should not have been surprised. What I saw that night in Rio practically said it all.

As an example, backstage after the show, the Brazilian fighter Antonio Rodrigo Nogueira, who'd scored a knockout in his first round, came up to me and said, "Bruce, thank you so much. Thank you for that energy! It made me feel great to hear myself introduced this way. Please, I must take a picture with you."

That night made me feel wonderful. Brazilians have such a beautiful, unified passion for sports that it leaves you breathless. Thirty million Brazilian homes watched the fights that night, and they were so important to that nation's spirit and culture that the fights were shown for free. I will always remember the trip, and look forward to many returns. It's a beautiful country that has given a lot to the creation of MMA, and I thank them for teaching us all that you can always go deeper in service to the things you love.

Although I've since seen fans in other nations do the same thing, I will always remember that visit as the time I learned that my catchphrase really meant something to people.

Another standout experience happened an ocean away. Back in 2002 I got invited to announce at the Inoki Bom-Ba-Ye in Kobe, Japan. It's a New Year's Eve fight event organized and promoted by a much-revered Japanese wrestler named Antonio Inoki. He's a steel-jawed master showman who is in his early seventies now. His claim to fame, among other things, is that he's the only wrestler ever to have fought Muhammad Ali. The two men had tremendous respect for each other, and Inoki's Bom-Ba-Ye is actually inspired by the chant *"bumaye!"* which crowds used to cheer Ali when he fought George Foreman in Zaire in 1974. The phrase means "Kill him!" "Do it!" "Beat him up!" or "Take him out!" depending on whom you ask for a translation.

At the same time the Bom-Ba-Ye was going on, there were two other massive MMA events taking place in Japan, all within 500 miles of each other, the K-1 Premium Dynamite and the Pride Shockwave event. All three were on TV, fixating more than half the population of Japan. All three events had about 40,000 people attending them. The stadium where I was announcing had 43,000 people, which was the largest crowd I'd ever faced prior to the 55,000 people who showed up for UFC 129 in Toronto. Shows you how much the Japanese love martial arts. Imagine half the U.S.A. tuning in to three MMA events on major TV networks on New Year's Eve!

For me, it was a great event just because of the fighters on the card, such as Lyoto Machida, who was once managed by Inoki. Also there were Rich Franklin, Josh Barnett, and Aleksander and Fedor Emelianenko. But the transformative moment came at the end, when audience members left their seats and came streaming down the aisles straight for us.

What's this now? I thought.

They were coming up into the ring so the great Inoki could slap them.

You heard me: they wanted this titan of Japanese wrestling to slap them across the face. Inoki is renowned for his *Toukan* slap. To receive it from him is considered a high honor in Japan. The story is that in the 1980s, Inoki visited some schools in Japan where students tested their strength by taking turns punching him. While a news crew watched, one kid punched him in the gut and Inoki slapped him. You can watch this now-famous video online. The kid falls, but then gets up and bows to Inoki. That scene captured the imagination of the Japanese; it epitomized so many things about that culture. Stoicism. Respect. Masculine strength. It just became a thing where people asked Inoki to slap them. The word *Toukan* comes from Inoki's nickname, Moeru Toukan, which means "fighting spirit that burns."

Well, let me tell you, it does burn. Inoki was about sixty years old when we met, but he was brutal. I watched him slap Josh Barnett, and I thought, *Wow, the guy can slap.* I'm always up for something new. So I went over and asked to receive the slap of respect. He whacked me loud and hard. I went with the slap, which spun my head to the right. I balanced myself, then smiled and bowed. Inoki did the same.

But Josh is a fighter and I've had years of martial arts training.

We knew what to expect, sort of. I watched the mass of people coming down out of the stands. There were mothers, fathers, little kids, pregnant women. Since so many of these people weren't fighters, I was sure Inoki would pull his punches, so to speak.

Well, if he did, he hid it well.

I watched as these Japanese fans stood up stoically to the slap of the great fighter. Some took photos as their loved ones took the hit. Others broke down in tears, more from the honor, I suspect, than the pain, though that must have accounted for some of it. It was a gut-wrenching emotional experience. I had never seen such a massive outpouring of affection for a fighter.

Naturally, given the size of the crowd, it quickly became unruly. People were coming from all sides and I thought we would be mobbed in a matter of seconds.

Look, I said to someone, we need to organize this or someone's going to get hurt.

Inoki took the microphone from my hand and began to speak. I have no idea what he said. But a few words left his mouth and the crowd coalesced beautifully into a single line formation in a matter of seconds. I was blown away.

For the next forty-five minutes, people were silent as they accepted their slap of respect.

Oh, and I should probably tell you about my brush with death. Later that night, the organizers threw a swanky New Year's Eve after-party. Free port and champagne. Lobster. Shrimp. All-you-can-eat Kobe beef. At the party I was hanging out with Rico Chiapperelli, Rich Franklin, Jorge Gurgel, Matt Hume, Josh Barnett, and the other fighters. I spotted two Russian women I couldn't keep my eyes off. They were identical twin redheaded ring girls who were working the fights that night. I saw these girls and sauntered over, intending to strike up a conversation.

BUFFERISM NO. 9

"STAY SINGLE AND
YOUR POCKETS WILL JINGLE!"

When I hit age forty-five, I realized that more than 80 percent of my friends who had married were now divorced and paying alimony and child support. Enough said.

I didn't get too far, because Aleksander and Fedor Emelianenko came over.

The brothers smiled and each of them took one of my arms and locked it into an armbar, without applying the pressure. It's as if they were saying, "Here. Your arms are straight. We can break them at any time."

"Bruce," Fedor said in his accent. "Do we have a problem?"

My brain's going, *Uh-oh. He's serious.*

I smiled. The last thing I needed was a "problem" with these two bonebreakers. The last thing I wanted was to get the signals crossed because of the language barrier. I didn't crack a joke. I was completely deadpan. "Hey, guys, no problem here. Happy New Year!"

"Good," he said. "I like you."

He then said something in Russian to his brother, who grunted, released my arm, and walked away like it was just another day at the office. Fedor and I shook hands, wished each other Happy New Year, and went our friendly ways.

I wandered back over to Barnett and the guys, who were just laughing.

"What's so funny, guys?" I said.

"Do you realize how close you came to being a double arm cripple?" they said.

I said, "Where were you guys?"

They were like, "Over here. Not over *there*."

And who knows if Fedor wasn't kidding the whole time? But I didn't want to find out. If I was right, it would have been a bad start to the New Year.

WHEN we were in Sweden for the Gustafsson vs. Silva fight in April 2012, I had this moment when I was looking around during the prefight party and marveling at what an accomplishment the UFC was. We were all being treated to multiple magnums of Cristal, and I just had to think back . . .

As I'm writing this, I've missed only two UFC fights in sixteen years: one in December 2012 where I would've had to be in two time zones at once, and a Japan event in the early days because the UFC didn't have the budget to fly me over.

The fact that these are the only blank spots on my UFC record is pretty amazing. As yet another cork popped on a bottle of Cristal, I thought, *How far we've come.*

And I thought it again in spring 2012. I'd been studying the UFC 2012 schedule at home and had spotted what I thought was a potential snafu. UFC on FX: Maynard vs. Guida was scheduled for June 22 in Atlantic City. And the very next day we were scheduled to do UFC 148 in Rio de Janeiro. Well, that was a problem, as far as I could see. Philly to Rio was easily a fourteen-hour flight if I flew direct on a commercial flight. In some cases it's taken me as many as seventeen hours! But if there were any flight delays or stops along the way, there was a chance I'd miss the show. I could not let that happen. I couldn't risk ruining my stellar record.

I mentioned this to Lorenzo and Frank Fertitta at one of the shows, making them an offer. "Is there any way I can fly down with you on your jet? I'm willing to give up a paycheck. Take it and put it toward the fuel or whatever, because I don't want to miss that show."

Lorenzo smiled at me. "Bruce, we'll get you there, don't worry."

A few weeks later, after the third Fox network show in East Rutherford, New Jersey, I was told that the travel issue had been resolved: management would fly me from one show to the next via private jet. That weekend I needed to pack two tuxes, because within two hours of landing in Brazil, I was on my way back into the Octagon—a hemisphere away from where I was less than twenty-four hours before.

How far we've come.

14

THE NATURAL

On another visit to Japan, I stood on the outside looking in, watching as a series of men fell to the power of the monster on the mat. One by one, each of these guys tried to take him on. And one by one, he shrugged them off.

When all of them were licking their wounds, Big John McCarthy looked around to see if anyone else was left standing. His eyes lit on me. He smiled. "Come on, Bruce," he said. "It's your turn."

"Who, me?"

"Yeah, you," John said, nodding toward the mat. "Get in there."

It was December 1997. I was hanging out in a gym in Yokohama, Japan. The next day I was going to announce UFC Japan: Ultimate Japan 1. This afternoon, though, a bunch of us were just blowing off steam, visiting various locales, and had ended up at a local dojo where one of the UFC fighters was training for his main-event fight.

And now Big John had issued a challenge. He wanted me to get on the mat and do takedown attempts with the guy who had just beaten six or seven men in a row. *Okay,* I thought. *I can do this. After all, he's just taken on everyone in the gym. He must be tired.*

The monster on the mat was Randy Couture.

I got up and walked onto the mat to do my part, which was to keep him pumped up for his big fight like everyone else. And like everyone else, I got completely manhandled in seconds. Later that night, as I introduced him to 14,000 fans, my voice cracked as I said one word: *COUTURE.*

It was terrible. That rarely happens, and when it does, it's embarrassing.

Hmm, I thought, *I wonder if it's because he just kicked the crap out of me on the mat.*

UFC 13 was our baptism by fire. My first official UFC and Randy's debut. I was there when he took on Tony Halme, the so-called Finnish Viking. Randy stormed him like a bull and knocked the Viking to his back. Halme hung on for dear life, but Randy twisted his head free, slipped around to Halme's back, and sank into a rear naked choke. Remember: this was old-school UFC. The Finnish giant had a hundred pounds on Randy that night, but fell to Captain America in a minute's time. Randy's second fight, UFC 15, was one of the most memorable wars I'd ever seen. He was the underdog, going up against Vitor Belfort, whose hands seemed to deal nothing but knockouts in those days. He was coming off four wins, two against men he'd fought in the *same night*. But Randy just wore him down and finished him off. Eight minutes. Boom. Done.

Success as a fighter does not consist of getting into the Octagon, punching and grappling and hoping for the best. At least it shouldn't. Smart fighters come in with a strategy. If it works when they face their opponent, they stick with it; if it doesn't, they must be nimble enough to try something else. Couture is the most thoughtful, strategic fighter I've ever known, and I think younger fighters would do well to learn from his attention to detail. He tailors his prefight training to his opponent's strengths and weaknesses. If the opponent is a famed puncher, Couture trains himself so hard that he could shrug off a locomotive if it hit him in the face. He calculates how to get that guy to the mat as quickly as possible, because his own strength is in wrestling. If he can get the man down, he'll succeed, and he usually does.

Couture was a great wrestler who'd evolved over time to become a phenomenal MMA artist. He knew just how to strike and move his body in an unorthodox manner that confused his opponents. He could break down and defuse strikers. He could defuse wrestlers. The third round was occasionally tough for him, but he always came back and won. I'm not privy to his thought process, but from the outside it seems as though he has every fight planned out, as every fighter should, but he's nimble enough to shift and adapt as the fight progresses. The great Muhammad Ali used to be able to predict the round he'd win in. If Randy were as cocky as Ali was, he could probably do the same thing. In sizing up opponents, he was a very experienced general, mapping out strategy on the battlefield. I'll lose a thousand men, a general might say, but I know I'll take that fort.

I used to know a Russian fighter who didn't like to get hit. You can always tell when fighters are like that. It's their tell.

They turn their heads away from the punch if they see it coming, and they lose focus and control. You can't do that. Randy doesn't. He seems to relish it. You have to keep watching your opponent. I mean, if you cook bacon, you're gonna get stung by grease.

Once upon a time he got a lot of flak for retiring, then coming back. And there was controversy another time, because the UFC wouldn't let him out of his contract. Anyone on the inside understood what was going on. Randy was hugely popular with fans, and his agent had lined up a number of Hollywood projects and commentating gigs for him. He had a chance to make big money, and why shouldn't he? Who could fault Randy for leaving under those circumstances?

But watch what happens. Randy is in retirement, and he's in the commentator's booth and says he wants to come out of retirement to fight Tim Sylvia, who was the reigning heavyweight champ. Why? To me it's obvious. Watching Tim fight, Randy saw a chink in Tim's armor that Randy knew he could get through. What does that tell you? He's watching fights as a layman now, but he's analyzing them far more perceptively than anyone else can—commentators and fighters alike. He perceives the man's weakness, his curiosity gets the better of him, and at the age of forty-three, he proceeds to go in and take the guy apart!

He put Tim on his butt with one punch in the first few seconds of the fight. He was an 8-to-1 underdog. At UFC 15 in 1997, he beat Vitor Belfort as a 6-to-1 underdog. In UFC 44, he had Tito Ortiz upside down, with his butt in the air, and spanked Tito on the butt on camera before taking the man's title. Imagine having the composure in one of your most important bouts to lighten up and say, "Okay, this is one for the camera, guys."

The first time I ever saw him on the fence was at the hands of the Brazilian fighter Pedro Rizzo, in UFC 31. It was the first UFC under Zuffa, and one of the most brutal fights I've ever seen in the Octagon. Five five-minute rounds. Hugely intense. The two fighters inflicted serious damage on each other, and in the end Couture was chosen by unanimous decision. That was controversial at the time, and the controversy triggered an immediate rematch: UFC 34. Randy won *again*, this time by TKO in the third round. It was incredible. Pedro was eleven years younger than Randy, and a ferocious kicker. I remember, back in the late nineties, hanging out with Tank Abbott in Brazil. The poor guy limped so badly after a fight with Pedro that I thought I was walking around with a wounded King Kong on a leash. And Randy took Rizzo on at the age of thirty-eight, and *won*?

Back in the early days, Randy and I never really hung out together. But that changed the more we saw each other at fights and a couple of poker events. A boxing promoter once invited a bunch of us to come to Australia for one of the first MMA events ever held there. We were there for five days with free time before and after the show, during which we also went to an Australian football game where Randy addressed the players before they hit the field. Later we visited them in the locker room for celebration, laughs, and beer. Let me tell you, Australian footballers are some tough mofos!

Randy had a few beers and he was having a blast. He's not one to have too many, but he does have his moments. I'd never even heard him curse until that night. We were walking back to the car, and for some reason, something had pissed him off and he went off on this witty, foulmouthed rant in the parking lot. "F—this, and f—that!" I whipped out my camera and started videotaping him and he was hamming it up now for the camera because he realized how hilarious he sounded. So believe it or not, I actually have a video of Randy Couture cursing his head off in an Australian parking lot. No one's ever seen it but me, and I'd be a fool to release it, because I certainly don't need Mr. Couture to come knocking on my door.

Sometime in 2011, I ran into him and we were talking. He said, "You know, Bruce, I don't know how many more wars I have left in me." Shortly afterward, he left the UFC for good. He left in style. Every fighter wants to leave on his own terms. Randy did.

And unlike other fighters, he took the time to prepare for his after-fight life. Other fighters think the money will last and it doesn't. Randy took acting lessons and lined up work in commercials, TV, and film. He'll never be Laurence Olivier, but he's got a commanding presence that's great for many roles. He did two of *The Expendables* movies, he launched a bunch of products in his clothing line, and best of all, he's got his own gym. What wrestler wouldn't give his right nut to have a personal training session with Randy Couture? Who would turn that down? Is there a better teacher? It's like taking a basketball class with Michael Jordan. Guys like Randy and Tito can really teach, too, because they have the head for it. Plenty of great fighters just don't know how to get the knowledge out of themselves and put it into words in order to teach it.

I kid Randy a bit because he's been married a couple of times, but he's always been a good role model, probably the best the sport has ever seen. His example says to younger fighters, hey, you don't have to give it up too soon. If you have the edge, you can extend this into your fourth decade.

It saddens me that I will never announce his name in the Octagon again. I always enjoyed doing it, because it's wonderful to announce someone with incredible credentials.

"LADIES AND GENTLEMEN—

"HE IS THE ONLY FIGHTER TO WIN TWO UFC CHAMPIONSHIP TITLES FIVE TIMES AND IN TWO DIFFERENT WEIGHT CLASSES—

"PRESENTING THE FORMER TWO-TIME UFC LIGHT-HEAVYWEIGHT CHAMPION—

"THE FORMER INTERIM UFC HEAVYWEIGHT CHAMPION—

"THE FORMER UFC HEAVYWEIGHT CHAMPION—

"THE LEGENDARY UFC HALL OF FAME OCTA-GON WARRIOR—

"RANDY 'THE NATURAL' COUTURE!"

When I introduced him at UFC 102 in Portland, Oregon, in 2009, I knew that this great warrior's days were winding down. I didn't know when he would call it quits, but I didn't want to miss the chance to do something I'd wanted to do for so long.

I bowed as I announced his name.

I've never bowed to anyone before, and it'll be a long time before I do it again.

You only do it in the presence of MMA royalty.

15

IT'S A GAMBLE

My father taught us to play blackjack when we were kids, and I was always pretty good at it because I had a head for numbers. I even skipped a grade in math in school. I'm not Rain Man, but I'm pretty good. But I never really got a chance to play for real until I was twenty-one years old and starting to help my parents out with those gun and collectible shows where they exhibited at the legendary Riviera Hotel & Casino in Vegas. It was one of the top hotels in Vegas back in the day, and still lives large in American culture as the backdrop of movies such as *Casino*.

I loved those days. My father was what they called a boss gambler. Not a whale, exactly, but a guy who was well known enough to be comped and occasionally get the Frank Sinatra Suite, with everything paid for by management short of tips and play. He'd say to us, "Hey, you want to see a show?" Then he'd turn to Louie, the pit boss, and say, "My boys want to see a show." Louie looked like a guy out of a Scorsese movie. He'd make a call and cup the phone to his huge chest. "Hey," he once said to Brian and me, "Elvis is at the Hilton tonight. You wanna see Elvis?"

"Nah," we said. "We want to see Shecky Greene."

"You saw Shecky last night," Louis reminded us.

"So what?" Brian said. "He was funny."

"Yeah," I said. "We can see Elvis anytime."

Stupid us. It would turn out to be one of the last concerts Elvis played before he died.

After a while, people knew us and no one ever questioned the fact that I was gambling at such a young age. There was one glittering night when Brian won $8,000, I won $12,000, and our father $20,000! Our mother was ecstatic: $40,000 in one night!

Another time, when I was twenty-four, I had a huge win at the blackjack tables. As soon as I called it quits, the pit boss came out, congratulated me, and told me I could never play there again. He claimed I was a card counter. I was stunned. I don't have the head for counting cards, and was offended. Card counting sounded easier than what I was doing.

I persuaded them to let me stay by agreeing to play the six-deck shoe. Your odds are terrible on the six-deck because the casino is literally shuffling six decks and you have less of a chance to hit the high cards.

But guess what? I continued to win!

After a while, I started running my own weekend gun and collectible shows in Los Angeles, at the Hollywood Park Casino. When the show closed for the afternoon, I'd hang out in the casino. They didn't have blackjack, so I started playing poker, mostly seven-card stud or, better, high/low and a new game, No Limit Texas Hold 'Em. This was the game everyone was playing, and I became infatuated with it. It's the game you see played on the World Series of Poker, where the top champions get a gem-encrusted gold bracelet, the most desired prize in gambling.

It seemed only natural for me to keep playing, and as I got older, poker became a second or third career for me. From time to time I've dabbled in other forms of gambling. For a long while, like a lot of people, I became obsessed with following and betting on football. I became very good at handicapping the bookmakers' point spreads, and I was at my best when I stuck to my guns and my own analyses about who would win. When you bet like this, you can win even if you bet on the losing team. The trick is to beat the point spread.

I remember running into a very famous professional athlete—you'd know him, believe me—in Vegas on Super Bowl weekend, 2009. The Steelers vs. Cardinals game. I was in town for UFC 94, GSP vs. Penn. Right after the fights, I watched this sports star lose a million dollars at the high-roller roulette table. That's a lot of chips to lose on a game that depends not on skill but pure luck alone.

The next morning I ran into him at the gym, where he told me that he'd used up his $1.5-million credit line with the casino but still wanted to bet on the Super Bowl. He asked me if I knew anyone in Vegas who could extend him some credit. I couldn't help. Before he left, he told me to bet on the Steelers, who were the favorite. Well, I'd already placed a bet on the Cardinals. My VP Kristen was from Arizona, and I thought we'd have fun together cheering for her team. I changed my bet on the big man's advice, though. Wouldn't you know it, the Steelers *did* win, but they didn't cover the point spread, so I ending up losing. Had I stayed with my gut and gone with the Cardinals, I actually would have won money and retained my perfect record. Until that day, I had never lost money on a Super Bowl bet in nine years. The lesson there is not so much never to listen to a losing bettor, but to always trust your instincts over someone else's. And to stick to games where you have some control over the outcome.

That's what I like about poker. It's about your personal skill, not taking a chance on what an athlete or what a ball in a roulette wheel is going to do.

BUFFERISM NO. 10

"IT'S LEGAL TO LIE AT THE POKER TABLE."

I never lie in life. I tell the truth or I don't say a word. I love poker because I can get all my yah-yahs out and it's not only okay, it's expected.

Poker ultimately pushed football out of my life. My career really started with a poker tournament at the Borgata in Atlantic City. I was in town to announce UFC 53 in 2005, and decided to play my first tourney. I made it all the way through to the final table. The fever took hold of me. I realized I had the skills to play—big. Then, later in 2005, I made the televised final table again at the World Poker Tour's Celebrity Tournament. It's the dream of many players to be at that table, and I got in on my second outing. It was only my second tournament, and I came in sixth! I got invited to appear in an instructional poker DVD and started doing more tournaments on the pro circuit. I got world-class rated and became a player with a team called Full Tilt Poker. The more you win, the higher up you go in the annual professional rankings.

Well, as soon as I was playing for Full Tilt Poker, I decided to make some changes. I was becoming obsessed with poker, and I was already obsessed with football. I was a winning football season bettor for the last seven seasons, but I realized that between playing poker during the week, and spending Sundays and Mondays glued to the set watching football, I was spending way too much time on gaming and sports. It robbed me of my social life and ate into activities I loved, such as surfing, brunch dates on weekends, and time with my loved ones.

Screw it, I thought. *Football's out. I'll stick with poker.*

10 TIPS FOR MASTERING POKER

1. Watch hundreds of hours—seriously!—of poker TV shows and read a poker book.
2. Watch the instructional video *Final Table Poker* starring poker pros and yours truly.
3. Eat right, sleep right, exercise right, play right.
4. Don't play with the rent money!
5. Never have your girlfriend sit beside you and watch.
6. Learn the math. In school it cost you a grade, but on the felt, it can cost you your bank account!
7. Don't fall asleep at the table.
8. If you want to win, you should never drink more than one drink every four hours, if at all.

9. Leave the uppers and Adderall at home.
10. Win like you're used to it, and lose like it doesn't bother you.

So I stopped betting during the football season. These days, I only bet on a few playoff games and the Super Bowl when in Vegas. (There's always a UFC in Vegas on Super Bowl weekend.) The funny thing is, once I stopped betting on football, I pretty much stopped watching games in their entirety. Having a little action on the games always made it more fun for me to watch the whole game and cheer away. Ultimately I think my decision was a good one. I knew in my heart when too much of a particular vice was too much, and I quit in favor of the sport that gave me more control over the outcome.

I approach poker with the same attitude that I approach fighting, competition, business, and life itself. In a way, I guess it's a substitute for what I used to get out of surfing or fighting. These days I can't train or spar, much less fight, the way I could in my thirties. I can't go three rounds and have a great sparring match in kickboxing anymore. The arthritis in my shoulder has made it so that I can't and shouldn't paddle out more than a hundred yards or into dangerous waters when I surf. I just don't have the range of motion, so I have to pick my surf spots more carefully now.

I *can* play poker for the rest of my life. I *can* travel all over the world and do this wherever I go. I *can* sit at a table in combat with someone, and use my mind and my God-given talent for making my own luck. And guess what? Poker has a lot in common with fighting. It's the same strategy, the same mental attitude, the capacity for bold opportunism.

When you fight in the ring or the Octagon, you're

one-on-one. When you fight, you derive tremendous satisfaction from knocking an opponent off his game and triumphing. Poker's only slightly different. You start out navigating a group dynamic, but as people drop out and you ascend to the higher echelons, you're soon playing one-on-one with the better players. And you win by knocking someone off the table and taking their chips. And the whole time, you have to be thinking three steps ahead, the way you do in chess, backgammon, or fighting—all things I love.

At a poker table, there might be nine other guys sitting there. But it's not really nine guys. Your true competition is the weakest man at the table. Your goal, should you choose to accept it, is to knock that guy out. But to figure out which one you're going to pit yourself against, you have to watch everyone like a hawk. What are their personalities? Who's passive? Who's aggressive? Who's passive-aggressive? You begin to feel like a Jedi master, trying to feel the Force and determine whom to take out.

You watch how they put their chips out. Do they shove them out, or slowly put them out? Do they raise mediocre hands? Are they raising with every hand just to be in, and throwing out half-assed raises? Are their chips neat or untidy? If they are low on chips, you know you can pick on them. You always pick on the weak players, just the way a canny fighter knows to pick on a wounded warrior. You kick them on the wounded leg and keep attacking. If they have a cut on their eye, do you punch the other? No way! You beat them where it hurts until you make them break.

Poker isn't as strenuous as fighting. But it does tax you mentally and physically. Some of the competitions run for twelve hours a day and you need to stay alert, well fed, and well rested.

It gets very exhausting sitting at a table with a bunch of clever men and women waiting for you to show some sign of weakness. When I enter these tournaments, I follow practically the same regimen as I do when I announce: I wake up, work out, have a power breakfast. It's not about which girls I'm going out with tonight, or which clubs I'm going to. It's about staying focused. I meditate to get my head in the right place, and then I go downstairs and go to war.

Until that Black Friday, April 15, 2011, when the U.S. Department of Justice effectively shut down online poker, I enjoyed playing the sport online. I remember one time arriving at my hotel room in Abu Dhabi and dipping into a little online poker. I was doing really well, but I'd just been flying for more than twenty hours and was jet-lagged. Next thing you know, I dozed off in the middle of the game! I woke up three hours later and looked at the screen. I was still in the running, because I'd done so well earlier in the game and had built up so many chips. To stay awake, I was slapping myself in the face to finish the game. It was hilariously nerve-racking, and a hell of a lot of fun. I ended up finishing third and winning $11,000—not bad for a guy who almost slept through the tournament.

I wouldn't want to give the impression that I never lose. Everyone loses.

You can't win every night. You can't let it affect you. If it does, you have to leave poker. If I let my loss from a couple of days ago get me down, it's going to affect my success *today*. Ergo, I have to ban loss and failure and negativity from my psyche. How else can I move forward?

I see a lot of similarities between that mind-set and the fighters I see. In the Octagon, you have to stay positive, you have to stay fit, and you have to stay mentally alert. If you make one mistake in fighting, you're knocked out. If you make one mistake in poker, you're knocked out.

Do you remember UFC 31 in 2001? Pat Miletich was winning the fight. Carlos Newton got him into a bulldog choke, and Pat lost the fight because of one mistake. He ended up losing by submission with only ten seconds left in the second round. That's exactly what can happen if you slip and lose your concentration. I remember looking at Pat's face after the fight; it pained me to see the frustration that was etched onto it. He was so mad at himself that he ripped out his mouthpiece and flung it away. He knew he had it. Only ten seconds to go!

Or more recently, you probably remember that UFC 112 bout in Abu Dhabi, where we all watched the challenger, Chael Sonnen, go against the legendary Anderson Silva. Chael hit Anderson well over 200 times with strikes and kicks, all the way up to *the last two minutes of the fifth round*, when Silva made Chael tap to submission from a guillotine choke. Until that moment, Chael was winning convincingly on all the judges' cards. These things happen, and every fighter has to make his peace with them.

My uh-oh! moment came in 2010 during the World Series of Poker. When we started the series, we all started with $30,000. In the span of five days, I'd built that up to $512,000. (Please bear in mind that these figures are not "real" money, but tournament chips. Everyone starts with the same number of chips in a tournament—and winner takes all.) Now, on the fifth day, the 7,500 players had dwindled down to 478. On the last hand before first break, I was on the button, meaning I had a decision to make. My opponent was a young hoodie-clad poker warrior. He raised the chip blind from $8,000 to $25,000. I peeled back pocket aces, the most powerful opening hand in the game.

I raised his $25,000 to $75,000 in chips.

He went in the tank, which means he had to think. He zoned out for two minutes, which is an eternity at the poker table. Finally he called my bet and put out the $75,000.

The dealer now hit us with the flop. Three cards hit the table: eight, ten, eight.

In my hand I held aces and eights, the notorious "Dead Man's Hand," which legend says was held by the gunslinger Wild Bill Hickok when he was shot in the back in 1876.

I did the numbers and I figured the range. Whenever you play poker, you have to figure out what range of cards a player would typically raise a bet on. Everyone's got different thresholds. Me, I'll play any two cards, whether it's a ten and eight suited, or king and jack suited, or a four and five suited. Other guys will only call bets or raises when they're holding "premium" hands, such as an ace and a king, a king and a queen, or any pair. You've got to hack the code, and figure out how each player works, and go after them accordingly. So now I asked myself, *Why would my opponent raise the bets? Does he have a pair of tens? Or a pair of eights? Why would he call my $75,000 chip raise?*

I did an insane thing. I bet $100,000 in chips.

My opponent went in the tank again, and then finally, grudgingly, pushed out a stack of $100,000 in chips to meet mine.

The dealer gave us the turn card—the king.

I started strategizing. Okay, a king. What does that mean? I figured if my opponent had an ace and a king, or two kings, in his hand, he'd be aggressive as hell in his betting.

I bet $130,000 in chips.

I waited for him to make his move. This was his chance. Was he going to jump on it or not? He didn't. He went in the tank for over two minutes. *Okay,* I thought. *He doesn't have kings.*

When he came out from under that hoodie, he shoved his entire stack at me, going all-in.

I looked at the chips in front of me. I'd started with a little over a half million dollars. I was now down to $150,000 in chips.

The chips in the pot were worth $1 million.

Do I fold or call, hoping my opponent has a king, and he maybe doesn't realize I have aces? What do I do? If I win, I'll be in the top ten–chip leader count of a tournament that pays $7.5 million in *real money* for first place. The tournament's buy-in—the money we all put in to enter and get our first stack of chips—was $10,000. If I lost now, I'd win $27,500—a net gain of $17,500. It was a fall from grace, but a soft fall.

I called. My opponent turned over two eights. He flopped four eights on the table, what we call quad eights.

I lost.

The cameras were on me. I had just played five days straight, playing the best players in the world, playing my best game ever. And all that was taken away from me. All gone in the flip of a couple of cards.

All the air left my body.

But how do you feel after that?

I recalled something my father always told us: *Win like you're used to it, lose like it doesn't bother you.*

Wise words, but tough to live up to—in the heat of the moment. But hey, I wasn't going to live in failure. Okay, I made the wrong call, but it was the right one at the time. It took ten minutes to recover from that loss after I started breathing again. But don't think I didn't play that scenario over and over again in my head more than a hundred times. I saw it as an opportunity to learn. I now have a love/hate relationship with pocket aces whenever I peel back my cards. Statistics show that if you're facing more than one player, you will lose with pocket aces 66 percent of the time when going all the way to the river, or last card. These days I try to push all players out of the hand by the turn card, the fourth card dealt by the dealer. Lesson learned.

I went home with $27,500 that day. And about two weeks later, I won first place and another $75,000 in the main event of Larry Flynt's Grand Slam of Poker at the Hustler Casino. The two events together made it my winningest month ever: $100,000-plus in a single thirty-day period.

It's hard to feel bad about a loss when that happens.

There's an old saying: where there's a chip and a chair, you can win. As long as I have a few chips in front of me, I know I can win. As long as I have bullets in the gun, I know I can shoot. As long as I can stand, I know I can throw a punch.

One of these days, I'll win that bracelet. And when I do, I *will* flaunt it.

You'll see it in the Octagon.

It'll be on my microphone arm.

16

THE ICEMAN

The funny thing about MMA guys is that in their street clothes they don't always look like the monsters they are. At an event in the American South once, after the fights were over, a bunch of us hit the bars. I was standing at this divey watering hole having a drink with some of the fighters when it became obvious that the guys closest to us had probably been drinking since noon. The music was cranked. People were screaming and dancing, and someone shoved us. We told the guy to watch it, and he mouthed off to us.

Well, not to me, exactly.

To Chuck Liddell.

How crazy do you have to be, right? Now, granted, maybe if you've never watched an MMA bout in your life and you saw these guys in a bar, you might be thinking, hey, I can take them. Well, no, mincemeat, you can't. I call you mincemeat because that's what you're about to become.

Some MMA fighters don't look that big, but Chuck Liddell is actually much bigger in person than most people think. My father once said that Chuck was one of the most naturally tough-looking men in the UFC.

I'm looking at Chuck and there's this look in his eyes like, *Okay, I'm going to take one more sip of beer, and when I put this down, someone's losing his head.*

You'll remember from my description of the London street brawl that I watched Chuck defending himself in an alley. We were definitely not feeling any pain that night, and he was still one of the most dangerous human bulldozers you could have encountered in that alley. Watching him work a public street brawl was like watching a movie without the flashy sound effects. He was just swatting people. Swat. Swat. Swipe.

So this night down south, B.J. Penn and I looked at each other and nodded, knowing that we had best back Chuck up, as something was about to blow up. B.J. stepped in right behind Chuck, glaring at these guys. I took Chuck's right.

We just looked at these guys, and watched the threat evaporate from their eyes like sweet tea on Alabama asphalt in June.

And Chuck turned around and thanked us both.

There must have been something in the air that night, because as I left the club, a hellacious brawl broke out between two girls at the front entrance. There were so many swinging punches and so much hair-pulling that even the bouncers hung back, not wanting to get caught in the middle of it. They didn't get involved until the blood started flowing; then they had to step in and shut it down. But still—that's not a common sight in my neck of the woods on a Saturday night.

I think sometimes that the secret of Chuck's success might

be his disarming toughness. He worked as a bouncer in San Luis Obispo, where he's from, and I'm sure he learned to defuse situations and always be ready to throw down. He's not cut like a bodybuilder; that's not his physique. But so what? He's one of the most steel-muscled men you'd ever want to meet. With his iconic mohawk and the Hawaiian Kempo tattoo on his arm, he's a true original. He's created trends with his haircut, his partying style, his legendary prowess with the ladies. But he's absolutely authentic. He doesn't copy anyone; people copy him, down to the hair.

Early in the sport's history, the bosses figured out that certain fighters captured the imagination of the fans. Guys like that were assets to the organization beyond their box-office appeal, if you will. You could trot them out to meet the press. You could put them in a suit and have them promote the sport. You could put them in gloves (or not) and put them on your next poster. They were very visible ambassadors. Early on, guys like Royce Gracie were the face of the sport. Tito Ortiz, when he showed up, was one of those poster boys. You could say that a guy like Tank Abbott was a controversial face in the early days. Chuck Liddell, who started fighting in 1998 with UFC 17, quickly became one of the sport's biggest icons of all time. Not just for the UFC, but for the sport of MMA as a whole. Even today I'd argue that Chuck is still one of the most familiar, visible faces of the sport internationally, though he retired in 2010.

He's a true fighter in the way that B.J. and Randy are. There are guys who fight because they have tremendous skill and they know it will earn them a good living. God bless 'em. There's no shame in that. They fight the way most of us work to get a paycheck and provide for our families. But if you told Chuck,

"We're no longer paying fighters. Will you still fight?" in a heartbeat, Chuck would probably say, *"Yes, because it's fun!"*

I know this because he was accepting fights in the old days when none of us were making much money from the UFC. He's a fighter's fighter. He will take on anything. I can't say enough to compliment his toughness.

He's a guy who shuts down other athletes. I first met Chuck's wife, Heidi, the mother of their baby girl, when she was dating the baseball player Jose Canseco, as Jose and I played a number of poker tournaments together in L.A. Jose and Heidi remained friends after they stopped seeing each other, and Canseco would call from time to time. If she was with a new boyfriend, he'd always sort of mock them to her over the phone. Just joking, you understand. But, funny thing: Heidi told me that she noticed he stopped doing it when she began dating Chuck.

You can trace the origin of Chuck's toughness by looking at his fight training bloodline. His trainer, John Hackleman, owner of a California dojo called The Pit, is one of the toughest men I have ever met. Hackleman was a professional boxer who happened to have a love for martial arts. His skill and life experience are amazing enough, but he somehow manages to infect his students with his spirit—if he sees that they have what it takes. John is one of the most sincere men I've ever met. A fighter never gets a compliment from him unless John means it.

Chuck was in hog heaven with the UFC, where he could indulge his love for fighting. In my opinion, the money was always an afterthought for him. Once when we were in London for an event, he invited me to a nightclub to meet after the UFC show—*not* the infamous Chinawhite—where he was making an "appearance." I got there and where was Chuck? He was up on the balcony hanging out with some friends. I went up to join him, and there were crowds of MMA-loving Londoners shouting his name up from the street; some were even shouting mine. Here we were, far from home, and they knew this fighter by sight.

That doesn't surprise me. I love our UK events. The UK fighters (and sometimes the fans) always come ready to fight. They are a naturally tough people, always ready to throw down, especially after a pint or two.

Looking out over this London street scene now, Chuck leaned over and said, "They paid me a lot of money to come here and drink tonight. But you know what? I'm having a good time!"

People love being around him in social settings because he puts them at ease. I remember spending a Sunday afternoon with him hanging out at the pool at the Vegas Hard Rock Hotel, site of the hotel's famous Rehab party, which was even the basis of a reality show on TruTV. It was great fun, great girls in bikinis and thongs, and we're checking everyone out. Chuck's standing there with his four-pound Chihuahua and his jet-black-painted toenails. That's Chuck: the world's toughest man, petting a Chihuahua and showing off his painted toenails. He's just himself. And who's gonna tell him otherwise? He can do whatever he wants.

BUFFERISM NO. 11

"I'VE NEVER MARRIED, BUT I WAS ALMOST DIVORCED TWICE."

Twice in my life I considered marrying. Thank God I didn't. It would have ended in divorce, without question. I wasn't ready for marriage. I probably would have fooled around on them. Today, I will not enter into a marriage if I have even the slightest thought of cheating. It's not fair to her, me, or the institution of marriage.

His persona aside, I think Chuck will always be remembered as a formidable fighter. The skills come first, of course. He was a striker first and foremost, but also a top wrestler. His ability to get up after someone shot on him or went for a takedown was incredible. He was like the Terminator; he just kept getting up. It was amazing to watch him get pinned against the cage, and then see that leg of his just come up out of nowhere and propel him to his feet, where he could shrug off an opponent. I've seen very few fighters who can "sprawl" and evade the takedown so handily.

One of the first times I saw him fight, in 1999, he refused to tap against Jeremy Horn, who had more than a hundred MMA fights, more than anyone on the planet, probably. Horn got Chuck in an arm-triangle choke. And the fight ended only because the referee realized that Chuck had gone to sleep.

To sleep.

They pried away Horn's arm and there was Chuck, out like a light on the Octagon floor. I wondered: Did it happen before he realized he should tap? Or did he refuse to tap? Probably the latter. Crazy, I know, but that's Chuck.

He also had the ability to land devastating strikes from impossible angles. He knocked out Kevin Randleman with one punch in UFC 31. It happened in such a weird way that if you watch the tape, you're left wondering, *Wait—where did that punch come from?* Chuck knew just how to turn his body, even when he was trapped in bizarre positions, to get the leverage he needed to deliver a punishing blow. He reminded me of guys like Muhammad Ali or Sugar Ray Robinson, who could throw punches even as they were stepping back from their opponents. Sometimes you have to both retreat *and* attack at the same time. That's really hard to pull off. Most fighters get it confused and end up leaving themselves open to attack. Not the greats. Chuck once knocked down Vernon White with a straight right hand while walking backward, and his blow carried so much force that it cracked White's orbital bone in the process.

So what happened? Chuck retired following UFC 115, after losing in a horrendous knockout. I look back on that night, and I still think he was winning that fight up until that final blow from Rich Franklin, who is a powerful striker.

Chuck was coming off a crushing number of fights. Of the last six bouts he'd been in, he'd been TKO'd three times, KO'd twice, and had won only once. Something happens to fighters when they start getting knocked out. They still have the confidence, they can study the fights objectively and see all the ways it could have gone the other way, but it's still too much of a risk to get back in the Octagon. You can win and *still* get hurt. You can get hurt in that six-to-eight-week buildup to the fight. Guys like Chuck don't spar lightly.

Some said he should have retired a while ago. But it was up to him to decide, and I'm glad he finally did.

As a rule, MMA people don't get hit in the head as much as people think, because so many MMA fights are taken to the ground. But strikers get hit a lot because their style naturally forces their opponents to defend themselves on that level.

I was worried about him because he's not just a fighter to

me. He's a friend. All it takes is one fight to mess things up for you forever. Many boxers suffer from pugilistic dementia, a condition of declining mental prowess found in those who have suffered concussions. I didn't want to see that happen to Chuck. I want him to have a great life and go on to the bigger and better things that await him, especially after all the years of blood, sweat, and honor he displayed in the Octagon.

I was so happy when I heard Chuck was joining Zuffa as a vice president. It was a smart move by Dana and the Fertitta brothers. Chuck's approachable and soft-spoken. He can speak intelligently to the press about the sport, he is loved and respected by all UFC fans, and he can educate fans because he knows the history cold. At the time of the announcement, everyone was asking, "Well, what's he going to *do*?"

Listen: all he has to do is be Chuck Liddell. Like Tyson, like Ali, he'll forever be an ambassador of the sport. And the best thing is, he doesn't have to take anyone's head off to do it.

17

FANS

One December, a young man wrote me from the UK hoping that I'd be able to help him give his girlfriend a Christmas gift that she wouldn't be able to get in a store. She was a roller-derby skater who had chosen to roll under the nickname "Bruise Buffer." Her number? One-eighty, of course. She had registered the nickname with the International Roller Derby Committee, so no other RD girl could use the name.

The boyfriend wondered if I'd be willing to write her a letter of endorsement. Nothing fancy. Just a note to say that I'd heard the story and was cool with her use of the nickname.

When I read the letter, I chuckled. I couldn't resist sharing the accompanying photo of the young girl in her roller-derby jersey with a few friends. I liked the pun, and it made my day that a young athlete would want to honor me in such a way. I wrote back with my thumbs-up, and added, "Please wish her my best and to be safe, tough, and relentless on the track and to Skate Like a Warrior!"

Another time, I ran into a trio of brothers at a UFC event in Chicago who had driven through a snowstorm that dumped three feet of snow on their home in South Dakota. I heard them calling my name early in the show. When I looked up, I saw three guys walking down the steps from the upper tier of the stadium in camo-colored T-shirts, each emblazoned with the word BUFFER. We took some pictures together, and a few weeks later they were nice enough to send me one of the T-shirts in the mail, along with photos of the snowstorm they had braved to make the show. I cherish the photo of all of us because it was such a compliment.

If you'd told me thirty years ago that people would some-day be selling T-shirts with my name on them, I would have laughed in your face. Even after I became an announcer, I fig-ured the attention of the fans would be forever focused on the fighters, and rightly so. They're the ones doing the hard work. But I was stunned to discover that some of the fan love has spilled over onto me.

Their attention honors me. Flatters me. Humbles me. And sometimes just plain cracks me up.

All of life is a pyramid, and the fans are the base of the UFC. *Without fans, the pyramid crumbles.* All of us are jobless without the fans. The fans keep the organization afloat. Dana and the Fertittas know this well, and their genius has been to help the fighters and the support staff understand it as well. When we're on the road, there are these die-hard fans who literally camp out twenty-four hours a day in the lobbies of the hotels where we stay, hoping for a glimpse of their favorite UFC celebrities. It sometimes looks like the lines you'd see snaking out of a theater to see *Stars Wars* or some other giant movie premiere. I was once approached by some fans who'd been at our hotel all weekend long, who asked for my autograph, then asked if I knew when Dana was coming down. They hadn't seen him all weekend. "I hate to tell you this, guys," I said, "but Dana isn't staying at this hotel." They were crushed. No one in the group had considered that possibility.

The UFC is so smart that it actually holds training sessions to teach fighters how to use social media—free Internet applications such as Twitter and Facebook—to reach fans, excite them, interact with them, and grow the fighters' followings. As an incentive, the UFC has even paid a bonus to the fighter who lands the largest number of new followers. Look at the six-figure Twitter numbers of guys like Randy Couture, B.J. Penn, Jon "Bones" Jones, Chuck Liddell, Rashad Evans, and Georges St-Pierre, and you begin to see how well they're connecting with millions of fans with the flick of a button on their phone. I love Bones Jones's Tweets in particular. He'll ask people what their favorite motivational quotes are. Or, instead of treating his fans to an endless stream of his own thoughts, Jon will try to get fans engaged. "What can you tell me today, people?" he'll ask. That's generous of him, not to mention smart.

Beyond the realm of the digital, though, the UFC arranges autograph and meet-and-greet sessions with the fans on weigh-in days and before fight nights. It amazes me to watch how fighters who are dehydrated and have been cutting weight like crazy to drop twenty pounds will stop in a hallway on their way to and from a weigh-in to give a fan an autograph. How easy it would be to say, "Not right now. I'm busy." But no. They do it selflessly every time.

We're in a long-tail business. The payoff, for us, is way down the road. If a fan feels welcomed by the UFC, he or she will tell their friends. And so on, and so on. Good karma will always come around.

If someone writes me via e-mail, Twitter, or mail, I write them back. I usually take time after the UFC events to check my account. On a Sunday night after a show, it's often brimming with the warm wishes that have poured in from the fans during the show. I always get a kick out of those days when I'm trending on Twitter. I have no idea what sets it off, but it's nice to be noticed.

BUFFERISM NO. 12

"BE HONEST. WHY LIE? IT'S TOO HARD TO REMEMBER WHAT YOU SAID."

I've always been scrupulously honest in business and dating. I'd rather date different women at once and be honest than tell each of them we're exclusive and then find ways to lie about seeing someone else on Thursday. Lying takes work and saps your energy. Why not use that energy to get what you really want?

And let's face it: I'm human too, and although it's rare, I *have* made mistakes. If and when that happens, you'd better believe the fans let me know. One time I introduced GSP as being five feet tall, not five-foot-ten. I didn't know I'd done that until

I watched the replay. *Oh Lord,* I thought, *did I really screw that up?* I apologized to Georges later, and he admitted jokingly that he had a lot more on his mind at the moment than to notice or care. Another time I mispronounced the city of Decatur, Illinois. "We love you, Bruce," citizens of that city Tweeted me, "but it's pronounced Deck-kay-tur, not Deck-uh-toor."

One night, I flubbed Rashad Evans's introduction to the main event. I got the name of his home city wrong.

I was sitting in my living room that Sunday after getting home, and I see there's a text from Rashad:

LOL How many years have you been introducing me? No worries. It's cool . . .

I dialed his number immediately.

"Who's this?" he said groggily.

"Bruce!"

"Bruce, man, thanks for calling. But it's like, twelve-thirty in the morning."

Oh, shoot, I thought. I thought he was still in Vegas. Turns out he's lying in bed in Michigan and I just woke him up.

I stammered out an apology. "Geez, I screw up your intro and now I'm waking you up!"

He cracked up. "It's okay, man. How's it going? Good to hear your voice."

Beyond Twitter, when a fan asks for a photo or an autograph, I happily comply. But what a lot of people don't get is that I'm not just doing it for them. Some of that good feeling feeds me, nurtures me, lifts me up on days when I'm maybe feeling down. That's the beautiful thing about fandom.

A woman once sent me a photo of her two-year-old niece holding a teddy bear, and told me the story behind the image.

Turns out that bear, whose name is Bruce, has a voice chip embedded in its fluff. Squeeze the bear and it says—you guessed it—*It's Time!* Think about it: For this little girl to receive a gift like this, it must mean that everyone in the family is watching the UFC. All it takes is one member of the household to tune in, and the rest are converted to the sport, down to the littlest toddler.

Some of my fans have actually educated me. A while back, one fan wrote me via Twitter to say that he couldn't help noticing that my tuxes had three buttons. I guess he worked in a men's shop. He wanted to give me the heads-up that three-button jackets were no longer in style. Believe it or not, I had actually heard this previously from my brother Michael, the dresser of dressers. But I hadn't researched the issue. But now, with this fan's Tweet fresh in my mind, I asked around in the shops where I was buying my clothes in Los Angeles, and it turned out that Michael and my fan were right.

Fans often write with requests for personalized Bruce Buffer voice recordings, which they intend to use for weddings, birthdays, and special events. Honoring those requests takes time out of my workday, so I do charge for that service, but I try to keep it affordable. I don't want to gouge couples who are spending so much on their special day, or families who are springing for special events such as birthdays and anniversaries. The thank-you letters I have received after weddings, in particular, are always awesome. I've watched some wedding videos that my fans have posted on YouTube, and frankly I've sometimes been reduced to tears that these people have incorporated my work into their special day.

One day I got an inquiry from a high-school basketball

team in Illinois. The coaches asked about our rates because a lot of the kids on the team were UFC fans. It moved me to think that my voice would be kicking off these young athletes on their home courts; I sent them a recording for no charge. They sent me a signed photo of the entire team.

Occasionally, some fans just don't know how to respect the boundaries. One time I accidentally Tweeted my personal mobile number, thinking I was sending a private direct message. Next thing you know, I started to get these phone calls.

"Hello?"

A timid voice on the other end would say, "Yeah, um, hi. Is this Bruce Buffer?"

"Yeah, who's this?"

"Are you the *real* Bruce Buffer?"

"*Yes*, now who is this?"

"Oh, you don't know me. My friends and I were wondering if you would just say 'It's Time!' for us. Just once."

I laughed, and then complied with what seemed at the time to be an innocent request. What the hell. When I was done, I heard the fans on the other end giggling. They politely thanked me, and I hung up.

Over the next few days, I started to get a couple of these calls—"Can you say 'It's Time!'?" "Can you say 'We Are Live!'?"—and I began to suspect that these clowns were taping the call so they could make use of it in every way imaginable: ring tones, voice mail messages, you name it. Technically, such a use infringes on my trademark and could lead to painful legal action. (You hear me, guys?) But okay. I let it slide. It wasn't important enough to sic on them the big, scary lawyers who spit flame and eat adolescents for lunch. (They really do, guys!)

I ought to have changed the number, but it was one I'd had for thirty years in the business, and I just didn't feel like breaking with tradition. For a while I basked in the glow of some pleasant calls from fans. But then the calls devolved into some dangerous, foulmouthed stuff, with one individual in particular calling and threatening to do unspeakable things to my non-existent wife. I saw red. I turned the matter over to the police. The next time the guy called, I was ready for him.

"Listen, shit-for-brains," I said. "The FBI has all your information. You might want to change where you live. Oh, and one other thing. If you ever come near me or my family, I will beat the living hell out of you."

Never heard from the idiot again.

See? There's a fine line. You can be a fan or you can be an A-hole. Piece of advice: don't be an A-hole.

One fan who means a lot to me is a young man I've watched grow up. Stephen Quinn is a differently-abled young man in his twenties who is the UFC's regulatory affairs coordinator. It's his job to make sure that the fighters have all their medical and other requirements met so they are licensed to fight. He's always sitting Octagon-side near Lorenzo, a family friend, and waves to say hi to me. Some years back, he made my day when he told me that he was getting a dog and was going to name it Bruce. At UFC 129, the night we had our largest attendance to date, he told me, "Bruce, I'm praying for a three-sixty tonight!" I said, "I don't know about *that*, Stephen, but trust me, if I go off, it's gonna be amazing!" Well, I didn't know then just *how much* I was going to go off. That was the night I blew out my knee.

Through Stephen's efforts, we have been honored with visits from kids from the Make-A-Wish Foundation from time to time. Some of these children, I am told, have to get an organ transplant every ten years to survive. That's something grown men don't go through. And they don't complain about it. They don't carp or criticize. They don't inflict their disappointment on others. All they want when they're with us is a photo and the fan experience. The fighters and I are honored to help them achieve that wish. Years ago, such organizations would never have thought to bring their kids to the UFC. But look how much we've grown, to be embraced as role models for these young kids.

At one UFC a middle-aged couple came up to me in the hotel lobby after the show, as I was signing for a number of happy fans, and asked if I would say hi to their son.

"Sure," I said. "Where is he?"

The dad pointed down and to my right. Their son was disabled and got around in a wheelchair. He couldn't move his hands, which were in UFC fighting gloves, and his head was bent to his chest. I could tell that meeting me made him happy because he was beaming happily. I kneeled down and made eye contact with him and thanked him for coming and asking to see me.

Our encounter made the whole family very happy, and we spent a few minutes together shooting some photos. I probably gave them more time than I usually give to fans. The whole time I was doing so, I could see out of the corner of my eye that other fans were congregating on the side, waiting to talk to me. But I gestured to them that I would be just another minute.

I found it hard to keep my composure in the presence of the young man and his parents. We who have our health and the full use of our bodies forget how blessed we are. This young man's heroes were the men of the UFC. I was grateful that he included me in their number. And I was touched by the efforts his parents had made to indulge his interests and take him to these events.

I was close to tears when they left me.

The other fans rushed over and I just couldn't deal.

"Sorry, guys," I said. "I just need a moment."

So I went off to the side and took a moment to feel what I was feeling. Then, after a bit, when the tears stopped coming, I dried my eyes. I've never been afraid to cry. I think it's one of the things that make a man.

When I was in Atlanta for UFC 145, I had the honor of meeting Lance Corporal William "Kyle" Carpenter and two other U.S. Marines who had come to watch the fights. Carpenter is a Medal of Honor nominee who threw himself on a grenade in Afghanistan to protect a fellow soldier. He's a young man, barely into his twenties, who has lost an eye, many of his teeth, and the use of one of his arms as a result of this heroic action. His face is covered with scars engrained with gunpowder debris. (Since we've met, Carpenter has regained the use of his arm, thanks to dogged rehabilitation.) At the UFC, I spent a few minutes speaking to Carpenter and another wounded Marine. They were attending the UFC with a sergeant who was dressed to the nines in Marine dress blues.

At four-thirty the next morning, when I returned to an empty hotel lobby after a night of after-parties, I got on the elevator and held the door for a young man who was walking with his head down. When the doors closed, the young man asked me if I was Mr. Buffer. I said I was. The young man, still looking at the floor, said, "Thank you for such an exciting night of announcing."

I thanked him. And when he looked up and I saw his one eye and that the right side of his face was marred with scars, I realized that he was the other young Marine I'd met that evening.

I thanked him and we spoke for a little while. When we reached my floor, I said good-bye and uttered the phrase I'd learned from my father: "Semper Fi!"

"It was an honor to meet you, sir!" the young man said.

When I left the elevator, tears filled my eyes. I have met many soldiers in my life at UFC events held on military bases and elsewhere, but this experience affected me more than any other. I call our fighters warriors and heroes, and I believe that they are. But they would be the first to admit that they are no substitutes for the true warriors—young men and women who put their lives on the line every day for the nation they love.

I give everything to my fans because look at what they have given me: the chance to feel connected, the chance to peek into their lives and understand their stories. You can't buy that. You have to earn it.

18

RAMPAGE

"**M**y nose hurts," Rampage Jackson told me. "My jaw hurts. My leg hurts. Every part of me hurts, and I *won* the fight."

"That's right," I said. "You did."

The two of us were settling into our airplane seats for the flight back to the West Coast following one of the most controversial UFC fights in recent history. The fight between Quinton "Rampage" Jackson and Lyoto Machida had been the main event of UFC 123 in Detroit. We hadn't had a fight in that city since the old days, since UFC 9. But what had transpired tonight would keep tongues wagging in Detroit and elsewhere for years after.

It was definitely a fight people wanted to see. Machida has this invincibility about him; he's great at keeping a distance between himself and his opponent with his style of karate and

MMA. And here was a classic puncher in Rampage, who is a monstrous warrior.

The main event didn't look like much to start. The men danced around the Octagon for what seemed like an eternity, with not much action. But in the second and third rounds, Jackson opened himself up just enough to get knocked to the mat. The Dragon pounced, and tried unsuccessfully to get Rampage into some kind of a submission hold. Rampage twisted his way out of everything Machida threw at him. Those on-the-mat moments were frustrating to watch, because you could see both men still had a lot of fight in them, a lot of energy. But nothing was gelling for either of them. When the fight ended, the image of Rampage struggling on the mat through most of those rounds had been seared into everyone's mind—including Jackson's. Before returning to his corner, Rampage lifted Machida's arm as if to say, "Here's your winner right here."

But the judges had a big surprise for this heavyweight monster and victor of more than thirty fights: They declared him the winner in their decision. The crowd of 16,000 seemed shocked. Hell, even Rampage seemed shocked. He gave one of those Scooby-Doo looks, eyes bulging with almost comical disbelief, when I announced the decision.

Anytime a close fight ends in decision, you're going to make half the fans happy and half the fans pissed. That's a fact of life. People tend to hate decision fights, and I understand where that comes from. We'd all prefer that a fight end in a spectacular knockout or submission, a clear, inarguable sign that one fighter utterly dominated the other. But life isn't that simple, and you wouldn't want it to be. I don't want to get too philosophical, but it seems to me that when we have to go to decision, it means those fighters were so evenly matched, and fought such a close fight, that neither one was able to get it over on the other. That, to me, is a great fight. It may not be a great spectacle, but it's an awesome display of skill, of technical maneuvering, of fighting prowess.

Now, if you're going to hand decisions off to judges, you have to be willing to accept their calls. Nothing heats up the Internet faster than fans who think their favorite fighter's been robbed. You could practically hear the fiber-optic cables sizzling all night. How could it be that Rampage spent so much of the fight on the ground, in the all-too-careful grip of Machida, and walked away the winner? It didn't make sense.

But now, away from the cameras, here I was, sitting on a plane with the man at the center of this amazing controversy, and he was confiding in me that he, too, was puzzled by the outcome. He hurt all over. Wasn't winning supposed to feel a little . . . *better*?

"Of course you won," I told him. As the plane raced down the tarmac, I enumerated a couple of the things I'd seen that night that convinced me that the decision was a fair one. Later, I was even more convinced. In the days that followed, Rampage was telling the press that he now saw it that way, too.

For my money, what I saw that night was pretty much confirmed in the replays I watched in my den. Again and again, I was impressed by the way Rampage controlled his space. For a lot of the standing moments of the fight, he kept Machida where he wanted him, at the fringes of the Octagon, on the outside looking in. It reminded me a little of walking a dog on a very tight leash so the animal only marches down the narrow patch of sidewalk where you, the master, want him to be. He can't even think about going beyond those bounds, because he just doesn't have enough play in the leash to permit him to go there.

Later, when Machida got him on the mat, Rampage proved to be an elusive quarry. Machida may have been able to keep him down, but he couldn't do anything to him. He couldn't lock him down. Couldn't shut him down. And he sure as hell didn't get him to tap out. The fight never escalated into the danger zone for either man. Whatever Machida, the presumed dominator, pulled, Rampage was able to handily evade and slip out of.

He won because he controlled the space. This is only one reason why Rampage is one of my all-time favorites. We go back a ways, to the King of the Cage 4 in June 2000, which he lost to Marvin Eastman. He went on to win all the other matches he fought that year—all *six* of them. That's what fighters had to do back then to make a living. He was probably fighting for $1,000 a fight, $5,000 if he was lucky during that year. He was legendary during those Japanese Pride competitions for his body slams. He fought Chuck Liddell twice and TKO'd him both times—no mean feat.

As for myself, I came to appreciate him for his striking ability. I've got a lot of love for boxing ability in MMA fighters. Very few UFC fighters have the boxing skills needed to compete in the squared ring against a boxer. In the Octagon, often you don't see fighters use the jab effectively. It's a strike that is hugely valued by boxers, and by MMA fighters who capitalize on it to set up another punch or a takedown. UFC lightweight champion Frankie Edgar, for example, is a fighter who could compete in boxing, as he works the jab and moves like a boxer, making him one of the most complete fighters pound-for-pound in MMA history.

Outside of the fights, Rampage and I bonded, and for a little while he was dating one of my old girlfriends, a beautiful young Asian woman. Because of this, he sometimes jokes that we're "blood brothers." If so, we didn't have to cut our hands to prove it.

BUFFERISM NO. 13

"FUN TO PLAY WITH, NOT TO STAY WITH."

I use this to remind myself that there are always fun people to date who might ultimately be wrong for you. If you detect that the person's selfish, say, maybe you need to give them a pass. But you can still have a couple of great dates and beautiful nights together. Just be honest with yourself and your partner about where it's going.

I've always admired his ability to crack jokes. That's one reason I think he has clicked with fans. He has a quick wit and a great sense of humor. When I see him on Kimmel or Leno, I have to marvel at his easygoing manner, and the hilarious facial expressions like that moment in the Machida fight. When he appeared in the film remake of *The A-Team*, playing Mr. T's old role of B. A. Baracus, I thought he was the best thing in the movie after Liam Neeson.

Rampage sometimes also takes the yuks a little too far. Early in his career I noticed that every time he gave an interview with the press, he was dropping a few choice curse words, often seconds after announcing how religious he was.

Now, I'm no angel when it comes to that stuff. If I get pissed, I swear a blue streak. But I do think I know when to zip it. The one time I didn't, as you'll recall, Pat Miletich offered to rewire my jaw for me.

I never said anything to Rampage about this until the day in 2001 when we were both attending Bas Rutten's wedding. At the time, Rampage had not yet begun fighting in the UFC; he was up-and-coming, having done King of the Cage fights and now embarking on his foray into Pride in Japan.

As we were enjoying the reception at the couple's recommitment ceremony, I turned to Rampage and said, "I have a lot of respect for you, brother. I'm not religious, but I *do* have to comment on something. I'm watching you, and you're making a grand career for yourself. You watch: the sport is going to blow up. You gotta prepare for this, Quinton. You've got to stop the cursing. You don't want to appear like you just came off the street. It's cool up to a point, but you have to try to handle yourself with class outside the cage. Sooner or later, the Cokes, Pepsis, Nikes, Burger Kings, Budweisers, are all going to come into the sport. They're gonna be looking for role models. You want that. You don't want to be stuck with the short-money sponsors. Think about it, Rampage. Think about the future."

Funny thing: back then, the sport was so underground that fighters would actually be sponsored by businesses in their communities that coughed up a little cash for the fighter in return for wearing the store's logo on their trunks. It was a far cry from Bud and Gatorade. One of the early fighter sponsors, which locked down real estate on Tito Ortiz's trunks in his early fights, was a chain of stores that sold adult videos and sex toys.

I didn't know how Rampage was going to take what I was saying. In one of my favorite movies, *The Shootist*, John Wayne plays a dying gunslinger who is known for his foul language, among other things. One scene I love, between Wayne and Lauren Bacall, goes like this:

WAYNE: Damn.

BACALL: John Bernard, you swear too much.

WAYNE: The hell I do.

I pictured Rampage having a similar reaction. But he didn't. He thanked me and said he'd think about it.

I don't like to play the part of insufferable Uncle Bruce, but I think I'm permitted to speak the truth with my blood brother. None of us is perfect. These guys are practitioners of an emotionally and physically demanding craft. When the fights are over and the relief washes over them, the first thing most of them want to do is cut loose.

But the money guys are always watching. I don't think a lot of people are thinking about this. The assumption is that the sport has arrived, but we still have a ways to go. And there are still critics who are looking for any reason to take MMA down a peg.

Well, lo and behold, a month later Rampage told me that he had taken my words to heart and he wanted to thank me. He was working to clean up his act, and he has. I rarely see him curse on camera anymore.

When he fought Ryan Bader in Japan—the fight that pushed a lot of his buttons—Rampage showed up five pounds overweight and with two injured knees. He didn't back out, because he didn't want to disappoint his fans, and he pushed the UFC to let him fight on this card. The fight didn't go well for him; Bader finished him by unanimous decision. We went out afterward in Tokyo, and I stayed an extra two days to hang with Quinton. He was limping much of that time, but we had some fun together. Later he elected for knee surgery, and went public via Twitter about his disappointment with the UFC. And Dana was his classic self: "You have one fight left in your contract; do it and leave if you're so unhappy."

He may be unhappy, he may not be ready to retire, but he has always shown gratitude toward me. In Denver the night he got submitted by Jon "Bones" Jones, Rampage came up to me at the after-party he was hosting and thanked me graciously for my opening words. "That introduction was wonderful. Thank you so much. That really got me going. You got me going, Bruce."

I had to smile, because this is the side of Rampage people rarely see. The sweet, humble side, the man who expresses thanks for the little things people do for him.

What the fans see is the performer, the guy who marches into the arena with the thick chains around his neck and howls at the moon. Fans are in awe of the masterful staredown technician who seems to shoot daggers from his eyes at his opponent.

Standing in the Octagon with my mic under Big John's or Herb Dean's arm, and watching as Rampage glares at the man he's about to battle, is one of the biggest thrills of my life. There's nothing like being in the Octagon at that moment, when both men begin to smell each other's blood.

Once, after I concluded Rampage's intro, I started to turn to the other corner. Rampage didn't want to break character, but for a second our eyes met and he managed to give me a little wink.

I've never told anyone about that.

But I guess I just did.

19

GREAT FIGHTS

I love driving to work, but I don't get to do it that often. On November 11, 2011, I got my chance. The weigh-ins for the long-heralded *UFC on Fox1* were being held at the Santa Monica Civic Auditorium, just down the road from where I live. The place was packed, standing room only. I was delighted to see that L.A.'s Latino population had come out to watch the event and later storm the trucks hawking UFC merchandise out front. Junior Dos Santos and the heavyweight champ, Cain Velasquez, had no doubt been a huge draw. The next day at the Honda Center in Anaheim, the two were slated to go at each other like a couple of elk locking horns in a *National Geographic* special. It was going to be a great fight. Dana said that it would either be over in thirty seconds, or we would be treated to five rounds of an intense battle.

Everyone who had anything to do with the UFC was champing at the bit, with good reason. The fight marked the beginning of what everyone knew would be a game-changing relationship with Fox Sports. The deal had been simmering on the back burner for a while before being announced early that year. The organization had had offers in the past, but whatever popped up just wasn't working for them. HBO wanted the UFC, but reportedly also wanted production control. No way were Dana and the Fertittas going to relinquish control.

But Fox was another thing entirely. It's like the world's biggest funnel for potential viewers. TV's weird: you can receive 300 channels, but people still stick close to the top of the dial. The big four networks are your most-watched channels. If the UFC wanted to win converts, they had to get in that range. But Fox had a whole lot more under the hood. They could use that front-and-center real estate to direct eyeballs effortlessly to their multiple cable channels.

For me, making that switch from deep cable to the top of the dial felt like kismet. In 2001, when I arranged for my brother Michael to appear on *The Best Damn Sports Show Period*, my contacts later led to getting Tito and me on the show as well in January 2002.

Before Tito and I went on that day, we were back in the green room and I was talking to *BDSSP*'s producer, George Greenberg, who asked me when the UFC was coming to L.A., because they would like to cover it. At the time, the sport was not sanctioned in California.

"But hey," I said, "why not do one better and really make TV history by showing a *live* UFC fight on Fox for the first time in free TV history?"

"How do we do that?"

I set up a conference call with Dana and Lorenzo Fertitta to see if it could be done. After that one call, Dana, the Fertittas, and George followed through to create UFC 37.5, which was held at a ballroom in the Bellagio Hotel in Vegas, approximately two months later, during sweeps week. Fox and *BDSSP* realized its largest viewing audience ever, as a result of airing the Liddell/Belfort main event. (The decision was ridiculously close, but the judges scored for Liddell.)

Now, as I sit back realizing the current seven-year deal, worth an estimated $100 million a year for the UFC, it is obvious to me that Fox is the best and only network for the UFC to grow with. In a roundabout way, that relationship all started that day in the green room with George Greenberg, who is now a top dog with Fox.

Fox had had the UFC swimming in its bloodstream for nine years. It was only a matter of time before they owned up to it and let it bubble to the surface.

The first UFC show on Fox heralded such great things. We all knew it. We all felt it. It was a game-changer. Earlier that week, the *New York Times* had run a front-page article about how UFC "dips toe into the mainstream"—their words. In talking to the press, Dana was a complete mensch, pointing out that it would be a stellar night for fight fans. After the UFC bout was over, fans would easily be able to catch the Manny Pacquiao/ Juan Manuel Marquez boxing match.

Backstage before the show, we could all feel something big, seminal, and life-altering was about to happen. The eyes of the world were watching us.

10 WAYS TO BRING CLASS BACK TO FIGHTING

1. All commentators and announcers must dress with style.
2. Jeans are okay on camera; just make sure they're neat.
3. No cursing during the interviews . . . especially any word beginning with an "F."
4. Avoid licking an opponent's blood off your gloves when on camera.
5. Don't forget to thank your mom during the victory speech.
6. No biting!
7. Never hit the ring announcer—unless he hits you first.
8. Sign every fan autograph and take every picture requested, except in the bathroom.
9. Send a thank-you note after every staredown—not.
10. Potted plants in the corners of the Octagon.

Everyone I saw that night was stepping it up a notch. I went backstage to the green room to grab a bite, and in walked Joe Rogan. Normally he's very casual in jeans and an untucked shirt. Tonight he was dressed beautifully in black slacks, black shirt, and a Dolce & Gabbana belt. His shirt was tucked in. He looked great. He was dressed to impress.

"Oh," he said when I asked why he skipped the jacket. "I look like a monkey in a jacket."

"I bet your wife bought the belt."

"Nope," he said. "I went shopping. Got it myself."

I looked around outside, and there was Chuck Liddell in a

designer suit and tie. I'd never seen him in a suit and tie. Mul-timillionaire that he is, he doesn't really flaunt the style. I turn around and there are Carlos Condit and Dominick Cruz and GSP. All in suits. Rashad Evans and Jon "Bones" Jones were dressed to the nines as well, but they always are when they're not fighting. They can be bigger fashion plates than I am.

"Geez," I said, "if you guys stopped fighting, you could be models." They all chuckled. "Seriously," I said. "You ought to tell your managers to get your images out there."

It was as if the sport had suddenly grown up, from shorts, sweats, and hoodies to the full-out style of champions.

Outside, at the top of the show, they ran a clip of my voice saying, *"This is the moment you've all been waiting for!"*

Next, Fox segued into a kind of *Monday Night Football*–sounding intro. That moment said it all. It told the world that the UFC had arrived. We were no longer an underground sport. We were no longer a cable TV sport. We belonged in the pantheon of all great sports. We had earned the right to be in the world's living rooms, free and live. Get set: it was just the beginning.

SOME things had changed in the world of sports to get us here. One was that MMA had simply grown to the point that it couldn't be ignored. The other was a more subtle shift in the way Americans viewed the fighting sports.

In 2012, Lorenzo Fertitta paid $1.1 million for the gloves Ali wore when he defeated Floyd Patterson in 1965. The truth is, a lot of us in UFC love boxing. When I was a kid, boxing was king. You trained in boxing first, then moved to wrestling and the martial arts if you had the interest.

But MMA rarely gets props in return from people in the boxing world. Instead we get Bob Arum calling our fighters and fans skinheads or saying UFC fights consist of "rolling around like homosexuals." We get sportscaster Jim Lampley denigrating the skill level of our fighters. It's embarrassing. It's like a badminton player putting down tennis.

I ran into the champion boxer Floyd Mayweather in the high-roller room at the Mandalay Bay Hotel a few years back. I've known him for years, and he's a phenomenal athlete who has always been nice to me. He came up to me, tailed by several bodyguards, to say hi and some other nice things. He said he'd been watching me from afar and was proud of my success. Flattering stuff, and very nice to hear, coming from a five-division world champ.

"So were you at the fights?" I said, referring to the UFC event I'd just announced.

"No," he said, "I'll never go to a UFC fight. I have no interest."

"I understand," I said, "but thanks for the compliment, Champ."

I think he's missing out on some great fights, but I've come to understand that kind of response. WWE's John Cena once told me the same thing, which surprised me. Clearly, a lot of people feel threatened by the sport of MMA and its skyrocketing popularity. I see their reaction as comparing apples and oranges; boxing and pro wrestling are *not* MMA. But a lot of people simply don't know how to respond to the rise of MMA other than to take potshots at the sport.

I believe MMA has surpassed boxing in the eyes of young fight fans here in the U.S.A. Boxers, their fans, and the boxing press will deny this, of course. And in Europe at least, boxing is still huge. An event there will fill a 40,000-seat stadium. I'm booking Michael in places like that all the time overseas. But I daresay that when Floyd Mayweather and Manny Pacquiao retire, you'll be hard-pressed to find an eighteen-to-thirty-four-year-old in the U.S.A. who will be able to name a champion in boxing. Today's young people are entranced with MMA. Maybe it's because so many of the hot new sports must be extreme to catch their attention: extreme skating, extreme snowboarding, extreme motocross. But that does not bode well for the future of boxing.

The best example I've seen of a boxer changing his tune came from Bernard Hopkins. I saw him ringside at an Octagon bout in Philly in 2011. I was shocked to see him there, because he'd knocked MMA in the past, comparing it to gay porn.

"I'm glad to see you here, Bernard," I said, "but I thought you didn't like MMA."

He said, "Bruce, I've trained with these guys. Once I trained with them, I realized how highly skilled and trained they are. I have nothing but respect for them."

That impressed me. At least Bernard took the time to get to know the fighters and their work, and his feelings had evolved as a result. And he is not alone; clearly the world has changed. But those who had to be persuaded didn't change their minds overnight. Great fights helped them get over their prejudices.

IT'S hard to talk about what makes a fight great. There are lots of nuances, lots of little factors that need to be considered. The night of the big Fox event was hugely historic, a major turning point for the sport—but it wasn't a great fight. Dos Santos hit

Velasquez on the temple, one of the worst places to get hit, and we had a new world champ in a little over a minute.

Outside the stadium, Fox had erected a massive white tent with full-on security, luxurious couches, and a bountiful spread of all-you-could-eat beef, Mexican food, and sushi. Free drinks everywhere you looked. DJ Samantha Ronson was spinning. Massive TVs in every corner allowed the VIPs to watch replays, the main coverage, and, later, the boxing match. They spent seriously big coin on this thing, and people were having a blast. I was watching the Manny Pacquiao fight with Chuck Liddell and actor Mickey Rourke when someone told me that both I and my brother Michael were trending on Twitter. Both of us at once? *That* was a first.

It was a glittering night. Fox had done wonders for our ratings. Nearly 9 million people watched at the height of the fight. We broke a record for the highest-rated MMA fight ever on TV. Everyone was stoked.

But despite the huge buildup, the main event turned out to be a quick, decisive fight that disappointed a lot of the fans. "Don't blink when you watch the UFC," a fan Tweeted me afterward. And yeah, I barely had a chance to get back to my seat. It was over that fast. In one sense, the fight was cool: it showed people the power of the mastodons in the heavyweight division. All it takes is just one punch to put your lights out.

When Joe Silva, UFC matchmaker, puts together fights, he's thinking very carefully about the skill factor. How can I pick fighters who are evenly matched? Who's got to fight whom for the sake of the record books? And who deserves the right to have a shot at the title?

But if that were all there was to it, we'd set up a camera to record the fights for posterity and leave them to duke it out in an empty stadium.

Great fights have drama, drama, drama.

Either the fans bring it in the door, or the fighters deliver it by surprise.

Human beings love emotion. They crave stories. What's the story between these two fighters? What's the excitement all about? Why should I care?

Sometimes the drama is built into the fight's DNA from the beginning. The two warriors have met on the field of battle before, and they hold a grudge. Going into UFC 40, that incredible Tito Ortiz/Ken Shamrock fight, we had two guys who were fan favorites. Tito was in his prime, and Ken was on the tail end of his. It was a fight so hot you could smell blood in the air. Ken had his wrestling prowess and his penchant for getting pissed and going nuts on the mat. Leading up to that match, you knew supreme dislike was brewing between these two guys.

Dislike, anger, hate—audiences love grudge matches. I get that: we're all emotional beings. But when fighters feel the hate, the fight's about to become hugely unpredictable. Will these guys lose themselves or stay in control? Are they too mad to fight?

That night, Ortiz beat Shamrock by TKO. It was a tremendous fight, one that cemented the sport in the minds of fans. When the fighters walked out into the MGM Grand Arena, the fans displayed the most excitement I've ever felt at a UFC. A boom of voices rocked the house. I had to look down at my card for a second because I had forgotten Tito's height. The card was trembling in my hand so much that I actually had to steady it. The energy was not to be believed. During the match I felt like yelling "Stop!" because Ken was taking such a beating to the face, but he fought like a warrior. That was a pivotal fight for the organization as well. It happened within two years of Zuffa taking over. They would still have to fight their financial battles for a number of years to come, but this event said, "Look and listen, folks. We can't be missed."

The rematch, UFC 61, was fun, too, watching as their personalities collided further. As I was announcing the fight, Tank Abbott was in the audience Octagon-side to my right, in the first few rows. Just as I was getting into the swing of things, Tank threw a small Ken Shamrock action figure into the Octagon, which landed near my feet. Uh, okay, Tank.

In contrast to his foster brother Frank Shamrock, Ken has a temperament that can go off at any time, if necessary. He's intimidating when he wants to be, but otherwise can be a very cool cat. He has a grand ability to hype a fight, and only those who know him know what's really simmering under his skin.

One night after Tito had won a fight, he was talking to the press in the Octagon when Ken, who was pissed at something Tito had said during his interview, bolted up the stairs suddenly to confront him. I was the first to body-block his rush.

There are two sides to Ken's personality: the WWE promoter side and the serious, "let's do this" side. That night, Ken was all business and a little more than serious. All I could think to say then was, "Ken, don't fight for free!" He calmed down, all right, but his actions made the evening that much more memorable for the fans, and their next rematch more marketable.

What else makes a great fight?

Fighting styles.

If you have a fight between two strikers such as Chuck Liddell and Rampage Jackson, you just *know* they're going to slug each other. You can guess that there's probably going to be a pier-six brawl and *somebody's* going to go down in dramatic fashion, which is just how Chuck went down in that UFC 71 rematch.

What makes a great fight?

Fighting styles—and their inevitable *evolution*. You can never predict this. It just happens in front of your eyes, and only then do you realize the sport has undergone a powerful shift. It's another one of those subtle shifts in MMA that you can only talk about after it's happened.

The monster known as Matt Hughes, a wrestler, meets Royce Gracie, a jiu-jitsu artist, on the field of battle and completely dominates and controls the man who practically birthed the sport. When that happens, a legendary fighter becomes an old-school fighter. Matt Hughes was not just Matt Hughes that night. He was a symbol of the new guard of mixed martial artist.

And then, lo and behold, Matt fought GSP, who put another style in play. GSP became the new school and Matt became the old school. GSP is a dedicated and gifted martial artist who excels at every style he trains in to become the supreme MMA fighter he is. He is so gifted athletically that if you gave him a basketball and a great coach, he'd probably be playing in the NBA in a year.

The same thing happened the night Jon Jones fought Rampage Jackson. We'd never seen Rampage be dominated in this way before. Wow—look, it *can* be done, and *this* is how you do it. Jon showed himself to be the standard-bearer of a new generation, a new school of fighter, the new supreme mixed martial artist.

What makes a great fight?

Well, I can tell you what *doesn't* make a good fight:

predictability. When James Toney stepped on the scales at the UFC 118 weigh-in, he looked like a guy who had not really trained for an MMA bout, especially one against Randy Couture. Toney had spent his whole career as a boxer, and had only recently decided to try his hand at MMA. I'm the first to say that a boxer will probably beat an MMA warrior *in the boxing ring* 99.9 percent of the time. I absolutely believe that. But I *also* believe that a boxer will have his ass handed to him 99.9 percent of the time in the Octagon unless he's committed himself to learning a new way to fight. The fight started, and out came Randy. Toney didn't land a single punch. Randy took him down and got him in an arm triangle in the first round. Toney looked like a turtle on his back. Absolutely no idea what to do. He tapped. End of story. It was painfully uneventful because we all knew it was going to happen.

Then there are fights that you never expected to be that interesting. When that happens, you want to kick yourself. When GSP fought Matt Serra in UFC 69, people were wondering, "Gee, will Matt survive an encounter with GSP?" There was a size difference between the two men. Matt's a tremendous fighter and jiu-jitsu artist, but there was this expectation of defeat in the air. What happens? Matt whacks Georges on the temple much the same as Dos Santos did to Velasquez. Boom. It's all over. A complete shutdown, and GSP loses his welterweight championship in a minute. The classic puncher's chance reared its head. And when those two faced off again at UFC 83 in Montreal, Georges completely dominated Matt, no question. *C'est la vie.*

What kind of fights do *I* love?

The perfect storm, in terms of buildup, high emotion, and keenly matched ability are the Silva/Sonnen fights. Chael Sonnen is the most cerebral and humorous trash-talker on the planet. For better or worse, he knows just how to build a fight and he always goes too far. Look at his long-standing rivalry with Anderson Silva, the Brazilian fighter. At a weigh-in Q&A, someone asked Chael how many languages he spoke. "Three," he said, "maybe four, if you want to count Portuguese as a language." Another time he told a variant of the old guy-walks-in-a-bar joke: "Anderson Silva and his friends walked into a bar. They turned the stools upside down and they sat down."

They love Anderson Silva in Brazil, and this is the second-most-watched sport in that beautiful country. When a man starts bad-mouthing an entire nation, think of the hate that creates. Emotion enters the Octagon, and fans become personally invested. At one point I told Chael, "You should never set foot in Brazil again. You won't be able to walk down the street. Someone's going to take you out." He agreed with me. You'd think he would simply have trained and shut up, but he kept bad-mouthing Silva relentlessly.

Their first fight was five rounds of war, all on Anderson. He was getting the crap kicked out of him. We were worried that he might have a cracked rib, but, great fighter that he is, in the last two minutes he slapped a triangle on Sonnen and practically put him to sleep. Silva turned the course of the night and retained his championship. The drama in that fight was unbelievable.

But later, Chael was already sowing the seeds of hate for the rematch. On my radio show he said he was looking forward to defending his championship. "Wait a second, Chael," I said. "What championship are we talking about? You lost your championship fight to Anderson Silva."

"Welllllllll," he said. "I don't know if you can call that losing when you hit a man three hundred times and he hits you eleven times and he lies down and puts his legs around your head and pulls you in and chokes you out. I would never lie on my back and let a man go between my legs."

Okay, Chael.

Their fight awed me, but like everybody, as much as I love the grandeur of a perfectly executed submission, I love to watch someone stand up and punch. One of the greatest fights of them all was the first Bonnar/Griffin fight. It rocked because it was a mix of fighting styles coupled with great striking. These guys kicked and punched and hit the ground and got up, going three rounds in a seemingly endless tumult. Our jaws were on the floor. Expectations were insanely high. Those guys delivered, but what if they hadn't? What if it had ended quickly? Would it still be one of the greatest of all time?

People constantly ask me, "What is your favorite fight of all time?"

Usually, it's reporters or fans who ask me this, and I always try to give them an answer, but damn, it is hard to say. It's like picking your favorite movie, your favorite food, your favorite beer, your favorite book. There's so much out there, how can you ever choose just one? Whenever I feel I have seen the greatest fight ever in the Octagon, another one comes along within months.

The sport is just that good.

20

BONES

The night of UFC 126, I was leaving the after-party at XS, a Vegas nightclub, at 3:00 a.m. As I was walking through the lobby of the Encore Hotel, I saw the fighter Jon "Bones" Jones trot in at a full clip, frantically looking around.

"Hey, Jon," I said. "What's wrong? Did you lose something?"

He explained that he needed to pay his cabdriver. "I don't have any cash," he said. "I'm looking for an ATM."

"Come with me, Jon," I said, throwing my arm around him.

We walked out into the cool night. The cab was parked in front, engine idling, the driver looking annoyed and impatient. I rapped on the window and peeled off a few bills. Sent the guy on his way. I turned to Jon and slipped a hundred-dollar bill in his front shirt pocket.

"What's this?" he said. "Thanks, Bruce, but I can't take your money—"

I turned and looked at the six-foot-four-inch man who, just tonight, had won the $75,000 Submission of the Night bonus after taking out Ryan Bader in the second round with a choke that resulted in a tap-out. It was Bader's first loss, and Jon was a rising star; in six weeks he would be challenging Mauricio "Shogun" Rua for the light-heavyweight championship. If he won, he'd be the youngest light-heavyweight champ in UFC history, only twenty-three years old. (News flash: He did.)

10 THINGS YOU SHOULD NEVER SAY AT A UFC AFTER-PARTY

1. I could have taken that guy.
2. Quit hogging the fucking dip, Liddell.
3. Dana, can I rub your head for luck?
4. Is Michael Buffer here?
5. Can you autograph my martini glass, eyeglasses, shoes, swizzle stick, etc.?
6. I've got a great marketing idea for you: the dodecagon. Run with it.
7. I was a high-school wrestling champ—bring it.
8. Want to take it outside, Silva?
9. I'm thinking you need a better nickname.
10. Do you work out?

"Look, Jon," I said, "you just won a main card event. It's a fight night, and there are fans all over the city. You are not to go walking around Vegas alone by yourself, without cash, without your crew, you hear me?"

He nodded. "Yes, Bruce."

I love Vegas. Know it like the back of my hand. But I'll be the first to say that you need to stay alert there, the way you would in any big city. Especially if you're highly recognizable.

I know fighters well enough to know that they are often so exhilarated on a fight night that they can't sleep. On that night, Jon's victory over Bader was still so fresh he could taste it. It was 3:00 a.m., but Jon could probably have stayed up till noon the next day. All he wanted to do was have some fun until he worked off that high.

Some people were coming up out of the lobby now. Some of them were my friends. "We're heading out to another party," I told Jon, waving over his shoulder to our limo driver. The sleek black ride pulled up. "Come out with us."

As the limo pulled away from the curb, I made a mental note to talk to Jon's manager about this. But for now, the night was still young.

I'VE been telling people for a while that my young friend Jon "Bones" Jones is a new breed of fighter. He's a whirling dervish in the Octagon, a spinning tornado of elbows, knees, and feet. He's got the longest reach of anyone in the organization. A well-proportioned, wonderful freak of nature, as so many great athletes are.

At UFC 135, he devastated Rampage Jackson to the point where Rampage couldn't do a thing. Jones is similar to Chuck Liddell in the sense that his long arms and legs are a huge asset for him over his opponents. He had ten inches on Rampage, who, being a striker, found it hard to land some damaging blows. Rampage did a great job early in the fight, but he just could not connect. Then, later in the fight, when Rampage finally hit stride, Jon changed the game up and submitted him with a rear naked choke—the first time an opponent had ever pulled that on Rampage. After the fight, a panting Rampage said he lost the fight fair and square, and that he had tremendous respect for Bones. He then proceeded to pay the victor a high compliment, saying, "I don't know who is going to be able to beat this man."

As I write this, the Bonesman is as yet undefeated, though he did lose one fight by disqualification, to Matt Hamill, for throwing an illegal elbow strike. Jon and Rashad Evans were friends and training partners who once said that they wouldn't voluntarily fight anyone they trained with. I respect that, but if you're a fighter, you have to fight whoever stands in your path. Taking on a teammate is tough because you know all of the guy's moves. When Jon's title came up between them, a match was inevitable. It was scheduled twice, but both matches were postponed due to hand injuries. In spring 2012, Jon beat Rashad by decision at UFC 145. A chilly rivalry sprang up between the two men building up to that battle. Bones could barely make eye contact with Rashad at a prefight press conference. And when Joe Rogan asked if the two had anything to say to each other, Jon said, in effect, "I'm just going to say very little." And then he walked off.

I understood that. I had taken some time to get to know Jon, and I know that he feels uncomfortable speaking ill of anyone. The first couple of dinners we had together, he struck me as a congenial, nice human being, a gentleman whose million-dollar smile lights up the room. He's capable of subtle, self-deprecating jokes, but he will not say anything negative about anyone. He always seems to be in a good mood. Not only is he a tremendous fighter, but his character virtually guarantees he will someday be an ambassador of the sport.

I started telling people that Jon would someday be the Muhammad Ali of the UFC, and critics knocked me for it, but I'll stand by it. Ali in his prime had a devastating wit and was a master of psychological warfare, but he also charmed millions of people because he had what Jon has: charisma. Jon's a gentleman outside of the Octagon, and a cyclone inside it. His technique is indescribable, graceful, yet stylized. He pulls off moves that you only see in the movies. Actually, they're better than the movies because he's accomplishing real damage.

Jon and I have spoken many times about his career and his future. While in Rio de Janeiro for UFC 142, we hit the beach together for a couple of hours of body surfing. I told him that the world was his oyster. The only adversary that could ever hurt him was himself. Moving forward, I told him, he would be a role model for the UFC. The eyes of the fans would always be on him, and some would even be watching for him to fail. I urged him to watch himself, to be careful, to think about cultivating his image.

That's why I was bummed when he wrecked his Bentley and was charged with DUI in the spring of 2012. I was relieved that he wasn't hurt. It was a foolish incident that could have easily been avoided. I believed then that the fans would support him, and ultimately forgive the mishap. But his perfect role-model record is tarnished. I hope that his trainers and handlers coach him well and keep moving him to the next level. Being in his early twenties, he's still got some maturing to do, as both a man and a fighter.

But he's luckier than a lot of the fighters who came up in the UFC only a decade ago. First, he practices the sport in a whole new way. Second, he's in the right place at the right time. The 2011 Fox deal propelled the sport to new heights and exposed it to millions of new fans. The UFC's gone mainstream, and Jon's in the perfect position to reap some of those benefits. He's already locked in seven-figure deals for himself with soft-drink and apparel companies, like the multiyear deal he inked with Nike to release his own signature line of clothing. Sneer if you want, but those deals go a long way toward ensuring the futures of fighters and their families. They also give fighters the luxury of training well and safely. When I look at the older fighters I knew, like Frank Shamrock, I lament that the sport was so underground at the time that they couldn't earn some big money this way when they were in their prime.

Another thing Jon has in his corner is a loving family. His dad is a Pentecostal minister in upstate New York; Jon was a church choirboy while growing up in this deeply religious family. He was the middle child, and though he wasn't exactly a shrimp, his older and younger brother were also tremendous athletes. Both played football at Syracuse. Arthur's now a defensive end for the Baltimore Ravens; Chandler was selected in the first round of the 2012 NFL draft by the New England Patriots. Jon tells me that when they were boys, Arthur and Chandler used to beat him up, and he'd always lose. He didn't have what it took to be a football player like them, but he did excel at wrestling. But it was only later, when he left college to support his girlfriend Jessie and their first child, that he discovered MMA and started training hard. When he took the belt from Shogun in March 2011, he'd only been practicing the sport four years. That's an amazing accomplishment, and I'll bet his brothers think twice before they pick on him now.

Like me, Jon's a big believer in meditation. In fact, he and his trainer Greg Jackson were heading out to find a peaceful place to meditate the morning of his pivotal UFC 128 bout, when they came upon that thief that Jon famously took down. The guy had just smash-and-grabbed a GPS device from an elderly couple's vehicle in New Jersey. Jon grabbed the guy, submitted him, and held him until the cops arrived. The luck of that crook, huh? What a terrible day to choose to loot a car. Hours later, Jon got himself together and took the belt as if he hadn't already had an eventful day.

So I don't really see any weaknesses in Jon's armor, save a hint of innocence. That's why the night I saw him alone in Vegas rubbed me the wrong way. People think I make too big a deal about fighters needing protection. Obviously, Jon can handle himself against anything life hurls his way, and his management team can't be there to protect him all the time, but a champion has bigger things to do than look for an ATM machine or guard himself against drunk idiots.

If you think I'm exaggerating, I should tell you that when the limo pulled up that night in front of the Encore, I got in first with my friends. Jon lingered on the sidewalk. "Jon," I said, "come on. Get in."

He did. And the second Jon pulled the door shut—the very second—someone in the crowd outside the hotel threw a punch and knocked a guy to the ground exactly where Jon had been standing a few seconds ago.

Jon looked at me, stunned.

"We should go," I told the driver, who hit the gas.

Life can change fast on fight night in Vegas. When the parties start winding down, drunk people suddenly find themselves bored and looking for something to do. You've got a lot of testosterone flowing. Someone mouths off, and *boom*, someone takes it in the jaw. If that's going to happen, I'd rather it happen to someone else, not one of our guys. They don't need that headache, and they don't need that publicity.

21

MMA HOLLYWOOD

My family was living in Dallas, Texas, the year the original version of the movie *True Grit* premiered. The opening-night event was taking place right there in town, and there was no way we were going to miss it. I was about twelve and my brother Brian was fourteen; we were obsessed with John Wayne. Our father drove us to the theater early, dropped us off, and we ran to line up for tickets.

The theater was packed with people waiting to see John Wayne play one of his greatest characters, Rooster Cogburn, the one-eyed marshal hired by a young girl to track down her father's killers. Brian and I managed to snag seats at the end of a row. I was perched right on the aisle.

Just before the movie started, who should walk in but John Wayne and Glen Campbell, who played the part of the Texas Ranger who tags along after Cogburn in the film. I'd heard of Campbell, but he'd made little to no impression on me. The future Rhinestone Cowboy couldn't hold a candle to the Duke.

I got excited. My eyes locked on Wayne and swiveled to keep him in my view. Finally, I couldn't stand it anymore. I leaped from my seat and yelled, "Hey, Duke!"

The audience seemed to take a collective gasp. Even in Dallas in 1969, you were supposed to act nonchalant in the presence of a screen legend. But no one had sent me the memo.

Wayne did a ninety-degree turn and looked at me.

"Hey there, little pilgrim," he said.

That was the first and last time in my life I was rendered speechless. That's what it takes, apparently. A howdy from one of the biggest movie stars on the planet.

People ask me sometimes if I have any hobbies, and this is my chance to bore them to tears with my knowledge of movies. I became obsessed with them as a kid. Like my father and brother, I enjoyed historical weapons and artifacts, but I was always more into collecting vintage movie posters and lobby cards. *It's a Wonderful Life. Frankenstein Meets the Wolfman. The Creature from the Black Lagoon.* James Bond movies. That kind of stuff.

Because I live in Los Angeles, it's inevitable that I see movie stars and celebrities all the time. On the road with the UFC, I meet and see tons of these people, too. Some impress me because they're stars; others impress me because they're stars who clearly love the fights, like the director Guy Ritchie, who trains in martial arts in Torrance, California, and his two *Sherlock Holmes* stars, Jude Law and Robert Downey Jr., who have often showed up at UFC events together. Ed O'Neill, the *Modern Family* star, worked for more than a decade to attain his black belt in Brazilian jiu-jitsu with the Gracies. The actor Jason Statham is another who is respected not only by me but by a lot of the fighters, because he trains incessantly, mostly jiu-jitsu. He's one of the few actors I've met who I believe could hold his own in a fight, and could be a real fighter if he wanted to be.

And there are "celebrities" who make no impression on me at all. I remember one time seeing Paris Hilton at one of the fights. She was sitting in two of the best front-row seats ever—seats fans would kill for—only to leave the event after watching a couple of fights. That impressed me about as much as a used Kleenex lying on the ground.

And today I'm proud whenever I see UFC fighters such as Randy Couture or Quinton Jackson transitioning to film. They bring a powerful, presold mass appeal that few other new actors have—but they have to be willing to work the call of Hollywood into their careers.

Hollywood people often phone my office to reach fighters because they know me from previous projects or deals. In 1999 I received a call from the offices of the famous director Ridley Scott. One of his casting people called to say that Scott was interested in having the UFC fighter Mark "The Hammer" Coleman for an upcoming movie. Could I get hold of him so they could talk to him about casting him?

It was an opportunity of a lifetime. Mark was at the height of his UFC fighting career, and would have been a perfect pick for any movie showcasing raw physical talent and strength. But when I called Mark at his training center, he was just not into it. The thought of switching gears from training to run out to Hollywood seemed like too much of a hassle.

"Mark," I said, "this is a golden opportunity. This is going to be a huge movie."

He passed.

Well, that movie was *Gladiator,* which went on to win five Academy Awards, including the Best Picture and Best Actor awards, the latter for Russell Crowe. Every time I watch it, I can just picture Mark Coleman playing a scene as a Roman soldier or gladiator with Crowe. Mark just has the look. But it was not to be.

After the film's release and amazing commercial success, Mark came up to me at a UFC event, expressing huge regret for not agreeing to meet with Ridley Scott. In so many words, he said I should have hit him upside the head to make him listen when the opportunity presented itself.

A lot of martial arts fans developed their love of the sport from watching fight scenes in movies. I was maybe too young to befriend the great actor James Cagney, who a lot of people don't realize was a judo practitioner. That fight scene in the 1945 movie *Blood on the Sun,* where he kicks the ass of the evil Japanese soldier, is such a classic. That was probably the scene that persuaded me to study judo.

In my younger years I always rushed out to see movies like *Enter the Dragon, The Octagon, Above the Law,* or *Bloodsport.* I loved Bruce Lee and Chuck Norris and really enjoyed Steven Seagal and Jean-Claude Van Damme movies, as did anyone who cared about martial arts.

It turns out that Jean-Claude lived near me; we both worked out at the same Gold's Gym. In 2006, out of the blue, Van Damme called me, politely asking if I would agree to meet with him because he was thinking of doing a fight movie and thought he might have a role for me.

I went over to his beautiful house and we sat down to chat. I had actually met Jean-Claude in the 1990s at a popular hot spot in Hollywood called Bar One. He and I played pool together with a bunch of girls, and I will always remember how he posed and flexed his muscles for the girls, who of course loved it. That night he was on top of his game, wearing a huge smile, and fun to party with.

But now I could not get over how the ravages of time and drug abuse had aged him from the handsome guy I played pool with that night some twelve years ago. At one point in the meeting he was pontificating about life in general and happened to say, "You see, Bruce, when you get to be my age, you will understand this."

"Jean-Claude," I said, "how old do you think I am?"

He shrugged. "I don't know."

"I'm forty-eight," I said. "You?"

"Forty-four."

It saddened me to see how this guy, one of my on-screen heroes, had been diminished by his past of drugs and depression. Nothing came of our talk, which is fine, but I was always struck by his kind, courtly manner. A true gentleman.

BUFFERISM NO. 14

"LIFE IS LIKE A PYRAMID."

In business, family, politics, sports, and entertainment, the leaders and authority figures sit on top, with the followers underneath. That can give you a big head if you're on top, until you realize the top can't survive without the base.

A few years later I went to see his new film, *JCVD*, about a washed-up action star who unwittingly becomes involved in a bank robbery. It's probably the only one of his films that actually garnered some critical acclaim and awards. I was blown away by one scene, a six-minute-long soliloquy in which the character talks about all the mistakes he made in his life—the drugs, the womanizing—and how he ended up a broken, defeated man. The film was regarded as a fictionalized portrayal of Jean-Claude. I had such profound respect for him when I saw that. It was probably the most honest thing I've ever seen on film. I thought it was Oscar-worthy.

As I write this book, Jean-Claude has just stormed back into Hollywood again, with his amazing turn in *The Expendables 2*. When I saw him up on the screen in that movie, I couldn't believe I was watching the same man I'd sat down with a few years before. It was like the charismatic Jean-Claude I'd known in the 1990s had magically returned. He's gotten himself back in incredible shape, throwing those amazing high kicks of his like a twenty-year-old, and he absolutely *owns* the screen in his scenes as the bad guy. I have to say, seeing the transformation he'd made was an emotional moment for me. Life's put him through some hard times, but in the end he's proven that, like the iconic characters he's played, he's a true warrior.

Chuck Norris is another of the great screen fighters who feel like they've been in my life ever since I was a kid. He used to come over to Steve McQueen's house to train him. I never met Chuck in those days, but I remember Steve McQueen and his son Chad always talking about Chuck, Chuck, Chuck. Later I would train with Chuck's fighting partners, Bobby Burbich, who taught Tang Soo Do, and Pat E. Johnson, who did the fight choreography in movies such as *To Live and Die in L.A.*, *The Karate Kid*, *Teenage Mutant Ninja Turtles*, *Batman & Robin*, and a bunch of other really popular films. Norris and his crew were all part of this tight-knit community of fine martial artists in Los Angeles who trained people to do authentic-looking fight sequences in the movies, and mentored a number of fight-loving celebrities as clients.

But I never met Norris until I ran into him one day at my dentist's office. I was doing the UFC by then and he recognized me. We enjoyed bonding over all the various missed opportunities we'd had to meet over the years.

"I'm going down to watch some kickboxing at the Palladium," he told me. "I might be able to get you some tickets. You interested?"

"Sure! I'd love it," I told him. "I'll bring my brother Brian."

"Great, if it works out, I'll leave you two tickets at the desk," he said.

So Brian and I get there and find our seats, only to discover that we are sitting dead center, front row, with Chuck Norris and his wife. We certainly didn't expect to be hanging out with the man himself.

Since then, Norris and I have become friends. If he's promoting a fight, he'll always make sure I get tickets. He often showed up at UFC fights in Vegas. I respect him because he's refreshingly free of Hollywood BS. Remarkably, for a gentleman who's reached his seventh decade, he trains every single day. He trains with another Hollywood martial artist, Bob Wall. In the great Bruce Lee film *Enter the Dragon,* Wall was the guy with the scar on his face who killed Bruce Lee's character's sister, only to be cut down by Lee at the end of the film.

Back in the day, an aikido master turned actor who showed up on the scene reportedly issued a challenge to all Hollywood martial artists that he could beat anyone who tried to fight him. The young man's name was Steven Seagal. All the great martial artists on Norris's team, after they became aware of his challenge, publicly offered to take Seagal on in an article that ran in *Black Belt* magazine. Bob Wall says that when he called Seagal's dojo to formally accept, the big man told him that he'd cap the ass of anyone who showed up at his place.

Gene LeBell, who is eighty years old as I write this, is probably the greatest living fight and martial arts trainer in Hollywood. He's famous for fighting while wearing a pink *gi*—the product of a long-ago laundry mishap that became his signature look. The man has trained wrestlers, judo fighters, stuntmen, fighters, and martial artists, not to mention numerous actors, and he has choreographed stunts and fight scenes for more than 300 films. He is often asked by martial arts fans to tell about the time Seagal claimed he was invincible to attacks and chokes on a movie set, and LeBell—who is twenty years older than Seagal—hopped on Seagal's back, got him in a choke, and held him until he passed out. I had heard the story thirdhand, so I once asked Gene whether it was true. He responded, "Steven Seagal is a fine man and a great actor." That's all he would ever tell me.

I like Steven. He's always been nice to me, and I had him on my radio show. He stands six-foot-six and weighs about 300 pounds. I know people like to mock him for putting on weight over the years, but I notice that they don't say anything to him directly. His closed fist is about the size of my face. I would not want to tangle with him.

In February 2002, when Anderson Silva took down Vitor Belfort with a front snapkick at UFC 126, it was one of the sport's more eyebrow-raising upsets. It rocked the world, people say, because never in the Octagon had we ever seen anyone dropped with a front kick to the chin. It was a hugely dramatic moment. Now, that's a basic kick you learn in yellow-belt tae kwon do. It later came out that Seagal was training Silva and took credit for teaching Silva that kick. There was a little controversy about it, because Seagal is still something of a polarizing figure who elicits snark from yahoos across the Web.

What convinced me that perhaps Seagal was teaching his tricks to younger MMA fighters was the night he walked out with Lyoto Machida at UFC 129 in Toronto, the same night I blew my knee. That was the night Machida took on Randy Couture and dropped him with the same kick to the chin. You could say that blow kicked Randy into retirement. That was only the second time I've ever seen anyone drop someone with a front kick like that, and both happened within three months of each other.

That's sort of what I like to call the family tree of a kick, from Seagal to Silva, and from Seagal to Machida. As I say, there's nothing special about the kick. It's one thing to throw the kick; it's another to land it in the way that both those fighters did. And yes, I really do believe that Steven Seagal in his own way had a little impact on the world of MMA.

But it wasn't until the spring of 2012, when I went down to Buenos Aires to shoot a Budweiser commercial, that I finally got a chance to separate the myths from reality. I was slated to appear in the commercial with Seagal himself, Anderson Silva, and Lyoto Machida. While we were hanging out in Buenos Aires, I got a chance to watch Silva and Machida train one-on-one with Seagal. They worked together on some interesting moves; two in particular are ones that I have *never* seen put into action by any Octagon fighters in all my years of announcing. Seagal focused a little on teaching how to keep kicks under the radar when thrown, so your opponent doesn't know what's happening until it's too late. Most fighters are taught, as I was, to lift and aim with the knee as your gunsight and kick *through* your opponent, but Seagal was training them how to keep the foot under the peripheral vision of an opponent. I also saw them using karate chops to the head and clavicle, and working with some interesting wrist submissions. At one point I saw Seagal lead Machida around helplessly because he had the young fighter in a wrist lock. Lyoto almost keeled over from it. Now, going forward, if I see Lyoto or Silva work effectively with any of these moves, I'll know Seagal made an impression on them. During the whole time, I saw nothing in these young fighters' eyes but obvious respect for a *sensei*.

I told Steven it was awesome to watch him work, and that I was impressed by his fluidity of movement, speed, and power at the age of sixty. "I'm faster than they are, but they are great fighters," he remarked with a tight-lipped smile.

Later, Seagal invited me to dinner and I got a chance to ask him about all these little rumors about his past. He denied Bob Wall's story of threatening to shoot anyone who came to his dojo. "What I said was, 'I don't fight in print,'" he told me. In other words, he would fight any challenger, but not for publicity, which is what Seagal felt Wall was looking for.

And he insisted that his original challenge did not arise out of any disrespect for Chuck Norris, which is what a lot of people thought at the time of these so-called dojo wars. "I said I didn't like Chuck Norris's *films*," Seagal told me, implying that he had a healthy respect for the man and his martial arts talents.

If you know anything about street fighting and you watch a lot of MMA, you probably spend a lot of time analyzing fight scenes in movies you come across. I'm the same way. Half the time what I'm seeing is really just the magic of the movies—great fight scenes, based in fact, that are designed to look beautiful on the silver screen. Other times what I see is just utter nonsense.

Knowledge of street and sport fighting can take the fun out of fight scenes in movies. The biggest movie "fight myth" is simply the idea of the movie punch. You hit a guy in the face, and he drops cold. Now, can that happen? Sure, you've seen it happen in the Octagon. Think of your famous KOs, guys who dropped with one punch, such as Matt Hughes or Chuck Liddell. But fans also know that fighters don't go down easy. If a man's trained to the point that he's pretty much immune to all punches but a perfectly placed shot to the temple or chin, you really have to wear him down before he's ready to drop. Another classic Hollywood fight standard is breaking a guy's neck with one fatal twist. In movies like *Salt,* we have the beautiful Angelina Jolie doing this to bad guys left and right. Now, can a neck be broken with someone's bare hands? Sure, it's *possible.* But not by a woman the size of Angelina.

On one hand, my love of MMA teaches me to love good movie fights and despise bad ones. I can always tell if the people throwing the blows have some boxing or MMA training. That's why I enjoyed movies like Seagal's *Above the Law* or Jet Li's *Romeo Must Die.* I can watch between the blows and see how they have adapted techniques from the real fight world.

Now, to be honest, I myself can even point out flaws in Chuck's movie fights. I have always felt Seagal's fight scenes were more realistic. Typically, the characters he's playing don't just drop their opponents—they maim them to the point where they can't get back up. That's exactly what you'd do in a street fight, terrible as it may sound.

I found Seagal to be a very intelligent, classy, and interesting man who displays not a hint of BS. We spent the night talking about a million little things: his work in law enforcement, the respect he has for the officers he works with, the great Bruce Lee and the tragedy of his early death, and our mutual love of guns. He's one of a few actors other than Steve McQueen and Lee Marvin, both former U.S. Marines, who always impressed me with their display of firearm expertise in film.

We had a great time that night. As we headed back to the hotel, I couldn't help thinking how often two of my biggest passions in life kept colliding.

I love movies. I love fight culture. When both come together, I'm a happy man.

22

360

When I set out to become an announcer, I never sat around thinking to myself, *Hmmm . . . if I'm going to this do, I need a catchphrase.* I was obviously well aware from the work I'd done with Michael's trademark that signature lines could be profitable if marketed correctly, but I wasn't about to consciously concoct one of my own. I felt there would never be another phrase as marketable in sports and entertainment as "Let's Get Ready to Rumble." I never wanted to come across as mimicking my brother, nor was I ever phrase-driven, as almost every other announcer is. I've always believed in the saying "It's not what I say, it's how I say it."

If it was going to happen, it would have to happen naturally, organically. It was going to have to spring out of who I was and what I was moved to do in the Octagon. That's why I never really rehearsed my announcing, and still don't.

In the world of sports broadcasting, aspiring sportscasters

talk about "getting clear"—perfecting their commentating voice so that they can call games or riff on the air without the very natural hems and haws of ordinary speech. Sometimes you'll see young people sitting in the stands at a baseball game, for instance, calling the game into a mic attached to a digital tape recorder. Later they'll review the recording and see how well they did. Good for them. They have a dream and they are taking steps to perfect their craft.

I just never did that. The thought of standing in my living room or in my home office practicing phrases like *WE ARE LIVE* or *IT'S TIME* or even reading off the names of the fighters I'm going to be announcing this weekend, just feels weird to me. Inauthentic. False. If you want to get deep about it, I think that doing such a thing would also set up two realities for me. The rehearsal voice, and the live-in-the-Octagon voice. I don't want those two voices in my head. Better to just do it live. I'm a professional. I've done it tons of times. I know how to pull it off.

I guess you could say that the way I practice my job is, I do my job. In the early days I sought out smaller venues and fights that let me have a chance to perfect my mannerisms, my diction, and my voice. That was my version of sitting in the stands speaking into a mic. Real fights immediately showed me what I needed to know to do the job. How loud I had to speak. How to pace myself. How to juggle the mic and cards. How to move around the ring or Octagon.

I'm the first to admit that the phrases associated with me— *IT'S TIME TO BEGIN, IT'S TIME, WE ARE LIVE,* or *THIS IS THE MOMENT YOU'VE ALL BEEN WAITING FOR*—are not hugely creative. But they're natural. They're exactly what you'd expect to hear in that moment and in that setting. The only thing that's special about them is how I deliver the words. My passion, you could say, speaks louder than the words themselves. My love of the sport elevates these simple words to something worthy of your attention.

5 ANNOUNCER CATCHPHRASES THAT DIDN'T MAKE THE CUT

1. It's *almost* time!
2. Everybody limbo!
3. Let's get ready to rhumba!
4. We . . . are . . . taped!
5. This is the moment some of us have been thinking about for a good long while now.

Early on, I discovered that I liked to move around inside the Octagon. If you stand in one place, someone is always looking at your back. Meanwhile, the fighters are in two different spots in the Octagon, approximately thirty feet apart. From the very beginning, it seemed only natural to me that an announcer would want to somehow "bridge" that gap and try to connect the two men in the audience's mind.

The audience at any fight, from boxing to MMA, is primed for motion, for action. But what happens at the start of most fights? A bunch of people stand in the ring or Octagon, and nobody really moves. But if I start in one corner, announce a fighter, then move *across* the Octagon to the other fighter, I'm drawing the audience's eyes to the second man. They follow me, and they're engaged.

One time I almost screwed up. I've forgotten which UFC event it was, but I was about to say:

"Introducing first . . . fighting out of the Blue Corner . . ."

I realized that because I was moving around so much, I was actually facing the fighter in the *Red* Corner instead. I had only a couple of microseconds to correct this. My left brain told my right brain that I had to move. Without thinking, I reverted to an old kickboxing move—the spinning bottom fist—and did a split-second, full-body spin as I belted out the word *FIGHTING!*

I was glad that I'd corrected myself.

But I noticed that the crowd perked up. I heard a chorus of approving sounds and murmurs ripple through the arena.

I had just done my first Buffer 180, though, in my mind, I called it a whip-turn until fans started calling it the Buffer 180.

Now, I could have dropped it after that fight and simply focused better on what I was doing. But I liked the way it felt, the reaction it got, and it seemed to broadcast more than any other gesture my energy and passion at that very moment. Moreover, like the words I had begun to say before each fight, the Buffer 180 grew naturally and spontaneously out of who I am.

Well, naturally, the Buffer 180 would eventually get people chattering on the Internet about the possibility of a 360. I frankly enjoyed the chatter. It showed that people were getting a kick out of what I was doing. The fans weren't just counting the seconds until the fight started. (Well, okay, maybe they were, and so was I.) The point was, I had taken what was typically an important yet static part of any bout, and injected movement, passion, and entertainment into it. The fans were responding.

Besides me, the person who is most responsible for the 360 coming into existence is Joe Rogan.

Joe and I go way back. He started working with the UFC back in 1997, with UFC 12. He's a cool guy, and he's got remarkable range. He's an actor. He does stand-up. He's a sports commentator who is extremely cerebral and quick-witted. And he's a true mixed martial artist in his own right. He's an original, and the fights would not be the same without him and his commentary.

I've always liked Joe, and with all we've experienced over the years together with the UFC, we've built a very cool and mutually respectful friendship. I'm a big fan of his comedy and have taken in his show multiple times on the road and in L.A.

He came on my radio show once, and we talked about sensory deprivation tanks. He has one in his home and is a big believer in their ability to combat stress and enhance quality of life. He even hooked me up with an installer near my home, and I went and tried one out. The experience was mind-blowing, or maybe I should say mind-relaxing. I found it to be a lot like meditation, which I've practiced for years. The water is loaded with Epsom salts, so you float in it with only your face poking out. You can't hear a thing and you just let your body and mind flow as you relax. Afterward, you feel energized and completely stress-free. If I had an extra room in my house, I'd probably install one, the way Joe has done.

Joe's obsessed with UFOs. He's probably read about and watched more TV specials about UFOs than anyone on the planet. We've also bonded over this because, believe it or not, I actually spotted a UFO when I was about nineteen years old.

It was 4:30 a.m. in Trancas Canyon in Malibu, where I lived. I was getting into my car to head to work at the telemarketing job when I saw a ball of light coming up from back in the canyon. It appeared right overhead where I was standing. I followed it to the coastline, where it went out over the water, turned south, and then just—ZAP—disappeared.

Later that day on the TV news, I heard that a woman in Palos Verdes, about fifty miles south of Malibu, reported seeing a UFO at around 6:00 a.m. that same day.

Coincidence?

On the way to work, I was still shaking inside. I had to tell *someone*. So I went into the sheriff's station in downtown Malibu and told the officers at the desk what I'd seen. I braced myself to hear them brush me off. Instead, they surprised me.

"We believe you," they said. "We patrol this coast every day, and we've seen some *very* strange things over the ocean at night. So don't worry, kid. It's okay."

That comforted me—slightly.

Somehow the *Malibu Times* got hold of the story. A reporter called to interview me, and then ran an article on the incident. My friends got a big laugh out of it, but many believed me. All I can say is, I know what I saw. Spielberg's *Close Encounters of the Third Kind* came out shortly after, and hit home with me. The SETI Institute, which conducts research on extraterrestrial intelligence, sent me a batch of paperwork to fill out and sign. Their questionnaire asked tons of questions. Was I abducted? Did I experience loss of memory? And on and on.

As I told Joe the day we talked about this, "If we are *here*, then why can't they be *there*?"

But back to the 360. I have to say that if I have any mystique at all, I owe a lot of it to Joe because he took the time to show fans that what I did in the Octagon was worthy of their adulation and interest. The hilarious videos he's done about me and my work have gone viral on YouTube, driving the legend of the 360 even further into the hearts and minds of UFC fans leading up to UFC 100.

You're probably seen the before-and-after videos. But here's what was going on behind the scenes building up to that moment.

As soon as fans started talking about a 360, Joe started nudging me about it whenever we ran into each other at UFC events. "Hey, Bruce, are we gonna do it or what?"

After having Joe nudge me so much, I began to think that maybe I really should attempt a 360. UFC 100 was drawing near. If I was going to do it, it should probably be then. For the first time ever, I actually did do a little rehearsal at home. Pulling off the actual move was a piece of cake. I'm a physical guy and I've pulled off far more complex moves practicing martial arts.

No, my real hang-up was the logic of the thing. The 180 had a clear-cut purpose: it helped me to transition from one fighter to the other with the maximum amount of energy and flair. But why on earth would I use a 360? If I'm facing GSP at a fight and do a 360, I'm back to GSP again. How does that propel the action forward? It didn't make sense. It would only eat up precious time.

But then it dawned on me. The 360 could be like adding an exclamation point to the end of anything I said. But it had to be used sparingly. Otherwise it would lose its meaning.

I had every intention of pulling it off at UFC 100 in July 2009, but I didn't want to jinx myself by scripting it too much.

Joe needled me about it as we went into the weekend, but I stayed mum about my plans, if indeed I had any. I only knew that if it was going to happen, it would come about the way all those 180s had: when the spirit moved me.

At the start of the main event, I introduced Frank Mir, the challenger, in the Blue Corner. Then I stalked across the Octagon to stand before the six-foot-three, 266-pound slab of muscle who was at that time the reigning UFC Heavyweight Champion.

"BROCK!"

Then I leapt in such a way that I was completely off the ground for a microsecond. When I landed, I began to roar *"LESNARRRRR"* while taking one step forward and punching the card toward Brock's face. He and I were beautifully in sync in that moment. I made my move just as he threw both his arms into the air. A true Hollywood moment! Later, when I watched the video, I saw that I did not simply do a spinning, grounded 360, but an *airborne* 360.

That, friends, was the birth of the Buffer 360. It's a move I did for the first and last time that night. People always ask me when I'm going to do it again, but I really can't say because, to my mind, it's gone forever. Joe happens to agree with me, by the way. We still have a good laugh about it from time to time, but we both know that's the way it should be. People ask me if I'll trot it out for UFC 200, UFC 300, UFC 400, and beyond. All I know is, I *will* do something special for those events, but not a 360. As always, I won't know what it will be until that given night.

Later that week, the biggest laugh I got came when I got an e-mail message from Joe. It read, YOU DID IT!!!! AND YOU DID IT IN FRONT OF THE BIGGEST BADDEST MOFO ON THE PLANET!!!!!

23

TO ALL THE GIRLS I'VE
LOVED BEFORE

I love women. I love tender, unpredictable moments, and I love falling head over heels in love. I love the ritual of planning a romantic evening, picking the girl up, taking her out, wowing her, and all that comes after.

I'm not a guy who kisses and tells. But I will tell you that the UFC has enhanced my love life. When you're on the road all the time, you meet amazing women everywhere you go. Hang out at the after-party some night and you'll see what I mean. No matter what city we're in, beautiful women come out of the woodwork, seeking out the fighters.

A lot of fighters enjoy those fringe benefits. I've been in clubs with Chuck Liddell in his wild-man days, when it wasn't unusual to see him partying with a bevy of beauties. How could he be so lucky? Simple! He's the champion of the world. That's hugely attractive to female fans. Look at a guy like UFC welterweight champion Georges St-Pierre. Not only is he blessed with handsome looks and a great physique, but he speaks both English and French, to boot. There aren't many women who can resist the allure of such a combination.

In the old days, you'd see women come to the UFC shows with their boyfriends, and conventional wisdom held that it was a "guy's sport." Wrong. Women love athletes. The sport just had to catch on and be more visible. Today we go to the shows and we see multiple women, groups of women coming to have a good time. And after the show, they're heading out to the parties and looking to meet fighters. They're so happy to meet the fighters, it's incredible. And to my astonishment, some of those women are even happy and excited to meet *me*.

Have I indulged over the years? Sure. Once, when I was doing a radio show with Frank Trigg, they were talking about the groupies on the road, and how you sometimes get cougars on the prowl for young fighters. Trigg joked, "Anything over twenty-one is a cougar to Bruce."

Okay, that was me. The temptation is always there, but I like to think I've wised up as I've grown older.

Some of the sexual escapades—or even just sexual innuendo—on the road have gotten crazy over the years. A classic example is the number of times a guy will stop me at an event to introduce me to his wife or girlfriend, and then ask if I can take a picture with her. You know my standard response: Absolutely, yes! I go into my patented Bruce Buffer smile and give them a shot that they will hopefully treasure (or throw darts at) for years to come.

But I have to say, sometimes these encounters get weird.

"Can I get a picture of you kissing my wife?" guys ask.

I decline such requests.

Sometimes guys up the ante: "Want to sleep with her?"

Uh, no, thanks, pal. I can get my own action.

Strangely, that has happened twice in the UK. I don't know why.

One female fan started e-mailing me provocative pictures of herself, after I'd recorded a special birthday greeting for a young child in her family. But that e-mail exchange quickly went from titillating to disturbing, and I finally had to break off all communication.

Once, after I'd finished a King of the Cage show, my phone rang at 2:30 a.m. I had an early flight the next morning. *Who's this waking me now?* I wondered. It was two young women calling.

"Hi, we're down in the lobby. Can we come up to your room and meet you?"

Because I'm a red-blooded American man, my first instinct was to say, hey, sure, I've got an hour to kill before I have to get ready to catch my flight. Why not have some fun before I blow town?

But I was wiped out from the day before, and, I think, a little older and wiser than the old Bruce. Old Bruce would have said, "Sure, come on up. Room 302."

New Bruce is savvier, pickier, and more careful. New Bruce thinks about these things in a way that a twenty- or thirty-year-old guy doesn't:

What if there's a guy waiting for me outside the door with a baseball bat?

What if I wake up tomorrow and I'm missing a kidney?

What if I do something stupid and I'm looking at a lawsuit when I get back to L.A.?

Nothing goes unseen in an age of technology, when everyone is carrying a cell phone equipped with cameras, video cameras, and voice recorders. Even if you're lucky enough not to have some embarrassing activity caught on tape, that doesn't mean the details of your misadventure can't come out in another way later. I've seen many celebrities go through the wringer with this stuff. These celebs have been forced to pay out hundreds of thousands of dollars in settlements to avoid scrutiny and being raked over the coals. Bad publicity can potentially damage careers, so you really have to be careful.

Besides, what if I invited these women up to my room, giving them the idea that I'm open to party, and then discover that they aren't exactly my type and they don't turn me on?

I was surprised that I was so cautious because, to tell the truth, there were times in the past that I wouldn't have blinked an eye.

I've mellowed. Calmed down quite a bit, and instituted rules. There have been times when I've brought dates to the UFC weekends, but I've come to realize that it's a bad idea unless I've been seeing the person awhile and know that she can occupy herself when I'm not with her. Otherwise, it's a lose–lose situation for everyone involved. In the first place, I'm working. My first obligation on this fight night is to my employer, to the fighters, and to the fans. Bringing a girl to the fight can potentially create problems, because they have to be willing to let me put my job before them. They have to be patient and understand that I am there to perform and do my job, which means interacting with fans. Whoever I'm with often has to stand on the sidelines as I pose for pictures and sign autographs, from the moment I leave my hotel room until I return to it at the end of the night.

Early on, when I wasn't exclusive to the UFC, I went to a non–UFC event down south and brought along as a date a beautiful young ring girl I had met while announcing a previous MMA event weeks earlier. She flew down to meet me at the hotel the night before the fight.

I was getting ready for my performance, going through my pre-show routine, when all of a sudden, out of the blue, my lady friend started flipping out in the hotel room. Until then, it had been a comfortable situation. Now she was sobbing, upset that I wasn't paying enough attention to her. This happened just as I was getting ready to go downstairs to announce.

What was the rest of the night going to be like? she demanded to know. Was I going to treat her like the queen she was?

I looked at her and said very calmly, "Look, we've had a great time together, but now I have to go to work. I'm sorry if you're not feeling good about us right now, but I have to prepare for the fight. You're supposed to be supporting me instead of making me a wreck. You have two choices: you can either fly home now or you can fly home in the morning. Either one is fine with me, but tell me now so I can make the call."

Now, okay, she was emotional and weepy. And I'd be the first to say there's nothing wrong with expressing your feelings. But it wasn't right, considering that she knew very well what she was getting into. She knew that this weekend was a work opportunity for me. I'm going on in a few minutes, and yes, I can't give you the attention you probably deserve. But you knew that before you flew down here. So let's work through this and make some decisions.

She stopped crying and pulled herself together. She washed her face, cleaned up, and made her decision: she was sticking around. And I don't blame her. If she had left, she was going to miss out on an otherwise fantastic evening and after-party. We had a great time hanging out with Frank Shamrock and going crazy.

But wouldn't you know it, the next morning, she started up again. Why couldn't she come back with me to L.A.? Why couldn't we extend the romance for a full week?

This was another situation that definitely pushed me over the edge with respect to dating women in my UFC workplace. It forced me to set up some ground rules for the women, friends, and relations that I bring to these events. Family members and friends stay in a separate room. If I have a young lady staying with me, I orchestrate it so that her flight comes in *after* I've prepared for work. I always arrive at the arena an hour or so before the show to finish my data prep and mentally prepare for the event. So, before I leave the hotel, I make sure keys are left at the front desk. The tickets are waiting in the room. I make sure she has a seat close to where I'll be on the floor. I say hi, we kiss hello, and then I'm in the zone until the job is done. After the show, we'll have a nice night of parties, and possibly a great Sunday together in the event city, but beforehand I need to maintain my focus.

Luckily my family understands this. "You have to work?" they say. "Go to work. We can take care of ourselves." Michael has never been to a show except for the three UFC events he announced (UFC 6, UFC 7, and "UFC The Ultimate Ulti-mate"), but my brother Brian and my VP, Kristen, have both attended, and we always have a blast, because they're reasonable and don't expect me to hold their hands everywhere we go.

In the early days, before I was an announcer, I'd watch

Michael perform and I just fell in love with the job. He looked like a million bucks up there, and I thought, *Man, he must be meeting a ton of beautiful women.* It was one of the reasons I wanted to do what he did! But over the years, such occurrences have helped me formulate my rules:

I never lie or make false promises. And I don't date Octagon girls in the UFC, although I dated some in the pre-Zuffa days, and I've dated some ring girls in the boxing world. It's like dating someone in the office. In the past, when I dated women who worked for me in companies I owned or managed, when the relationships failed, someone ended up either leaving or losing their job. The person with the lesser amount of power—typically the woman—ends up leaving. This has happened a couple of times in my life, and believe me, it's no fun for me or the woman. I don't like hurting people's work life or their ability to earn a living. It's a very selfish and ultimately inconsiderate thing to do. I don't want that mental duress on my conscience. I have too much respect for the female gender.

I like to tell people, "I've never been married, but I've almost been divorced twice." There were, in my life, three women to whom I almost got engaged. One was a beautiful, intelligent girl who was a Miss America contestant from Virginia. After nine months of a lovely, growing relationship, I realized that although I loved her, I was not *in* love with her, and decided it was best to let her go. I didn't want to waste her time or mine. If I couldn't see pursuing a marriage with her, it was best for the both of us to move on with our lives.

I thought this was very unselfish on my part, but this young lady went from loving me to loathing me. She couldn't understand why I didn't want to work toward marriage. The way she saw it, most men would *kill* for the opportunity to be with a woman like her. The fact that I was able to walk away incensed her.

She is one of the few ex-girlfriends to whom I have not spoken since we broke up. I'm still friends today with all my other serious girlfriends. We have what we started out with— friendship—and the only missing link is that we are no longer intimate.

How could I walk away from such a beautiful prize of a woman?

Simple: I was honest with myself, I was honest with her, and I knew in my heart that it would be best to wait for the true Ms. Right. And it was best for my ex to be free to find the right man, if it wasn't going to be me.

It was at a party that I met another girl who changed my life. In the days right after the O.J. Simpson trial, my good friend Darby and I went to a birthday party in honor of Al Cowlings, the former football player. Al was the guy who drove the notorious white Ford Bronco that O.J. used in the famous low-speed car chase.

Darby is an amazingly hot, Nordic-looking girl. We'd dated a few times, and had settled into being just friends. Yes, we went to this party together, but we both knew that if we got lucky and met someone tonight, it was okay to give out or get a number and try to follow up. Darby was a great "wingman," and I like to think I was the same for her.

10 WAYS TO BE A GOOD WINGMAN

1. Spot the girl making eye contact across the room and alert your buddy.
2. Be the "ice-breaker," not the potential "date-breaker."
3. Forget cheap pickup lines. Just start by saying "Hello."
4. Bring *your* "A" game to the table when your friend doesn't have it.
5. Don't go home with the girl your buddy wanted to meet.
6. Pay for the first round of drinks, but say it is on your buddy.
7. If the girl your buddy has his eye on asks if you're single, say, "No."
8. Keep *fresh* condoms in your wallet. They go bad.
9. Don't drink apple martinis or any other frou-frou drinks.
10. Carry plenty of cash, plus credit cards that aren't maxed out.

I was in the kitchen when in walked this vision of a girl who reminded me of Claudia Schiffer. And it was as if I suddenly went deaf, the music stopped, all sound died, and I was just entranced by this girl, whose name was Kristen. Her smile was so infectious and real and genuine that I fell in love with her at first sight. My instincts proved correct. I had just met the most amazing woman I would ever meet in my life, besides my mother.

On the way home that night, I told Darby that I'd spoken to

Kristen and that I had gotten her number and that I had to meet with her. Darby was touched by the impression this Kristen had made on me. All the way home, she was saying, "So . . . when are you going to call her?" That kind of stuff, needling me, getting me to take action.

Shortly afterward, I started seeing Kristen. Long story short: I probably should have married her, but I didn't. For whatever reason, we dated about six months and broke up.

Usually that's the end of the story, but this time it was a little different. We lived a few blocks from each other, and we'd keep running into each other as we'd go about our day running errands. It was a little awkward at first, but we got over it and I found myself having a different set of feelings for her. Not lust or sexual attraction, but genuine friendship. We spoke frankly about the people we were dating, and about work and life and family. I saw her as my pal, my confidante, my equal, and grew to love her as another human being and someone whom I was honored to have in my inner circle.

A few years after I started my business with Michael and needed to hire an assistant, I could think of no one more qualified than Kristen, who at that time was working as an assistant to the media mogul Barry Diller, one of the most powerful men in Hollywood and a founder of Fox Broadcasting. I lured Kristen away from Diller, and she came to work for me, first as my assistant and eventually as the VP of both Buffer Enterprises and the company I formed with Michael—the Buffer Partnership—which runs all of his affairs.

Kristen is my right arm. Without her, my personal life and the way I pursue business would definitely change. I can't fathom being without her and working alongside anyone else. I consider her not only my business partner, but the sister I've never had. She's been through everything I've experienced—the ups and downs—of my life, work, and family for more than fifteen years.

She married a great guy named Chris in 2002. They don't realize it, but *I'm* the one who profited the most by their marriage. You see, Kristen has since become the mother of two great sons, Henry and Rupert, who are both under ten years old as I'm writing this. From the moment they were born, Henry, my godson, and Rupert have been sharing my workdays with Kristen and me at my home office at the beach. And that's how the guy who never had a family of his own has been enriched by the love of two kids. In between phone calls and business deals, I changed diapers, dressed and fed them, and helped educate them. I'd lay them down for their naps and wake them up in the afternoon while their mother was dealing with our clients in the next room.

In fact, it's a joke to say that I've educated these kids, because *they* have educated *me*. They've taught this old bachelor what it's like to love two sons and to be loved in return. That's been an experience I wouldn't trade for anything in the world.

I think back and wonder if I wasn't too hasty in breaking up with Kristen. In a way, she's the one I let get away. "Typical me," I say in retrospect. "*Stupid* me. I didn't want to settle down, because I thought I had so much ahead of me to accomplish."

Well, guess what? Her love, and the love of her family, have changed me.

It's only recently that I've changed my tune. I don't even think that I was in the right frame of mind to get married until

I was forty-five years old. With all that was going on in my life, I just wasn't willing to commit fully to another person. Before that, I was dealing with a whole bunch of other issues that sucked the time out of my life and sapped my energies. My parents got older and needed attention. My responsibilities changed.

Life is interesting that way. In your twenties, you're out every night trying to conquer everything that moves. In your work life, you're beginning to have a glimmer of ambition. You want the chance to make a name for yourself in the work that you do. Your thirties hit, and you hardly notice because you feel just the same physically. You're still going out, still trying to conquer every woman you're attracted to, but your male and female friends are dropping like flies. Everywhere you look, people are getting married, if they haven't already. You're hot for women, hot for love, hot for success. The ambition hard-on is raging.

Then you hit your forties and people who have been in your life forever start dying. The friends you thought were so happily married announce they're splitting, and no, there's no chance of a reconciliation. Their perfect love has turned to perfect contempt. The children are traumatized.

All of this—it's a fact of life. Every decade of life brings its own challenges. The big, life-altering ones take you by surprise. If you want to be happy, you have to set your priorities.

I can't say I haven't been frustrated from time to time with my singleness. I fly all over the world and see amazing places. I look out at the harbor in Sydney and see that opera house and those great ships, and the waiter brings me some of the world's most spectacular wine. Don't you think I reflect on how nice it would be to share those moments with someone special? Don't you think I wonder what it would be like to take my wife to Vegas and share with her all those memories I have of growing up in that wild, unusual, fascinating place?

You bet I would.

Would I get married today? Absolutely. In a second, if I met the right woman. If that woman looked at me with love and said she wanted to have a child with me, I'd be more pre-sold on the idea than any other single guy on the street. Why? Because I already know what it's like to hold a sick baby in my arms. I know what it's like to change that child's diapers, to nurture him, teach him, love him. I would think about all the ways Henry and Rupert have enriched my life. If it's going to happen with Miss Right, I'd say sure.

But I have to be realistic. The life of a UFC man is hard because of the travel involved. In the early days we were on the road six weeks a year. Then it grew to twenty-four weeks. After the Fox deal in 2012, the schedule increased to thirty-one shows in a year, not counting my other appearances. Now I'm even turning down various other appearances because they fall on UFC weekends and my loyalty is to the UFC, first and fore-most. So I am here today, gone tomorrow, in Europe two weeks from now. I'm running my businesses. There's poker playing, side gigs, interviews, podcasts, and managing Michael and the Ready to Rumble brand. And on and on.

That's why I recently confided in Kristen that with this kind of schedule, I didn't think I'd ever have time to meet someone and have a normal relationship. It's great to meet some wonder-ful girls and have a few laughs, but it's hard to build a trusting relationship if they're always wondering where I am on a Saturday night.

As I tell people all the time: Don't cry for me, Argentina. This is what I signed up for, and I'm having the time of my life. But maturity and being handed the privilege of watching Kristen's children grow up have taught me that notches on the bedpost are not the way to take the true measure of a man. The mark of a man is how well he makes his relationships and his marriage work.

Trust me: I would be the most wonderful, loyal husband in the world if I had a wife. How do I know that? Because I had a great example. My parents were together fifty-seven years and loved and nurtured each other until the day fate parted them.

I'm a romantic. I hold out hope that it could happen to me someday. If and when I do get married, it'll be for the rest of my life. I'm old-fashioned that way.

But it's okay. I'll take love if it comes, but if not, I already have the world's greatest lifestyle. Every day I have a chance to go out to provide for myself and my family, which is everyone, including my brothers, my mother, Kristen, and my godson and his brother.

I give them everything I can, because they've given me everything. And what's more, they gave it to me when I didn't know I needed it.

24

INTO THAT GOOD NIGHT

I n 1999 I negotiated a tremendous deal for my brother Michael and our company. Warner Bros. had approached us about using the name *Ready to Rumble* as a movie title. It was a hard negotiation, because I was insisting on more money and a share of the movie profits. Think about it: How many times could we possibly license Michael's catchphrase as a movie title? Exactly once. It didn't make sense to accept a flat fee and never see another dime from a potential moneymaker. We had to receive a handsome fee, but we also had to get points, or the deal just wasn't worth doing. The producers could have just dropped it and walked away, but the director—a genius, in my eyes— kept insisting that he *had* to have the title. Finally the producers capitulated.

I was delighted. I had just checked something off my bucket list: a movie bearing Michael's trademark; a big juicy cameo in the film's climax, for which he was paid a huge fee; and profits to boot!

I called my dad, excited to tell him about the deal and get his approval.

"My first movie deal, Dad!" I told him.

He was initially very excited for me. But he used the opportunity to bring up one of his pet subjects: how I should manage the career of a young friend of his, a popular heavyweight boxing contender who was on the rise and who wanted new management.

"Look," I said, "how many times are we going to go through this?"

I'd tried managing fighters for a while, but finally realized that it wasn't for me. You have to be in the gym constantly, which makes it hard to focus on anything else. Your fighters have to be your chief concern. At one point, former UFC fighter Frank Shamrock wanted me to manage his career and build his brand in areas outside the world of MMA. I declined respectfully.

"That's not what I want to do," I told my father. "I'm about making the deals, not dealing with day-to-day personality issues slowing me down."

My father got disgusted with me, and we hung up. I was so angry I couldn't see straight. I thought, *What the hell just happened? Two minutes ago, I was happy as hell. But this guy just stuck a needle in my balloon and sucked the life out of me.*

Sometimes I was able to tell him how I felt. At other times I just didn't want to ruin my family's evening, so I squelched it. I knew without a doubt that my father was one of my biggest fans, but there were times when I could not be in the same room with him. The heat of two stubborn men duking it out in a war of the wills was just too much.

BUFFERISM NO. 15

"THE ONLY WAY TO FOLLOW A HORSE IS WITH A SHOVEL."

My dad said this all the time. The best achievements in life—like fighting and poker—require skill and professionalism. There's no skill in betting on horses, because you can't control the outcome. Whatever you do in life, you'll minimize your losses if you remember to apply your skill to endeavors you can actually control.

But there came a time when I began to notice that my father was losing his edge. Spirited as he was, he could no longer deal with the physical demands of traveling the country and exhibiting his fine collection of historical guns and artifacts, while buying and selling and dealing with the public at these trade shows. Driving back and forth to Vegas and elsewhere was taking a toll on him and my mom. And it was then that I caught a glimpse of the future. My father had turned his back on the corporate culture, on its pensions and retirement benefits. If this man and woman who had loved us so much were going to live in comfort into their golden years, they would need a new breadwinner: me. And Brian was going to step into a new role as well, watching out for our mom and dad. In fact, that's just what he did. When he retired from the force, he dedicated much of his time to helping them run their business, keeping things running smoothly, and making sure that the bills were paid.

We did all this because we were family. And because we were a team.

But, ironically, my father's life changed the day mine did. In 1996—at the very moment Robert Meyrowitz's office called to offer me my big break announcing UFC 10—my father and I were visiting my mom in the hospital. Later, as my father and I left to grab some sushi, he noticed a funny thing: his foot was acting funny. He'd take a step and one of his feet didn't lift; it dragged on the ground and he almost tripped. Strange. But it turned out to be the first sign of neuropathy, a gradual deterioration of the nervous system.

Over the course of a dozen years, he'd struggle with that and a host of other ailments. His short-term memory was going as well. At one point, as I was taking him, my mom, and their caregiver to the movies, my dad was telling us a story, and it suddenly struck me that nothing he was saying made sense. He was basically recounting for us a very far-fetched hallucination. I'd be having dinner with him and he'd insist that his father, the prizefighter Johnny Buff, had just walked into the room and sat down at the table to enjoy a meal with us.

In his lucid moments, which were frequent, he hated what was happening to him, hated to see his body turning against him, and of course he was too proud to accept people's help. If we were in a public place, he was especially self-conscious, and hated to have people see him walking with a cane, and then a walker. And so I indulged him far too many times, leaving the walker and, later, the wheelchair in the car, and coming around to take his hand or arm.

Once we went to Geoffrey's, a restaurant in Malibu that had a beautiful patio overlooking the ocean. I went over to take his arm as we left the car, and he said, "Son, you let me walk." I knew he was self-conscious with all those people around. Although it scared me, I let him do as he asked. I felt I had to let him have that moment. But the times I could let him do that were rapidly coming to an end. He walked all the way through the restaurant, and just as he reached the table, that thing happened with his foot again and he toppled. I rushed forward. But he caught himself and slipped into the chair unharmed.

My parents were luckier than most people who get to this point in their lives. When it became obvious that my father could no longer get up and down the stairs, Brian and I bought them a lovely single-story house within fifteen minutes of each of us in nearby Playa Del Rey, near the beach. After thirty-five years, they moved out of our beloved Malibu. I was able to hire two very loving caregivers to come live with them when it became obvious that my father was too much of a burden for my mother.

Caring for a parent or loved one this way is not cheap. When people hear me talk about money, the assumption is I'm spending my fortune on wine, women, and song, but that is only half true. Don't get me wrong. I *enjoy* the fruits of my labor; the last time I went to buy a new wardrobe, I easily dropped five figures on a half dozen new tuxedoes and suits. But a lot of my good luck has gone to care for my parents, too. And I would trade all my money and more to give them their health back.

I'm happy to do it. My parents deserve it. They cared for me once, and now it's my turn to return the love. I thank God every day that I have the resources to pull this off. My heart goes out to anyone who is caring for elderly parents. I don't know how Americans do it without vast financial sacrifice.

The public never knew this, but my parents' health was and is often on my mind when I leave town for a UFC show. On the road, I'm often fielding calls from my brother or one of our caregivers. There were always little crises that rattled me: a fainting spell, a drop in someone's blood pressure, bad falls, calls to the paramedics, trips to the emergency room, and Dad's anger bubbling to the surface again. To be able to do a UFC event, I have to be able to put it all out of my mind and concentrate on my work. I need to put on a shoeshine and a smile and give a hundred and ten percent in the Octagon. It has always been my ritual to find a quiet spot when the show ends to call my parents and relive the highlights. "Well," I'd say, "what did you think? Did you like the show?" I'd talk to them, get the update from the caregivers, good or bad, and then I'd hang up, put the smile back on my face, and head out for a fun evening.

One day in 2008, Mom and their caregiver Daysi went to a bakery to pick up some special desserts for dinner. They went into the store, leaving my father in the car. Minutes later, they heard screams. They looked out the window and saw a crowd gathering around their car. My dad had decided to get out. In the three minutes it took for them to go into the store, he experienced one of his dementia moments. He forgot he could not walk, and when he got out of the car, he crashed to the ground and cut his head open. He had to be taken to the hospital. He insisted that he was fine when I rushed over to meet him at the emergency room. But when I went to pick him up when he was released three days later, he looked at me, his head bandaged, and said, "That fall took a lot out of me, son."

It tore me up inside. I know that it humiliated him, as it would any of us, to be helped from the wheelchair to the bed, to the toilet, to the dinner table. There were days when he'd kick up a fuss and lash out at Daysi, her daughter Yohanna, who was his second caregiver, or my mom, who were only trying to make his life more comfortable. Daysi and Yohanna had come to love him, too, and they wanted him to enjoy his days and be the loving, caring, and funny man he always had been.

In one of the poems Dad read to us as kids, the poet Dylan Thomas wrote about the death of his father, also a military man. I'll never forget the words Thomas used, urging his father not to give up without a fight: *"Rage, rage against the dying of the light."*

My father raged, all right. Man, did he. And I was always the heavy who was brought in to smooth things over. One night in the middle of May 2008, after he had a particularly bad, angry day, I came over after work, went into the den where he was sitting in his favorite chair, knelt beside him, and spoke to him face-to-face.

"Look, Dad," I said. "Please don't get mad at me. Everyone here loves you. We know you hate this, but you have to understand that everyone here has feelings. The girls are just trying to help you out. You can't treat them like this. Now, can we work together on this as a team?"

He winced. Nodded. He knew I was right. "I'm sorry," he said, "I'll work on that."

"Good."

I went home that night, and later, just before his bedtime, he called. "Son, I just want you to know that I'm being my wonderful self. I'm behaving myself."

"I know you are," I told him. "I love you, Dad."

"I love you too, son. More than you'll ever know."

He went off to sleep, but it was a fitful night for him. At one point he deliriously told his caregivers that the devil himself was perched at the end of his bed, waving at him, urging my father to come with him.

About 4:30 a.m., Daysi called me. "Bon-Bon," she said, using the name she calls me. "I have to tell you something . . ."

She didn't have to finish. I rose in the darkness and got dressed. I drove over. My parents' house was silent. My mother was lying down. Daysi came out of my dad's room. I went in and closed the door. I stood beside the bed and looked at my father's body. Then I kissed him good-bye.

This was the man who raised us, fought us, fought *for* us, and taught us. Once, in service to his country, he had barked orders to troops and taught them to fight with their hearts, minds, and bodies. He had charmed CEOs, movie stars, and countless women. He had captured one woman's heart and never let it go. He had marched confidently through the glittering halls of those long-gone casinos in the desert, and played to win. He had pounded out thrilling adventure stories. He'd taught his sons all he knew in the hopes that they would become good men.

Lying before me was the same man, only not. The man I knew was gone. What I saw before me were the eighty-three-year-old remains of that warrior. And some days later, when his ashes were scattered along the Los Angeles County coastline, we sent that warrior out to sea.

My family felt great pain at his death. Brian and I had never lost anyone this close to us. But waiting on the other side of the pain was relief. He was a proud man, and we hated to see him suffer. We thanked God that he was in a better place.

In the days after he passed away, I put his death in the back of my mind and went about my business. I thought I was dealing well with the loss. But then it all came back to me in the strangest way. I went to see the movie *Gran Torino* when it came out six months later. Clint Eastwood is phenomenal in the role of a tough Korean War vet who bonds with a young Asian kid who tries to boost his beloved Gran Torino. In the course of the film, you watch this tough old soldier take on a gang of young men, ultimately sacrificing himself to save his newfound friend from becoming a killer.

Clint Eastwood's toughness, his rage, his guts reminded me so much of my father that I was a ball of tears at the end of the movie.

I was a wreck when I left the theater. I went to a bar and got a couple of boilermakers, a drink my dad and I used to like. Beer with Johnnie Walker Black. I sat in the bar and thought about the old days.

For some reason, my father and the movies seem to come together hand in hand in my memory.

In 1992 a controversial Quentin Tarantino film called *Reservoir Dogs* came out. Dad and I went to the Century City theaters to see it the Friday it opened. The theater was packed, and there in an aisle seat in the fifth row was a man laughing crazily at the scene where Michael Madsen tortures a restrained police officer, then callously cuts off the man's ear.

Everyone in the theater was quiet and stunned by the scene. But the sound of one lone man laughing maniacally turned my dad the wrong way. He didn't take kindly to the thought of authority figures being tortured. No doubt in the back of his mind he was thinking of my brother Brian, who was an active member of the force at the time.

My dad asked me for my keychain, which has clipped to it a kubaton, a small metal weapon that can be used for striking and submitting an opponent. I knew what he'd do with it, so I refused to hand it over.

He stood and walked down to the spot near the screen where the man was laughing incessantly. I saw a shadow loom across the screen as my father leaned over him and said something. The man was lifted out of his seat for a second, then dropped back down.

He didn't say a word for the rest of the movie. Not a peep.

When my dad returned to his seat, I asked him, "What did you do?"

My father had leaned over the man, grabbed him by his lower lip, and wrenched him off the seat by tugging on his lip. He'd looked him in the eye and said, "Do you think this is funny?"

The guy shook his head no.

"Then I don't want to hear you say a word for the rest of the film, or you'll be carried out of the theater!"

My father dropped him back into his seat.

Now, sure, that was crazy. A situation like that could have turned on my father, who at the time was sixty-eight. I suppose we should give him props for wanting to go up against a much younger man at that age. When he was still in his fifties he'd told me that his biggest fear about getting older was not being able to handle himself in a fight if he had to throw down. Well, he had done fine that day. How many senior citizens do you know who would have done the same thing?

But in our litigious society, he could easily have been sued, arrested, or both for his actions. It got to the point that whenever I went to the movies with him, I braced myself because I never knew what kind of crazy situation he would get us into. He believed in respecting others and was not shy about expressing himself. If you had your feet on the chair in front of you, then he would sit in front of you just to make sure you dropped your feet. Or he'd tell you to, even if you were the only two patrons in the theater.

The movies and my dad also came together in my mind for another reason.

A long time ago, when I was just a kid, after I had met the great movie stars Jimmy Stewart and Rosalind Russell, my father berated me for not taking a picture of that special moment. "When you have a great experience," he'd say, "you should always write it down or take a picture so you won't forget it." And he was right. Few of us realize the importance of memories when we're young. It's only later, when we start to see how short life is, that we begin to appreciate what a wonderful life we've had.

Do you see now why I go out of my way to help fans get the pictures they want? And why I try to instill in fighters I meet that this really is a special time in their lives, one that is brief and beautiful, and that they will never get it back? You can fight into your forties if you feel like it, as Randy has shown us, but after that, you have the rest of your life to think about. How will that be? What is the next chapter? How will you meet the challenge of the passage of time? When I'm friends with fighters, I try to share that wisdom with them. No one ever laughs when I say this. I think on some level all athletes know that their time in the sport is brief.

The Eastwood movie triggered a three-day period of mourning for me. My father was in my thoughts the whole time. And then, as quickly as the pain arose, it subsided again.

Even before that, I knew I had to get on with my life. I showed up for UFC 84 in Vegas on May 24, only days after my father passed away, and pulled off another great night and went out with everybody to celebrate. I ran into Dana at an after-party that night after the show. He came up to me and offered his condolences.

Then he said something to me that I will remember forever, as it solidified and justified the loyalty I swore to him and the Fertitta brothers to be their teammate and warrior through thick and thin. "I just want you to know that we know how fucking loyal you are," Dana said, "and we love what you do. We want you with us till the day you die."

RETURN TO THE OCTAGON

As August 6 approaches, I'm good to go. When I board the red-eye for Philly, I'm wearing two things designed to safeguard my health: compression socks and an incredible knee brace custom-made for me by Össur, an Icelandic company that specializes in orthopedic devices. The paralympian champion Marlon Shirley hooked me up with them.

I'm talking with Joe Rogan as we take our seats. He's funny as hell, and he reminds me that he's had the same surgery in *both* his knees, but he's amazed by my progress.

It's nice to hear that, even if he is the umpteenth person to tell me. This is the first (and I hope the last) time I've gone through such surgery, so I didn't know what to expect. Yes, I know it's a common procedure in sports circles, but my pain-free recovery is apparently nothing short of miraculous. The day the doc walked into the office where I was sitting, he was happy to announce that the graft was still in place and everything looked good.

Wow, I thought. So six weeks of pre-surgery workouts really *did* make a difference. Flavio worked me so hard during those sessions that I sometimes wanted to kill him. Three to four times a week, ninety-minute nonstop workouts. Thirty minutes of intense full-body stretching. Intense circuit full-body training, with special attention to my legs. Twenty reps a set, ten sets of three different leg exercises. He worked me harder with a damaged ACL than I ever lifted or trained with that leg when it was healthy.

He worked me to the point that I wanted to throw up and punch him, not necessarily in that order. It did occur to me that maybe, just maybe, it was too much, and all for naught. The leg would heal the way it wanted to heal. But that wasn't true after all. The crazy Brazilian had turned out to be a genius.

"You got any special moves for tomorrow?" Rogan jokes now as we settle into our flight.

"You want me to kill myself?" I say.

And we both laugh.

The truth is, I've been thinking about this a lot. How am I going to do what I do? How long will it take before I trust myself enough to pull off one of my signature moves? I have a few ideas up my sleeve, but I'm not going to worry them to death on this flight. I'll deal with them on the ground.

We talk about our favorite topics: the fights. Who's fighting? What are their chances tomorrow? Tito especially occupies our minds. It was just a little over a month ago that he took out Ryan Bader in a main-card event. And tomorrow night he'll be in the main event. What a short amount of time! How will he hold up? What are his chances against Rashad Evans? It feels as though we can talk forever about this stuff, but somewhere over Nebraska we're snoozing like babies.

The whole trip seems touched with memory and gratitude, no doubt spurred on by everything that's been going on in my life. I think my doctor got my wheels spinning a few months back when he gave me the bad news and happened to say, "Congratulations. You're getting back everything you did to your body when you were younger."

BUFFERISM NO. 16

"WINNERS CONCENTRATE ON WINNING. LOSERS CONCENTRATE ON GETTING BY!"

I believe this with all my heart. If you're thinking about how to win, how to work the odds, how to get better, how to strategize, you're going to win. If you're always thinking how you're just going to make your nut this month, you will always be scraping by. Think big. Think to win.

The younger me and the older, wiser me are tumbling in my skull that morning when the plane touches down in Philly. It feels like a homecoming of sorts. The City of Brotherly Love. The city of cheesesteaks. The city of America's birth. The city where I spent my formative years. I came to know these streets as a kid, riding the bus to town with my brother to have a blast, checking out the museums, seeing movies, stuffing our faces. Unknown to us, in another section of Philly, our older brother Michael was taking his first steps toward manhood.

These past few weeks, throughout my recovery, I've felt as

if I were living my life all over again. The ups, the downs, the challenges, the victories. I heard the music of the slots of Vegas, the crash of waves where I learned to surf, the shouts of my dad, the caress of my mom, the crunch of fists, the ecstasy of women, the tender words of loved ones. I remembered the fighters I've known and the fights I've seen. I've remembered everything that's made me who I am. And I've realized how grateful I am to have the life I have. I'm a lucky guy to belong to such a sport, to such an organization. It doesn't matter where we are: Philly, Chicago, Toronto, Milwaukee, Rio, London, Sydney, Tokyo. The UFC is a movable feast, and anywhere the Octagon is feels like home.

As the first rays of sun hit me, I realize something else: vacation's over and it's time to get back to work.

PEOPLE always ask me what my fight weekends are like: What do I really do? What's my schedule like? How do I prepare? A UFC weekend is like a three-day party for the fans who come from all over the world to watch the fights. They imagine that the rest of us who work the show are out partying, too. That's true, up to a point.

I always say I'm a nun the night before a fight, but anything goes the night after. Depending on the city we're in, there are a number of after-parties. In Vegas the official after-party is always at a nightclub like XS or Tryst. There's always a VIP booth where the fighters and I hang out. There's nothing better than hanging out with these men who've known the thrill of the fight and the shared bond of the road. And, of course, it's always nice to have a half-dozen or so ladies in the booth, too.

Fighters such as Urijah Faber, Jake Shields, GSP, and many

others have enjoyed joining me in my booth. (Jake now always makes it a point to ask me if the party's on when he's in town for a UFC.) I usually do the big shout-out intro to the whole club around 11:30 p.m., and then the party starts. Probably the wildest intro I ever did in a club was the time I introduced a VIP patron who had just ordered a huge bottle of Cristal. It cost him $150,000. They paraded it in with multiple cocktail waitresses carrying the champagne bottle like it was Cleopatra, while sparklers sputtered away. I thought it was a huge waste of money, but some people crave that moment of public recognition, which is gone about as fast as champagne.

I've become good friends with the internationally renowned comedian Russell Peters. He's a great boxing fan and has become a huge fan of the UFC. He invited me to dinner in the MGM after a 2011 show, where we ate with his friends. I looked up at one point and saw that I was surrounded by a sea of talented comedians. Joe's at the next table with his guests, who were all comedians, too. Dinner ends, and Russell offers his car to take us to the after-party. This vehicle pulls up, and it's an *armored* limo. Why? I don't know. I suppose I should have felt extremely safe. But it felt like we were driving to a war zone.

But, hey, that's Vegas. In other cities, the options may not be that far-ranging. In that case we have unofficial parties, and just snack and drink at the hotel bar. It sounds boring, but sometimes the biggest UFC faces you want to meet are hanging out just feet from the lobby, because we're all on a short leash at times.

As we touch down in Philly, I have low expectations. I don't think I'm going to be partying much, because I want to take care of my leg. I'd like to get a cheesesteak, but I figure that can wait until after the fight tomorrow.

I chill out at the hotel for a few hours, then work out, ice the knee, eat lunch, dress, catch a ride to the weigh-in. I see Dana and Lorenzo and everyone's asking, "Hey, how's the leg?" I pull up my left pant leg and show off my brace. Emblazoned across the front of it is the UFC logo.

"Hey, we should sell those," someone says.

Some of the fighters come over and ask me about my recovery.

For some of these guys, it's the first time they're hearing about my misadventure. It's nice to hear their good wishes. I'm touched by their concern. But I just need to get back in the Octagon. I need to feel that microphone in my hand, and then I'll know it's okay.

The weigh-in is fun. They always are. This is what the organization does well—the human touch, interacting with the fans. There have been some really tense situations at these events, where the fighters come together for the staredowns and things get out of hand. Once, one of the fighters pushed his opponent and the guy nearly fell off the dais, which was about ten feet off the ground. And there have been situations where Dana and I and a couple of the other UFC guys have had to physically separate opponents.

I'm usually invited to tons of parties Friday night. More than I'd ever *want* to attend. I usually turn them down. The best party I can have on a Friday before a fight is a good night's sleep. Tonight I go out with Tito, who's fighting tomorrow. We have a blast at that steakhouse in Philly, but both of us know what's ideal: get back to the hotel at a decent time and get some shut-eye.

The next day, Saturday, I go through my usual routine. I order a power breakfast from room service. A vegetarian egg-white omelet. Cottage cheese. Oatmeal with raisins, bananas, honey, and brown sugar. Tomato juice. Coffee. That gets me going for the day.

I always work out on the road, but I tend to focus more on cardio than anything else. Just forty-five minutes, nothing too strenuous. I don't want any surprises popping up when I step into the Octagon, like the time in January 2012 when my back blew out on me two hours before the historic UFC 142 in Rio de Janeiro, Brazil. That was my punishment for not stretching properly after a seventeen-hour flight. There I was, minutes before the start of the event, in my tuxedo, getting worked on, on the floor of the dressing room of fighter Rousimar Palhares, by his trainer/therapist.

These days my goal is simply to stay loose for the show. After the workout, if there's a quality spa at the hotel, I take a steam bath, which is excellent for my throat. I have a massage to loosen me up. Then I go back to my room and look over my fight cards to make sure that they're all in order. I've gotten this data from the organization in the week leading up to my arrival in our event city. I've created a template on my home computer that allows me to flow all the data into it as each fresh infusion is received, so I'm always up to date. Later, when I hit the floor of the arena, I'll make sure that the fighters' weights, stats, credentials, and home cities are all correct. I'll need to make sure that what I'm saying jibes with what the production team will be flashing on the screen in your living room.

This info *can* change, but it's always a good idea to familiarize myself with what I have. I want it to sink in and make an impression. I visualize myself saying those words, but I *don't* rehearse them. I don't like doing that.

I take some time now to sit in my room and meditate. I started meditating in my twenties, after being turned on to it by one of my business partners. I enrolled in an ashram in Los Angeles and studied there for two in-depth sessions before I learned my mantra. I do it because it's smart: a twenty-minute meditation session is the equivalent of a two-hour nap for me. I call it my Zen moment.

I shower, and put on the monkey suit. You're going to laugh, but I have fifteen or more tuxedoes. I have them custom-made. A while back I met with David August, a high-end tailor to guys like Sylvester Stallone, Mickey Rourke, and Rupert Murdoch, to name a few. Together the lead designer, David Heil, and I designed six new tuxes, which he created for my 2012 UFC schedule. I'd never spent so much on a tuxedo, but David's work was worth it. I look and feel like a million bucks, and he designed them to allow more range of movement in the Octagon. He knows just what little things make all the difference. For example, he removed the lining over the knees inside my trousers so I can easily drop to one knee without having the pant leg bunch or catch. It's the kind of thing most custom tailors would never think to do. And honestly, I don't blame them; after all, how many guys need to move like that while wearing a tux?

Dressed now, I sing a little Frank Sinatra to myself, usually "Strangers in the Night." All I'm trying to do is get some intonation going. The way Sinatra pronounces words is amazing. You never fail to hear and understand any of the words he's singing, because his diction is flawless. Doing this really relaxes me. It's like standing around and saying, "The rain in Spain stays mainly in the plain" again and again, twenty times in a row.

I'm heading out the door of my hotel room when something occurs to me. I close the door and come back. I move the chair aside and stand in the empty space. I *know* how I can do this. I point the tips of my shoes at the bed and align my knees with my feet. Then I gently twist my torso toward the opposite wall. I mime holding a mic.

I'm thinking, *Fighting out of the Blue Corner . . .*

I swing my torso 180 degrees to face the bed.

I think: *Fighting out of the Red Corner . . .*

I do it a couple of times till it feels okay. It does. It's not my classic move, more like a one-eighty "lite." But it might work. I'm not supposed to knock myself out with the physicality for a while. No side-to-side motion. No surfing. Doctor's orders.

I hit the lights and go downstairs. There are tons of fans in the lobby. They're asking the fighters and anyone else they recognize for autographs. I'm happy to oblige. In the back of my mind, I'm thinking, *Avoid the big crowds. Don't get jostled. Take care of the leg. Doctor's orders.*

I hop the shuttle bus and we get to the arena, the Wells Fargo Center.

About 12,000 people are attending UFC 133. The crowd is pumped. More people asking me for autographs on the way in. *Happy to, happy to.*

In the early days, I used to do walk-throughs, sort of like production rehearsals, in the arena on Saturday. How we're going to walk in, what music will be played, where the fighters will be, and so on. But now I don't have to do it, because we're such a finely oiled machine. Everyone's in sync. When those fighters walk in, the crew knows what to do.

First stop when I get to the arena is a visit with Suzy Friton, who applies a little makeup to my face. I know, it's dumb, but it's important for the camera, so I've got to do it. Suzy's a phenomenal woman and a lifesaver. I'll never forget the time I ripped my tuxedo pants, top to bottom, front and back, while doing warm-up stretches five minutes before I was supposed to go on, and Suzy whisked me back behind the stage curtain and sewed those pants up with her little sewing kit—*with me standing in them*—in five minutes flat. That's why I love working with this crew: they're the greatest professionals in the business.

Next, I visit the media room. It's a nice place to hang out with the Octagon girls, various other road friends, and media. There's always good food here. I don't want to load up, but I haven't eaten anything other than breakfast. I grab some chicken, anything light. Here, also, is where I snag a great balm for my voice: half a cup of honey that I can keep on my desk. A little spoonful works wonders for the vocal cords, and it's full of nutrients. If I want something to drink, I try a little warm water, not cold. I also keep a stash of Hall's eucalyptus lozenges in my pocket just in case. If I don't have them, I know I can bum one from Suzy. She watches after Goldie, me, and the Octagon girls as if we are family.

Then I go to the local athletics commission table. I get the missing piece of the data puzzle: a sheet with the names of tonight's judges, referees, and commissioners. I take some time to review that with the commission, and then I carefully transfer the data to my stash of cards. Unlike the world of boxing, I announce the names of the judges of the main event only.

I meet with the audio production man who hooks up my interruptible foldback (IFB) earpiece. From that moment on, the director in the production truck is basically in my ear for the entire show. We can communicate easily about special announcements and last-minute directives.

Next, I find the desk I sit at next to the Octagon, where I set up my water, my honey, various colored pens, and my cards. I rip each of the cards at the bottom in the lower left corner. Just about a half-inch tear is all I need to slip my pinkie finger in there. I learned a long time ago that I need to anchor the cards to my hand in some way. I'm so physical in the Octagon that I could lose the cards if I'm not careful.

Unlike other announcers, I do not flip the cards in my hands to get to the next one. Instead, I throw each card away behind me onto the Octagon floor, and the referee or the Octagon gate man moves in to pick them up while I'm still announcing. One time they forgot to pick up the cards, and when I sat down I saw one of my cards on the Octagon floor. Believe it or not, during the entire round, the fighters danced around that card, but not once did either of them step on it. I was grateful for that, because—who knows?—they might have fallen and I'd feel terrible about being in part responsible for that.

The fans are streaming in. Some of them see me and come running down to ask for photos and autographs. I make it a point to sign all autographs and take pictures when asked, but I have to stay focused when the show is about to start.

The music is starting.

I stick close to the desk, in my safe zone, and do some voice exercises and a few specific stretching movements to loosen my body up.

The fighters are flowing in. The early fights kick off the night. Chad Mendes and Rani Yahya are the first prelim. I prep the cards. Check.

I've never rehearsed in my life, but tonight is different. Too much water under the bridge. And if I'm going to do it—and I'd like to be able to—I need to give myself the time to run through it.

I find a quiet spot in the back and I try it out again.

Blue Corner. *Twist*. Red Corner.

Feels good.

I walk back out onto the floor. The music's starting. "Baba O'Riley," by The Who. They always play this song with video of past UFC moments for the ten-minute period before pay-per-view events or televised shows. The song pumps up the crowd—and everyone working behind the scenes. The song has become a staple for a hundred or more shows, and it really gets the blood flowing.

The crowd is loving it. I only need three things to make this happen: the mic, the cards, and the crowd. Everything else I carry inside me.

I'm about to ascend the steps of the Octagon to pay tribute to these warriors. But before I do, I stop and make one last tribute of my own. I make the sign of the cross. Although I'm a spiritual person, I'm not at all religious—but this is something I do from time to time to honor all fighters and all religions. Yes, doing this gets stares and a few giggles, but I don't care. When I look up and point my finger to the sky, I think of all those who have gone before me. My uncle John, whom I just lost. My German shepherd Buff. My two nineteen-year-old cats, Bogey and Rocky. And my father. I loved them all. They helped make me what I am, and I carry them in my heart always.

Every fighter knows that when you meet a man in battle, a piece of him stays with you forever. Some are scarred by their encounters. Some are just made wiser. All of them take the lessons of the Octagon away with them and vow to fight another day. Even if you're not a fighter, the same laws apply. Everyone you meet gives you something. A chance to learn, a chance to be better. They may delight you, enrage you, seduce you, cheat you, care for you. But you are changed by that meeting. You want to live life? Live it to the fullest. You want to fight? Then, for God's sake, fight and give your heart to the battle. If you want to live, shout, play, make love, dream, cry—do all these things with passion and the precious knowledge that your time on this earth is short. If you want to live, *now* is the time.

I stare at the sky. I think of my father.

Thank you.

I go up the steps. I feel the energy of the crowd. I lift the mic to my lips.

"IT'S TIME."

ACKNOWLEDGMENTS

I'm indebted to a great number of people who allowed me to have the wonderful moments and memories described in this book. Every one of them deserves a thank-you from a humble and grateful friend.

This book would not have been possible without the vision, determination, and enthusiasm of my agent, Yfat Reiss Gendell, her assistant Erica Walker, and their colleagues at Foundry Literary + Media. My appreciation to the crew at Random House/Crown Archetype—copy editor David Wade Smith, designer Maria Elias, production manager Phil Leung, production editor Patricia Shaw, and Tommy Cabrera, Ellen Folan, and Paul Lamb in publicity/marketing—for their care throughout every stage of publication, and to Julian Pavia, my editor, who coached me through this exciting process and thoughtfully polished my words. Thanks also to Andrew Lear, for pulling it all together.

My friends in the MMA and UFC world deserve accolades for sharing with me so many of the adventures discussed in this book, or giving me the opportunity to have them in the first place. Thanks to Robert Meyrowitz, for allowing me to take my first steps into the UFC Octagon. Sincere thanks to Dana White, Lorenzo Fertitta, and Frank Fertitta for your trust and friendship, for being the amazing maverick businessmen you are, and for all you have done for the UFC and our great sport of MMA. Special thanks to Big John McCarthy, Joe Silva, Mike Goldberg, Joe Rogan, Craig Borsari, Lawrence Epstein, Bruce Connel, Al Connel, Anthony Giordano, Marc Ratner, Burt Watson, Sean Shelby, Reed Harris, Jacob "Stitch" Duran, Herb Dean, Thomas Gerbasi, Kirk Hendrick, Greg Hendrick, Tim O'Toole, Donna Marcolini, Liz Hedges, Jennifer Hamilton, Stephen Quinn, Suzy Friton, and everyone in the UFC organization.

I bow respectfully to all the ring and cage fighters I have announced over the years, and especially to the UFC fighters I have had the honor of calling my friends, among them Chuck Liddell, B.J. Penn, Quinton "Rampage" Jackson, Georges St-Pierre, Tito Ortiz, Frank Shamrock, Bas Rutten, Randy Couture, Jon Jones, Urijah Faber, Rashad Evans, Michael Bisping, Lyoto Machida, and Anderson Silva. I and everyone in the UFC owe our thanks to UFC fans around the world. If not for your passion and support of MMA and the UFC through the best and worst times, we never would have made it through to the realm of mainstream sports and beyond.

Some superb colleagues and friends have supported me over the years. You have met some of them in the pages of this book, but I thank them here again: my attorney, Mark E. Kalmansohn, as well as Daysi Cano, Yohanna Mejia, Dr. Scott Bateman, Dr. Neal S. ElAttrache, T. J. DeSantis, Samy Phillips,

Damian McLawhorn, Flavio de Oliveira, Brad Lecraw, and Alex Cano. My thanks also to my dear friends Gary Randall, Joe Lear, Rosy Marin, and Darby Brakke.

Kristen Greulach—your support, spirit, grace, and professionalism have shaped our companies and taught me so much about love and family; I thank you and *your* wonderful "team": Chris, Henry, and Rupert.

Michael Buffer—thank you for believing in my dreams about where I wanted to take your career and your "Let's Get Ready to Rumble" phrase. That trust has paid off for both of us.

Brian Buffer—I know you'd take a bullet for me. Thank you for your love and support and for being one of the last, true White Knights I know.

My wonderful and loving mother and father—for all the worldliness, love, and chivalry you both taught and instilled in me. Walking through life with you has truly been both inspirational and an adventure.

Finally, I thank those living and gone who also helped make me what I am: my uncle John Cappelli, my aunt Betty Cappelli, my grandparents Pat and Mary Carota, and my loving pets, Buff, Bogey, and Rocky.

ABOUT THE AUTHOR

BRUCE BUFFER is known the world over as the official "Veteran Voice of the Octagon" for the Ultimate Fighting Championship (UFC), along with many other international mixed martial arts (MMA) and fighting events. He has announced hundreds of events and thousands of fights, and is also known for his exploits as a high-stakes poker player, businessman, entrepreneur, and motivational speaker. Connect with Bruce Buffer via Twitter (@BruceBuffer) and his website, BufferZone.net.